Salvador Witness

The Life and Calling of Jean Donovan

by Ana Carrigan

Simon and Schuster
New York

Copyright © 1984 by Ana Carrigan
All rights reserved
including the right of reproduction
in whole or in part in any form
Published by Simon and Schuster
A Division of Simon & Schuster, Inc.
Simon & Schuster Building
Rockefeller Center
1230 Avenue of the Americas
New York, New York 10020
SIMON AND SCHUSTER and colophon are registered
trademarks of Simon & Schuster, Inc.
Designed by Barbara Marks
Manufactured in the United States of America

1   3   5   7   9   10   8   6   4   2

Library of Congress Cataloging in Publication Data
Carrigan, Ana.
Salvador Witness

1. Donovan, Jean.   2. Missionaries—El Salvador—
Biography.   3. Missionaries—United States—Biography.
I. Title.
BV2843.S4D663   1984   266'.2'0924 [B]   84-14160
ISBN: 0-671-47992-X

"Arms," poem by Manuel Arce, reprinted by permission of North American Congress on Latin America.

The lines quoted from Thomas Merton are from *Thoughts in Solitude*, published by The Noonday Press. Copyright the Abbey of Our Lady of Gethsemane, 1956 and 1958. Reprinted by permission of Farrar, Straus & Giroux.

The epigraph by Antonio Machado reprinted by permission of University of California Press.

The extracts from the homilies, speeches and pastoral letters of Archbishop Oscar Arnulfo Romero reprinted by gracious permission of the Arzobispado of San Salvador.

The correspondence from Sister Dorothy Kazel, OSU, to Sister Martha Owens, OSU, reprinted by kind permission of the Ursuline Nuns of Cleveland.

Acknowledgments

Some of the research for this book was originally assembled for a documentary film about Jean Donovan—*Roses in December*—produced in the summer of 1982 for Public Television. I wish to thank my colleagues in the production of that film, Bernard Stone and David Meyer, for that portion of their original filmed interview with Raymond and Patricia Donovan that appears in this book. The quotes by Edward Fenton, Carlos Paredes, and Fred Taylor, as well as the description by Ambassador and Mrs. Robert E. White of the dinner party in the American embassy attended by Jean Donovan and Dorothy Kazel on the last night of their lives, are from interviews conducted for this film by David Meyer.

This book owes a great deal to the following people:

—To John Houseman for insisting that I write it.

—To my editor, John Herman. His patience, trust, and commitment to this project made it all possible.

—To Raymond Bonner, for his generosity in offering me access to a number of key documents from the remarkable file he had assembled for his own book, *Weakness and Deceit: U.S. Policy and El Salvador*.

—To Scott Greathead, Diane Orentlicher, Michael Posner, and James Zorn of the Lawyers Committee on International Human Rights, who provided me with essential materials from their files on "The Case of the Four American Churchwomen."

—To John McAward and Leonel Gomez, who arranged my interview with "the Colonel."

—To my friends Kathleen Keville and Pat de Angelis—who came constantly to my rescue with indispensable research assistance—and Davidson Lloyd, who painstakingly deciphered my handwritten manuscript and typed all of the first and most of the second drafts of this book.

—And to Marcel Ophuls, who taught me how to tell stories with other people's words.

ACKNOWLEDGMENTS

I owe a particular debt of gratitude to Timothy Allman, whose description of his brief meeting with Jean Donovan short weeks before she was killed, in his article on El Salvador, "Rising to Rebellion," in the March 1981 issue of *Harper's* magazine made Jean come vibrantly alive for me and triggered my investigation into her life. Allman's description of Jean spoke of "a big and cheerful blonde, the kind of girl whom the boys in Ohio would have called bouncy or peppy, never fat. Her bulk," he wrote, "like her talk and gestures, conveyed buoyancy and vigor." And his perception that "it was not the catastrophe all around her that Jean Donovan found astonishing. It was the possibility that she herself might actually be able in some way to help alleviate it that seemed to fill her constantly with amazement and joy" came close—or so it seemed to me—to a contemporary definition of the meaning of sainthood in our crazed and anguished world. It raised the question: What meaning does Jean Donovan's life and death hold for the rest of us?

This book is the result of my search for answers to that question. It could not have been written without the collaboration and the help of all those whose voices provide a large part of the text.

To begin with, there could have been no book without the generosity and support of Jean's parents, Raymond and Patricia Donovan, or her brother, Michael, and sister-in-law, Ellen. Their trust, their collaboration, and their friendship sustained me throughout, and I am especially grateful for their permission to publish excerpts from Jean's correspondence and diary. I am also deeply grateful to other members of the extended Donovan family, in particular to Jean's uncle, Jay Murphy, Jr., who shared many family reminiscences with me, and to her cousins Donald and Marietta Kelly, whose extraordinary kindness and hospitality provided me with a home away from home during the course of my research in Cleveland.

Others whose support was crucial, who shared generously of their time, their memories, and their experiences, are the members of the families of the other three Americans who died with Jean: Mr. and Mrs. John Clarke, the parents of Maryknoll

ACKNOWLEDGMENTS

Sister Maura Clarke, and Maura's sister, Judy Keogh; Mrs. Mildred Ford, mother of Maryknoll Sister Ita Ford, and Ita's younger sister, Rene Sullivan, and her brother, Bill Ford; Mr. and Mrs. Joseph Kazel, the parents of Ursuline Sister Dorothy Kazel, and Dorothy's lifelong friend and sister-in-law, Mrs. James Kazel. I am particularly grateful to the members of the Clarke and Ford families for sharing their personal correspondence with Maura and Ita with me.

In the writing of this book I have used materials concerning Maura Clarke MM, Ita Ford MM and Carla Piette MM and Maryknoll Sisters reports. These are contained in the unpublished biographical manuscript "As the Poor," written by Judith A. Noone MM. I am grateful to the Maryknoll Sisters for this privilege.

Jean Donovan's colleagues in the Mission Team of the Cleveland diocese, Father Paul Schindler and Sister Christine Rody, and her precursors, Sister Martha Owens and Sister Cindy Drennan, provided me with essential background and insight into the daily routines of Jean's work and experiences in El Salvador. I am especially grateful to Martha Owens for sharing her correspondence from Dorothy Kazel with me.

The contribution of former United States Consul to El Salvador Patricia Lasbury-Hall, who overcame her reluctance to talk about the traumatic events in which she was involved in the immediate aftermath of Jean's death in order to give me a firsthand account of those hours, speaks for itself in the pages of this book. As do the contributions of the man who was the single most important influence in Jean's life, her great friend and mentor Father Michael Crowley of Cork, Ireland; and of the man who loved her, Dr. Douglas Cable of Los Angeles.

I am grateful too for the reminiscences of Jean's high school friend Fred Taylor of Westport, Connecticut, and for those of her Irish friends Maura Corkery and Edward Fenton. Her cousin Colleen Kelly and her college roommate in Cleveland, Debbie Miller, contributed greatly to the portrait of Jean in this book, and her friends from the Cleveland Youth Ministry, Rita Mikolajczyk and Mary Fran Ehlinger, provided invaluable insights into that period of Jean's life just prior to her

ACKNOWLEDGMENTS

decision to go to El Salvador. I am especially thankful to Rita for sharing her correspondence and tapes from Jean in El Salvador.

My thanks also to Father Ralph Wiatowski, who became Jean's theology teacher and friend during her last year in Cleveland, and who was the recipient of one of her last, most important letters; to Gwen Vendley, who, among Jean's instructors at the Maryknoll Lay Mission Program, understood and appreciated her best and also shared wonderful letters with me; to her fellow students in that program, Pat de Angelis and Cindy O'Donnell, who became Jean's friends and maintained contact with her to the end; and to her friends Maryknoll Father Fern Grosslin and Gary Martinez.

Others who helped to place the events related in this book within the political and historical framework in which they occurred include Heather Foote; Padre Rafael Moreno, SJ, former Secretary to Archbishop Romero; Carlos Paredes, former Undersecretary of Economic Planning in the Second Junta Government; Carlos Parada; Monsignor Ricardo Uriosti, Vicar of the Archdiocese of San Salvador; Ambassador and Mrs. Robert E. White; and Dr. William Wipfler.

For
John Houseman

Contents

Prologue

DECEMBER IS HIGH SUMMER IN EL SALVADOR. FROM October to May hardly a shower disturbs the certain repetition of sunbaked days and warm, clear nights. In the western plain it is the harvest season. A time when the landowners reap the nation's export crops—coffee, cotton, sugar cane—and El Salvador's landless poor throng the roads each morning before sunup on their daily walk to the fields. In the evening, in the quick-falling tropical dusk, the long lines of men, women and children straggle home along the edges of the black-topped roads in an oppressive, exhausted silence.

For Antonio Ramos, migrant worker and cotton picker, there was nothing about that Tuesday in December of 1980 to set it apart in any way from all the other long, monotonous days of the harvest. It was only later that week, after rumors had begun to circulate in frightened whispers among the cotton pickers of the Dueñas ranch, that the old man remembered the apparition that had broken so crazily into the middle of his exhausted sleep. *Si Señor.* There, right there on the dirt road that runs past his daughter's shack. That one, Señor, leading up the hill.

To the questions of the *gringo* reporter the old man gives polite, shy responses. No, this is not his house, Señor. He is from the North. He comes to the coast each year, just for three months, to work the harvest. Who knows, maybe this year he'll stay a while. In his village there is such trouble. Much grief, Señor. Too many people have disappeared and turned up later . . . he makes a gesture with his finger across his throat. And so many of the young have left the village to go into the hills. He is too old, Señor, too tired for such things. . . . That night? The night he saw the white van? Well, yes, it had been a hard day. . . .

Each morning when he climbed out of his hammock it was still dark. Hearing him grope for his sandals, his daughter Carmen would light the lamp and bring the cup of sugared water and the tortilla she had laid out for him the night before. Coffee? No, Señor, they didn't buy coffee. It was still dark when he set out at four-thirty on the long walk to the Regalado-Dueñas cotton ranch, the largest cotton grower in the valley. And each day, at six o'clock, when the first rays of the sun struck the fields, he was already at work. He was an experienced picker, and by the time the siren blew for the ranch lunch (refried beans and tortillas) the large sack at his waist would be full.

And then? Well then he kept going until the second sack was full. It's true, the afternoon heat is brutal. You know yourself. . . . The old man smiles and shrugs his shoulders in a gesture as ancient as his race. So then? Then he waits with all the other pickers, an hour, maybe two, until it is his turn to get his cotton weighed. Sometimes he can even get home before dark.

And that night? That night in December? What precisely did he see? Were there soldiers? Guardsmen? The old man shakes his head. No soldiers. Only the van. You see he sleeps on the porch, outside. The house is small, Señor, only one room for his daughter and her husband and four small children and her husband's mother . . . so, he hangs his hammock outside. Earlier that night he heard a car pass that way. Shots? Did he hear gunshots? He can't be sure . . . forgive him, there were so often shots at night. But the van, the white van, yes. And what he remembers is the music. Dance music, loud and clear and filling the night air. That was what woke him, suddenly, brought him out to look. And here it came—a white van, swaying from side to side on the rough road as it raced down the hill toward him, with all the windows open and the radio blaring and all the lights on bright. Inside? The lights were on inside the van? Oh, yes. They were drinking. The old man raises an imaginary bottle and tilts his head back. Like this. Four, maybe five of them, in civilian clothes. Yes, yes, that he is convinced of, because he remembers thinking how strange they should be having such a party after curfew. Women? No, no women. Just the men. Drinking and playing music.

Morning

To find the Western Path
Right thro the Gates of Wrath
I urge my way;
Sweet Mercy leads me on,
With soft repentant moan
I see the break of day.

The war of swords and spears
Melted by dewy tears
Exhales on high;
The sun is freed from fears
And with soft grateful tears
Ascends the sky.

—William Blake

Caminante, no hay camino,
Se hace camino al andar.

—Antonio Machado

CHAPTER I

"Missing Today in El Salvador..."

Tuesday, December 2, 1980

FATHER PAUL SCHINDLER, PASTOR OF THE PARISH OF La Libertad and head of the mission team of the Cleveland diocese in El Salvador, saw no reason to be concerned when two of his American missionaries—Dorothy Kazel and Jean Donovan—did not return to their home base on the night of December 2, 1980. The ten-member team from Cleveland had bases in three small towns along the Pacific coast and it was not unusual for one or another of the missionaries to spend the night elsewhere than in their permanent residence. This was particularly true of Jean and Dorothy, both of whom spent most of their time on the road, transporting people and provisions from one end of this tiny country to another. They were an intrepid and energetic pair—Dorothy, an Ursuline nun with eight years experience in El Salvador, and Jean, a young lay volunteer, who had joined the Cleveland team in El Salvador just eighteen months earlier. With their white Toyota minibus, they were widely known as "The Rescue Squad" by the rest of the American Catholic Church people working in various locations and parishes alongside their hosts in the Salvadoran Church.

For that reason, when Paul Schindler returned to the small port town of La Libertad at around six o'clock on that Tuesday evening, after a busy day in the capital, the absence of Jean and Dorothy did not strike him as unusual or alarming. The night before they had all three dined together at the American embassy. Although it was common knowledge that following the recent election of President Reagan, the status of Ambassador Robert White, and any ability he might have to affect American actions in El Salvador, had been sharply reduced, it had been gratifying for his guests to discover that their host was genuinely interested in learning their views, their particular perspective and knowledge of conditions in the rural areas, where they were struggling to provide help and protection to a population in desperate need of both. It was late when their conversation ended, and the ambassador and his wife had insisted that their guests spend the night at the embassy to avoid the dangers inherent in being on the road after the nine o'clock curfew.

The next morning, after breakfast with Mrs. White, the dinner guests went their separate ways—Paul, whose day off it was, to visit friends in the capital; Jean and Dorothy to do some shopping for the children's refugee center that the Cleveland team had recently established in the hill village of Zaragoza, overlooking the port at La Libertad. They were then to drive to the International Airport to meet four of their closest friends and colleagues, Maryknoll Sisters returning from a regional conference in Nicaragua. The flight from Nicaragua was due to land at three o'clock, and as they parted on the street outside the embassy, Jean leaned out the window of the van to shout to Paul, "Don't be too late tonight! We'll all have a party with the Maryknollers to celebrate their return!"

Now, when he noticed that the white Toyota minibus was missing from its usual parking spot on the square, outside the schoolhouse where Jean and Dorothy shared an apartment, Paul Schindler made a quick check in the parking lot behind the church, where two of the returning Maryknoll Sisters had left their car for safekeeping while they were out of the country. As he had hoped, the Maryknollers' car was gone. That meant that they were back from Nicaragua, had collected their car, and left for their own parish of Santa Ana some fifty miles north of La Libertad. It also meant that Jean and Dorothy had completed their mission safely at the airport, and that they and their friends, Maura Clarke and Ita Ford, the remaining two Maryknoll Sisters, would not be far away. Meanwhile, he was needed in the church to say the six-thirty evening mass.

Later that evening, following the mass, after a meeting with a group of parishioners who wanted to discuss the celebrations for the coming fiesta in the town, Paul crossed the courtyard that separated the church from the school-house. He climbed the flight of stone steps leading to Jean and Dorothy's apartment, hoping to find a note from one of them, reporting on their whereabouts. There was no note, but on the kitchen table there were several packages with Nicaraguan labels—packages that seemed to belong to Maura and Ita, indicating that the two Maryknoll Sisters were still in the vicinity. Obviously, he thought, they must all be spending the night up the hill in the mission house in Zaragoza—it was the only house large enough to receive all four of them—and besides, it was a place to which they would always go without bothering to leave a message.

Relieved, Paul went home and placed a call to his friend and colleague, Father Ken Myers, in Zaragoza. He was out, and Paul left a message to have him call back when he got in. It was late when Father Ken got home, and he figured that Paul's message could wait until the morning.

That morning, December 3, when the Zaragoza and La Libertad members of the mission team gathered in the shady courtyard of Father Schindler's house for their weekly staff meeting, it took no time to confirm that Jean and Dorothy were missing and that no one present had spoken to them or to anyone in the two parishes with whom they would normally have left a message to say where they had gone. Paul, outwardly calm, felt his anxiety rising. It had happened so often, to so many people he had grown close to: "Padre—my son, my husband, my father, my brother

. . . 'disappeared.' He went to buy cigarettes . . . he went to visit his mother . . . he went into the capital . . . disappeared." Sometimes Father Schindler would find the missing one, in a jail, or a police station, or an army barracks. Sometimes on the side of the road, or at the bottom of a quarry, or on the beach. . . . . But nothing had ever happened to an American in El Salvador, he reminded himself. Besides, these women, these blond, blue-eyed American women, were universally recognized as the last best protection for anyone in trouble, from refugees to Salvadoran church workers, even to an American priest. Everone felt safe in the hands of "The Rescue Squad." Canceling all other business, Paul immediately began trying to trace the missing women's movements from the time when he estimated they must have returned to La Libertad from the airport with the four Maryknoll Sisters on the previous afternoon.

To be dependent for communication with the outside world on the tapped phones of the Salvadoran telephone system was one of the special frustrations in the life of an active missionary. Yet now Paul had no option. Shortly after ten that morning he placed four calls with the Libertad operator: The first was to San Salvador, to the Convent of the Assumption Sisters, where the Maryknoll Sisters, Maura Clarke and Ita Ford, usually spent the night when they were in town; the second was to the northeastern town of Chalatenango, where Maura and Ita lived and worked; the third was to the city of Santa Ana, where the other two returning Sisters, Madeleine Dorsey and Teresa Alexander, were based; the fourth was to the American embassy. Then he sat down to wait for the calls to come through. And while he waited he listened to the radio, which on that morning was filled with news reports of violence and roadblocks in downtown San Salvador, where tension was high as the hour approached for the eleven o'clock funeral mass at the cathedral for six much loved and respected opposition leaders, assassinated one week earlier by right-wing death squads under police protection.

In deference to the reputations of the slain men, and in recognition of the tragic significance of their killings, a sizeable foreign delegation of concerned American and Canadian observers had flown into San Salvador on the previous evening to attend their funeral. One of these visitors, with close ties to many in the Salvadoran Church, was Heather Foote, a staff member of the Washington Office on Latin America, a resource center for Latin American scholars in Washington, D.C. Early that morning, from her hosts in the Convent of the Assumption in downtown San Salvador, Heather Foote became aware of their growing anxiety over the whereabouts of Maura Clarke and Ita Ford. They had been expected to spend Tuesday night at the convent, where a meeting to discuss the refugee situation in Chalatenango had been scheduled for early the next morning. When Maura and Ita failed to arrive, the Sisters of the Assumption assumed that they had gone to spend the night in La Libertad with Jean and Dorothy. Then, as the hour for their scheduled meeting came and went, the Sisters became alarmed and tried to make contact with Paul Schindler in La Libertad.

At the opposite end of town, in the overcrowded and understaffed refugee camp which she ran, Sister Christine Rody, another Cleveland missionary, was anxiously watching the clock as she waited for the arrival of "The Rescue Squad." They had lunched together in the San Salvador McDonald's the day before—Chris, Dorothy and Jean— and Chris had mentioned a logistical problem that was bothering her: she was unable to find transportation for a group of refugee women waiting to be evacuated from Chalatenango in the north and brought down to safety in Chris's refuge camp, where their husbands and children were waiting for them. Instantly, Jean had volunteered to take care of it. To Jean Donovan such problems were simple. Someone needed help, needed wheels, you got up earlier, you drove longer hours, you provided a solution. If someone needed to evacuate nine people or nineteen, provided they could fit into the white minibus, it was all the

21

same to Jean. As she outlined her plan to Chris, she would leave La Libertad at six o'clock on Wednesday morning with Maura and Ita, deposit them home in Chalatenango by eight, load up the refugees, and be back in San Salvador at the refugee camp by ten o'clock. She would still make it back to La Libertad in time for Paul's staff meeting by eleven.

There was no sign of Jean at eight o'clock. Nor at noon. Nor was there any word from Chalatenango. And Chris began to worry. Paul Schindler must know where she is, she thought. At twelve-thirty, when she knew that the staff meeting would be over and the participants would all be lunching together at Paul's house, Chris went to the public phone booth across the street from the camp and made a call to La Libertad.

When she returned to face the anxious questions of the men whose wives Jean was supposed to be bringing out to safety, she heard herself passing along the same strained assurances that Paul had just given her. "We're checking up on them," he had said. "They probably went to Santa Ana with the Maryknolls for some reason." Without leaving word? "They probably told someone who forgot to pass along the message. We have calls out," Paul had said. "Call me back in an hour."

"I went back to the refugee center," Chris recalls, "I was teaching kids how to stand on their heads—for entertainment sake, you know—and the whole time I'm thinking, Gee. I wonder where they are? What can be happening to them? Why aren't they coming? So at two o'clock, I went back to the street to call Father Paul again and he said they still didn't know where they were, and maybe I should come to Libertad to at least . . . you know, be there with the rest of the team."

By then Paul had spoken to the Sisters in the Convent of the Assumption. He had heard from Chalatenango that the refugees were still waiting for Jean, who had not shown up there, and he had also spoken to Madeleine Dorsey and Terri Alexander in Santa Ana, and had discovered that

Sisters Maura Clarke and Ita Ford had not traveled with them from Nicaragua the day before. Unable to get reservations on the same flight, they had been forced to take a later plane, scheduled to land at San Salvador three hours after Madeleine and Terri, at six o'clock in the evening. According to Maddie, Jean and Dorothy had dropped them off in La Libertad and then turned right around and driven back to the airport to meet the second flight.

Paul told Chris that he had placed a call to the Maryknoll Mission in Nicaragua to find out whether, in fact, Maura and Ita had ever left Managua the day before. "We don't know," he said, "whether we're looking for all four of them or just for Jean and Dorothy." And then he added, "They're probably sitting in a jail someplace; the ambassador is on to it, so don't get agitated, just come on down here. At least when we do find them we'll all be together to go and get them out."

At the American embassy, Ambassador White and his consul, Patricia Lasbury, had reacted within moments of receiving Paul's call. Lasbury, who had frequent dealings with the commander of the National Police, Colonel López Nuila, called him now to report that the women were missing. White meanwhile placed a personal call to the minister of defense, Colonel Guillermo García, to request that he immediately send out an all-points alert for a white Toyota minibus and two, possibly four, missing American churchwomen.

It was early in the afternoon when Pat Lasbury spoke to López Nuila. Her memory of their conversation is quite specific. In particular she found it disconcerting that the colonel spent so much time questioning her about the women's dress. Were they wearing their nun's habits, he inquired? She told him that in all likelihood they would have been wearing something very simple—a blouse and skirt, or maybe jeans. She was puzzled by his reaction. It was, she later thought, almost as though he had some quite specific reason for not wanting to accept, or believe, her description. In fact, she found herself in an unreal argument over something that she knew he had to be perfectly aware of. American missionaries in El Salvador had long since abandoned wearing the traditional religious habits.

Later, Colonel López Nuila would deny that he had ever spoken to her. "Yes, there was a call," he remembered. "Some low-level embassy functionary. . . . But not at two o'clock—much later in the day. Just a routine call to report a stolen or missing vehicle . . ."

It was four o'clock in La Libertad, and still the phone call to Nicaragua had not come through. Frustrated by not knowing whether they were looking for two or four of their friends, Chris Rody and Sister Elizabeth Kockik, who worked with the refugee children in Zaragoza, decided to drive to the airport and find out for themselves whether anyone among the personnel in the airport or the airline offices might have any information. Maybe they could persuade someone to let them look at the manifest for last night's flight from Nicaragua. Or maybe someone would remember seeing the women in the airport the night before.

From La Libertad to the airport is a distance of about five miles. The road, a new one, turns inland from the coast and runs in long straight stretches through some of the largest cotton and sugar cane estates in the valley. The sun was in their back, casting long shadows along the road ahead of them, as Chris and Elizabeth, speeding along an open, straight stretch of the road about three-quarters of a mile from the airport, came upon the wreck of a vehicle abandoned on the opposite side of the road, facing back toward La Libertad. There was not a great deal left of the vehicle—no tires, no windows—but something about the shape caught their attention. "Stop!" said Chris. "I think that's our van."

It was a disturbing sight. The familiar battered form of a Toyota minibus, the white paint blackened, charred and peeling, standing on the rims of the wheels, reduced to a burned-out hulk. They forced themselves to stop, get out, and check it. Only there was literally nothing left to check. No license plate, no tools. Maybe, they thought, if it's ours we'll recognize a flashlight or something in the glove compartment. But there was no glove compartment —no steering wheel, no dashboard—nothing. Not a shred of anything flammable remained. Only the dents in the fenders looked vaguely familiar. And there was a streak of red paint on the front left fender that was new. Stunned and confused, almost certain that this desolate and ravished wreck was all that remained of the white van in which Jean and Dorothy had been traveling when last seen, they resumed their drive to the airport in silence.

The International Airport in San Salvador is a military installation, and as such it is heavily policed at all times by members of the National Guard. Wearing combat fatigues and armed with M-16 submachine guns or the regulation G-3 rifles, their presence around the parking area, at the toll booth, inside the customs and immigration halls and in the terminal lounges conveys an instant message to all new arrivals. For Chris and Elizabeth, who had long since trained themselves to ignore these constant intimations of menace, the sight of the guardsmen lounging around the airport terminal was of little interest. In the search for their friends, the last people to whom they would turn for help were the official security forces.

As they approached the desk of the TACA airline office they realized that it was exactly twenty-four hours since Jean and Dorothy should have arrived here to meet Maura and Ita. Politely, methodically, they made their way among the baggage handlers and ticket salesmen, showing snapshots of their missing friends to any who would listen to their story. Within a short time they had their answer. "The two blonds? The *gringas* with the white van?" Yes, he remembered them. The baggage handler was positive. He saw them park their van. Would they like him to show them where they left it? Just out there, near the curb. And this other one, Chris wanted to know, showing him a picture of Ita. "The dark one? Very little, like a boy? But of course, she came off the flight with another, older lady with glasses. . . ."

They drove back through the dusk to La Libertad to let Paul know that he could now forget about the call to Nicaragua. Approaching the site of the wrecked van, they observed a couple of police cars parked in the vicinity. Several plainclothes policemen, carrying submachine guns and wearing flak jackets were inspecting the vehicle. They did not stop.

That night in La Libertad Chris, Elizabeth, Paul, Ken, and Maddie and Terri, who had come from Santa Ana to be with them, tried hard to keep up their spirits. No one quite believed the optimistic scenarios they kept making up for themselves and each other. Paul thought it was a good sign that all the missing women's belongings had been stolen. "When people disappear without their belongings there's no hope . . . but when the belongings disappear with them, then they sometimes turn up in jail. . . ." At seven o'clock the National Guard sent for Paul to come and help identify the van. Taking the engine number along with him, Paul was able to confirm the identification.

"Wednesday night," Chris remembers, "as we were sitting around the table we were thinking, Gee, this is the second night that they're missing. . . . We started to try and perk up our own spirits by saying, 'Well, this will be a great story for Jean's repertoire . . . this will be her new favorite. . . .' " The phone kept ringing late into the night, but the fleeting stabs of hope that accompanied every call quickly evaporated. All night long, the embassy, the archbishop, the press—everyone was seeking information, but no one had any to give.

At five the next morning (Thursday, December 4) Paul said mass. In the crowded church the mood of the congregation was somber, tense. At six o'clock, the leader of the Christian Democrats and leading civilian in the ruling junta, José Napoleón Duarte, called to say that he had the personal word of the minister of defense, Colonel García, that every post and unit of the police and National Guard throughout the province was on an all-points alert, searching for any clue to the disappearance of the women. At six-thirty A.M. the ambassador called to tell Paul that he was on his way to an early breakfast meeting with a group of Canadian clergy who had arrived at the airport Tuesday night to attend the big funeral of the opposition leaders. They had contacted him to ask for a private meeting because they thought that they had information that might be helpful. For the first time, spirits in the little house in La Libertad rose. The ambassador promised to report back after his meeting.

Shortly after his conversation with the ambassador, Paul set out to accompany a patrol of the local National Guard in La Libertad on an investigation among the migrant workers who lived closest to the site of the burned-out van. It was a fruitless expedition. Terrified by the presence of the guards, the shack dwellers denied that they had seen, heard, or knew anything. Angered by the futility of this line of inquiry, Paul, accompanied by a Salvadoran priest, set off to ask questions of his own, closer to home.

The station of the Treasury Police at San Luis Tapla, located only three miles from the site of the wreck, was, Paul knew, officially responsible for security in the vicinity of the airport. They were also responsible for a recent series of particularly violent security sweeps in the area including a number of brutal killings among his parishioners. Nevertheless, in view of Duarte's recent assurances, when he walked into the station at eight-thirty that morning, requesting the latest information on the case, his reception by the overweight, sleepy-eyed commander took him by surprise. Women? What women? A destroyed vehicle? Where? An all-points alert ordered by Colonel García? Surely the Padre must be mistaken. . . . Of course they would look into it. . . . As Paul turned on his heel to leave, he overheard the commander demanding radio contact with headquarters in San Salvador to check out his story. Then, on his way out, something caught Paul's eye. Facing him as he walked back onto the street, parked immediately across from the station entrance, was a brand-new, red pickup truck, of the same color as the streak of fresh paint they had noticed on the fender of the wrecked minibus.

In the coffee shop of the Hotel Camino Real in San Salvador, the breakfast meeting between Ambassador White and the members of the Canadian delegation was coming to an end. Their leader, Father Greg Chisholm, had described to White how their group had been stopped by a roadblock on the road leading from the airport Tuesday night between six-thirty and seven o'clock. Unfamiliar with the uniforms of the diverse groups in the Salvadoran security forces, Chisholm did not know whether the roadblock belonged to the army, the National Guard or the police. What he did know was that they had all been ordered out of their cars and searched, and that particular attention had been paid to the women. "It was," said Chisholm, "as though they were looking for somebody." The officer in charge had wanted to retain the women for questioning, but had relented when the men categorically refused to continue on their way without them. The Canadians described how they had all chatted with Maura and Ita in the customs hall while they waited together for their bags. They had offered the women a lift into town, but the Sisters told them they were expecting to be met by friends. Chisholm estimated that he must have left the airport that evening not more than fifteen or twenty minutes ahead of the women's van.

It was nine-thirty. Across town in the Convent of the Assumption, Heather Foote, who on hearing of the disappearance of the women had postponed her departure after the big funeral the day before, was on the phone speaking to a Maryknoll Sister in Washington when a Salvadoran priest handed her a scrap of paper with a penciled message scrawled in Spanish. *"Se han encontrado los cuerpos de quatro mujeres llevando sandalias,"* she read.* "What does this mean?" she asked. "It means," the

* (The bodies of four women wearing sandals have been found.)

priest replied, "that these are probably your friends." Very few Salvadoran women, he explained, own a pair of sandals.

It was close to noon before anyone was able to reach La Libertad on the phone. When the call finally came it was the international operator who succeeded in making the first contact. Chris Rody has total recall of what happened when the phone rang: "It's like engraven on my memory, you know, everybody, where they were standing, what was happening. I was standing by the table and Father Ken Myers from Zaragoza was sitting at right angles to me at the table, and he picked up the phone, and he looked up at me and covered the mouthpiece and said, 'It's a call from Washington!' And I said, 'From Washington?' And he said, 'Yes.' And then he got real solemn and still, and he just sat there real quiet; of course everybody in the whole room got real quiet and we all fixed upon him—and he looked up at me and he said, 'Was one of them wearing sandals?' And I remembered the last time I saw them they had been wearing sandals, because I was going to tease Dorothy about wearing sandals to the embassy that Monday night. And I said, 'Yes, I know for sure that Dorothy was.' And he didn't say more to me, or to the telephone, he just said thank you and hung up; and he looked up and he said, 'They've found four bodies . . . four women's bodies, and they look like North Americans.' "

CHAPTER II

Growing Up American:
1953–1972

There was no one, I would say, for whom life was more sweet than Jean Donovan. She was a totally human person. She lived life to the hilt. She lived through the whole university scene in the States, and here in Ireland too —she knew everything about it—all the questioning and the confusion, the drink scene, the dope scene . . . the whole thing. But that's not the point. The point is, that when she left that scene, when she left the world, the society that she was educated to play a role in—and when she was asked to play her hand of cards her way—to say something that she personally was convinced of for the poor of South America, she did it in her own unique way.
—Father Michael Crowley,
     mentor and friend, Cork City, Ireland

SHE WAS BORN AT SEVEN MONTHS—AN ACHIEVEMENT FOR which she took full credit, insisting that she was so anxious to be out in the world, alive and kicking and making her mark, that it was simply not bearable to sit around any longer cooped up in her mother's womb. But then Jean Donovan was always a young woman in a hurry. Rushing headlong into life with all the overconfidence of a much loved, much indulged and privileged child. Open, curious, avid for experience, hungry for exposure to all those other worlds that lay beyond the confines of her own, inherited environment.

There were, of course, other darker dimensions to her personality that for much of her short life she worked hard to conceal, for they were not the stuff of which American success stories are made, rather the reverse—characteristics such as vulnerability, insecurity and neediness were not acceptable to Jean. But she was very bright and learned fast how to protect these weaknesses by projecting their mirror image—brashness, recklessness and a fierce spirit of competitiveness.

Part German, three-quarters Irish, Jean Donovan's family history seems a typical American immigrant success story. It was a history of which Jean was inordinately proud and felt intimately connected to in every detail.

In the family album a faded brown photograph of her great-grandmother shows a slim young German girl with braided hair and a shy smile standing on the shore at Ellis Island. Her few possessions are gathered in bundles at her feet. She is sixteen years old, speaks no English, and has made the journey to this country in the spring of 1898 quite alone. The softness in her expression belies the strength and courage that must have sustained her on this voyage and that would see her through the hard and lonely times ahead. On arrival in the United States she carried in her purse a letter of engagement from an American woman, in whose Brooklyn establishment she would spend the next two years as a cook. In exchange for her labor she received board, lodging and English lessons. Within two years she had married a German-speaking immigrant like herself. Johann Hefli was a butcher who had come from Zurich and practiced his trade in one of the largest slaughter houses in Brooklyn. They had four children, one of whom, their second daughter Marie, would break away from her German background to marry a member of an entirely foreign breed.

Jean's grandfather, Jay Murphy, American-born only son of Irish Catholic immigrant parents, was an ensign in the American Navy when he and Marie Hefli met on a blind date while his ship was docked in the Brooklyn Navy Yard shortly after the end of the First World War. Resplendent in his naval uniform, his photo shows an exceptionally handsome young man with hard, chiseled features. The smile flashes Irish charm, but the look in his eyes says, "handle with care."

Marie Hefli was twenty-one when she and Jay Murphy were married on the fourth of July 1923. Jay was five years older than his wife. He had parlayed his service in the navy into a degree in electrical engineering at Cooper Union in New York, but business, not engineering, was to be his field. On leaving college he went to work as a hosiery salesman for the Brooklyn-based firm of Julius Kayser and Company. It was the beginning of a lifelong association that would make both him and the company very rich. In spite of the Depression, in spite of Roosevelt (whom he detested) and the New Deal (which he despised)—"He was an archconservative," says his son, "he never could abide that socialistic kind of thinking. He used to rail that while American businessmen were putting money in the bank through the front door, Roosevelt and his cronies were taking it out the back" —in spite of all this the business career of Jay Murphy, Sr., never faltered.

There are two formal portraits taken for publicity purposes at the time Jay Murphy became president of Christian Dior Hosiery. Both the pose and the expression are decidedly smug. The hard, rakish good looks of the naval ensign have become blurred, coarsened by success. The eyes have developed a calculating shrewdness that masks the hungry ambition of the younger man. Certainly, at fifty, Jay Murphy had every reason to be pleased with himself. His native Irish wit, allied to his drive and a capacity for obsessive and exclusive concentration on his business affairs, had brought him wealth, corporate recognition and political clout within Republican party circles in New York.

He was also a patriarch. Many years after his death while in retirement in Key Biscayne, Jay Murphy's grandson, Michael Donovan, recalls that on one terrible December night, as he hung up the telephone after receiving word of the mysterious disappearance of his sister somewhere in far-off El Salvador, there flashed into his mind the image of the cigar-smoking, backslapping powerhouse of a man who was his maternal grandfather—a man who knew all the important Republican politicians by their first names; a man who would not have stopped twisting arms until he had the White House on the telephone. For within his own family circle, Jay was a legend, and invincible.

The girl in the next picture is twenty-three years old, and it is her wedding day, date 1947. She stands with her back to the elaborate marble fireplace in her father's New York home in St. Albans, Queens. The pose is a traditional one, the photographer is Bachrach, most popular chronicler of the contemporary New York social scene. Her gown is ivory and it sets off the glow of her complexion. Her veil, of Alsatian lace, is a hundred and fifty years old and was brought to this country by her maternal grandmother almost fifty years ago.

Patricia Murphy, the beautiful and willful only daughter of Jay and Marie, faces the camera radiant with expectation. For on this October day she is about to leave her father's house to marry an unknown young Irish engineer from Cleveland, Ohio. They had met six months before at a fashionable ski resort in Massachusetts, and in keeping with the contemporary fashions in love and courtship, their romance had moved with speed down a straight line to the altar. Raymond Donovan, son of the yardmaster on the Nickel Plate Railroad in Cleveland, was handsome, carefree and easygoing. At twenty-nine, just out of the service with a degree in engineering, he had plenty of self-confidence in his ability to make money and a career in the new field of aeronautics. In that spring of '47, dazzled by Pat's beauty and style, he had proposed on their first date.

Thirty-four years later, Patricia and Raymond Donovan sit beside each other reviewing the photographs of their wedding:

> SHE: It was an exceptionally beautiful warm
> sunny day for the middle of October.
> HE: Yes, it was a really gorgeous day. Bright
> blue sky . . .

The record of that October day, in all its lighthearted gaiety, has been flawlessly preserved. "That's you pushing cake into my mouth," says Pat. "Throwing the bouquet. . . . That's the traditional picture, looking back through the window of the car. Everyone had a picture like that in those days."

The reception at the old Garden City Hotel in Garden City, Long Island, had been a lavish affair. By the time that Mrs. Murphy and Mrs. Donovan had each drawn up their guest lists, there were over four hundred people to be invited. A champagne bar, dancing to two bands, Jay Murphy, Sr., standing tall in tails, with a glass of champagne in one hand and a cigar in the other . . .

> SHE: I was just twenty-three.
> HE: And I was—was I younger than you?
> SHE: You were twenty-nine.
> HE: Oh. Well, I guess not.

They both laugh. Humor plays a large part in the Donovan's marriage, as does a shared attachment to the moral values of an earlier, less ambiguous time. Looking

back today, from the vantage point of the eighties, Raymond
and Patricia Donovan recall the dream that inspired and
sustained their union:

> SHE: We wanted a big family. We were both
> crazy about children, and we expected
> to have about six. I used to think about
> babies and little children. I never got to
> the adult part.
>
> HE: We weren't thinking about President of
> the United States or anything like that.
> Just normal, healthy children with good
> moral judgment. A good family life. Like
> regular people.

Pat gathers up the wedding photographs. "The world
looked awfully good in 1947," she sighs. "We'd just won the
war, solved all our problems," Ray agrees. "You just could
not envision your children getting involved in anything bad
back then. Everything looked very up. Very upbeat. It was
a good time to think of bringing children into the world."

The pictorial record of life in the Donovan family begins with snapshots from the summer of 1951. Pat, beautiful
as ever, a glowing young mother in a deck chair, holds a
new baby in her lap. Ray, shirt-sleeves rolled up, looking
lean, sunburned and very Irish, carries his son—Michael
Raymond—in is arms after a day at the beach. "He didn't
have a job when the baby was born," Pat explains, "so he
made the most of it—working on his designs at night, and
spending plenty of beachtime with the baby. He really got to
know his son very well that summer."

And then there was Jean.

Her story begins in Westport, Connecticut. There, in a
traditional ranch house at 55 Woodside Drive, set amid
flowering dogwoods and tall shade trees, Jean and her older
brother, Michael, had a childhood that was straight out of
the mainstream American dream. Echoes of that childhood
linger still in the snapshots collected in their hundreds in

family albums and in the framed photographs that cover almost every available space of open shelving in the living room in Sarasota, Florida, where Raymond and Patricia Donovan now live. Patricia Donovan picks up a black-and-white photograph of a little girl in a white frilly dress and curly blond hair, seated on the ground in earnest conversation with a good-looking older boy. The inscription reads: Wells Studio, Westport, 1954. "She was just a little over a year then and Michael was three. It's a typical pose. She's already telling him what she thinks he ought to do. Like all kids they had their fights. They teased one another. But God help the person who took off after the other one. If somebody went after Jean, Mike would be after him, and the other way around. Only they could yell at one another. Nobody else could."

Mike and Jeannie. Older brother, kid sister. Devoted, competitive and intense, their relationship was to be extremely important to both of them. According to their mother, sibling rivalry while they were growing up worked in their favor. "Michael was exceptionally bright and did awfully well in school, while Jeannie was very athletic; but Michael wouldn't let Jeannie get ahead of him, so he made himself into an athlete too, a good one; while Jeannie couldn't stand Mike having all the A's so she would knock herself out at the books until she got A's too."

Michael was twenty years old and a college track star when it was discovered that he had Hodgkins disease. "Jean really came apart at the seams when she heard about it," her mother says. Her brother's close brush with death had a profound effect on Jean; her innate seriousness was stirred for the first time. When Michael fell ill, he was a senior at the University of Pennsylvania in Philadelphia, while Jean was in her freshman year at Mary Washington College, the women's division of the campus at the University of Virginia in Fredericksburg. Every other weekend she would travel to Philadelphia where Michael was undergoing painful chemotherapy treatment to be with him. "I think she was down to see him even more often than we were," her mother recalls.

This quality of mutual protectiveness was a powerful element in their relationship from the beginning. In the earliest childhood pictures in the family album, Michael, the quiet, studious one, something of a loner, an observer of the scene, maintains a careful, protective gaze upon this strange new sister, whose flamboyant temperament is destined to be so different from his own. For her part Jean was always rushing headlong to catch up—assertive, boisterous, fiercely independent. "DO BY SELF," says her father, were the first words he ever heard her put together. "She was a tomboy," he explains. "Always climbing trees, falling out of trees. We were constantly rushing to the hospital because she was always in some emergency." She was also always taking center stage, with a mischievous mix of exhibitionism and sheer devilment that would frequently antagonize and charm people in the same, exasperating moment. Those who knew and loved her best claim she never lost that childish habit—nor the confusing capacity that went with it of provoking both hostility and affection in the same breath.

Jean was five years old when she developed her first passion. His name was Irish Lad, and he was a large, fat, rather lazy, palomino horse that belonged to a local riding school. A housing development now stands where the riding school used to be, but the Fairfield County Hunt Club, with its manicured pastures and brightly painted show fences, its wealthy membership dedicated to the scrupulous preservation of all the outward forms of dress and presentation, flourishes still. On any Saturday afternoon, from a vantage point on the road beside a sign that reads, "Keep Out— Private," you can still observe their stylized rituals.

Into this world—competitive, traditional, conformist —Jean in tandem with Irish Lad rode to conquer. There was never any doubt in her own or anybody else's mind that she had a way with horses, and for the better part of the next fourteen years they would occupy her energies, her talents, her time and her devotion. Today, the photos and the trophies displayed in Pat and Ray's living room furnish a solid record of her daring and skill.

Jean grew up during the sixties. In the larger world, beyond the confines of the riding school and the secure, ordered existence of the family circle at 55 Woodside Drive, the America into which she had been born in 1953 was no more. The campaigns for civil rights in the South, the urban despair that exploded into riots in the ghettos of the northern cities, three major political assassinations and the debate over the Vietnam War—all this and more had demolished the complacency of the country's prevailing self-image during the Eisenhower years.

To the inhabitants of the insulated, sheltered world of Westport, Connecticut, however, the new America being formed in pain and turmoil represented a foreign, essentially hostile environment, whose most turbulent manifestations of upheaval and dissent it was tempting to dismiss as a temporary aberration, to be observed and criticized from the safe distance of the living room television screen. Jean's father was doing very well. In 1963 the family had moved from the ranch house on Woodside Drive to an impressive, four-bedroom mansion, standing on one and a half acres of its own land. Now an executive at United Technologies, Ray Donovan and his colleagues were kept busy by the Vietnam War, designing and producing Huey helicopters at the Sikorsky plant just down the road in Stratford.

As a family, Ray and Pat sustained particularly warm, close-knit relationships with their children. Whenever they went away for vacations, they took the kids along as a matter of course. "In fact we probably took the dog most of the time," Ray says. Since the existence of good schools is one of the features of life in Westport, both of the children attended public elementary and high schools where Pat Donovan played an active support role in all of their extracurricular activities. "I think we had the most fun as a family, the four of us, in their high school years," she says. "I hated to see high school end. Jean and Michael were both very active in school; they got involved in things that we could participate in—even if it was just as spectators. We were always up at the crack of dawn for some reason, for a horse show or a track meet. Everything had to start at four in the morning for some reason, but as much as we all complained about it, I think that's the part of our lives we'd like to live over again."

The fact that they were practicing Catholics, who never failed to attend mass on Sundays and feast days, undoubtedly affected the moral climate and contributed to the sense of obligations that the children absorbed throughout their childhood. "A Catholic child," says their mother, "discovers early on that when, for example, you go away, on vacation or wherever, there is always another church waiting for you. A Catholic child notices and feels that they do have certain changeless obligations from a very young age." From the perspective of the Donovan family, religion was simply a part of life with certain rules and regulations which were neither questioned nor much dwelt upon. Ray was a regular reader at the church; the parish priest was a good family friend; but there was nothing overtly religious about the family atmosphere. "There was nothing out of the ordinary about our family," Michael Donovan insists. "We were not unusual in any way."

Nevertheless, something about growing up as a child within the Catholic tradition had a profound influence on Jean's subsequent development. For Catholics the universality of their religion creates a link to something older and larger than themselves. For Jean, who as a small child took the routine regulations governing the practice of her religion with an unquestioning seriousness and commitment, as she grew older, her membership in the Catholic Church provided the means whereby she was able to open the door to ideas and concepts that extended beyond the social and professional norms by which her family and friends lived.

During their formative years, the strongest influence on both of the children undoubtedly came from the expectations of their parents. "I don't think we ever sat down and lectured them," Ray says, "but we didn't have any dissension in the ranks either." Pat agrees. "We were lucky. They very definitely got the message that as long as they lived at home they did things our way. Once they were old enough to support themselves they could change if they wanted to."

In an age of acute generational conflict they never rebelled—at least not overtly. When Michael went away to college he did manage to horrify his mother's relations by becoming the first member of the Murphy clan to vote Democratic in the 1972 congressional elections, but his defection was short-lived. As for Jean, her earliest strivings toward independence took the conventional route—clashes with her mother over dress and appearance and a general distaste for anything that resembled formal or ladylike behavior. As a teenager, grubby fingernails, unwashed jeans and a weight problem all contributed to a rejection of the glamorous image that Patricia Donovan's only daughter could have been expected to fulfill. But the bonds of family loyalty were immensely strong, and much of Jean's early struggle to establish her own identity shuttled between an overdependence on her parents, with all of the yearning to maintain their approval which this implied, and her own at times frantic efforts to acquire independence.

Jean's hunger for life ran counter on many levels to the accommodations and compromises inherent in her family's comfortable, mainstream life-style. Inevitably, this clash of opposing needs became one of the central conflicts of her young adult years. It led to the development of a striking, idiosyncratic personality, full of rough edges and disarming vulnerabilities. There could be no easy resolution to a struggle in which her emotions were so deeply engaged and divided. For while she never fitted comfortably into the culture to which she belonged by virtue of her inheritance and her upbringing, she also never lost a deep and abiding love and respect for her parents. She retained also a strong sense of connection to the members of her extended Murphy-Donovan family—grandparents, uncles and cousins—by most of whom she was ultimately perceived as something of a beloved maverick.

As a child, this nascent conflict was easily sublimated through her addiction to horses. Her parents encouraged and supported her passion, and the riding school at Fiddle Horse Farm, where under the careful instruction of the owner, Susie de Palmer, Jean developed into a star performer on the show circuit, became virtually her second home. Horses not only provided Jean with a private world of her own where the tomboy and risk-taker could legitimately dominate and excel, they also, as she grew older, afforded a safer, more comfortable background for social life than her everyday surroundings.

Fred Taylor was Jean's first romance. He still lives in Westport, where he is now married and works in a printing firm. He and Jean got to know one another at the riding school where Jean worked after school and on weekends, cleaning the riding gear and straightening out the barns in return for extra riding lessons. "She was twelve and I was fifteen," Fred remembers. "I was working as a groom at the stable where Jean was riding. My older sister taught horseback riding there, and Jean ran all the girls at the barn. Told them what to do and how to do it . . . they were almost like her troops. She was a very strong-willed young girl." The tack room was Jean's domain, and she organized it and ran it, and ran the kids who used it, too, with a ferocious efficiency.

At the age of twelve Jean didn't have much time for boys or dances, and she certainly did not enjoy dressing up for formal occasions. But her mother was a sponsor of the Cranberry Ball at Staples High School, which was not only a formal dance, it was also a Sadie Hawkins affair, which put pressure on the girls to invite "a boyfriend." And Jean didn't have one. "She asked my older sister if I would go, and my older sister asked me. I said yes. I liked Jeannie. She was a good kid. And it was nice to go to a dance where one of the parents of your date was the main sponsor of the dance—that made you in with the in crowd." So Fred Taylor took Jean to her first dance and they became buddies.

Later, when Jean was about sixteen, they began dating. "We were now boyfriend and girlfriend. She still bullied everyone around her except myself. It's hard to put into words what Jean was like. She was different. She was strong-willed . . . but she was also shy. I think being strong-willed was to cover the shyness. I liked going out with Jeannie because she did run everything around her. She was so in control of everything. That was nice. I could relax."

The romance with Fred lasted only until Jean went away to college, for Fred found that allowing Jean to run the show had its drawbacks. "She had definite ideas of what I should be doing and what I should be earning. I should be making $10,000 a year before we got engaged, and I should be getting a position in the corporate chain of command where I would be advanced on my abilities. Her father had done so. Her father was extremely successful, and she admired him greatly and wanted the same thing for me. I felt that eventually Jean would take over my life." So the life which at eighteen Jean had mapped out for herself, as the wife of a successful business executive, living in Westport, Connecticut, and raising children and horses, was not to be hers. Fred married someone else.

This was her first defeat, but no one was supposed to see the hurt. One of Jean's closest riding-school companions, who had been locked in a constant power struggle with her for ten years, recalls how complicated it was to have a close friendship with Jean during those high school years. "You didn't ever know how much she really needed somebody. You'd say to yourself, 'Well, Jean always muddles through. She's got all the support she needs, just in herself.' I didn't think she'd ever get married because she was so strong. She probably drove some people away that she might have preferred not to—I know that hurt her in her relationship with Fred. When she lost Fred, even then she responded with toughness. She didn't cry, or break down or anything. She responded by being very nonchalant about it. But it was so obviously fake. At the time I sort of interpreted it as, well, Jeannie missed a conquest—because she was into conquests.

But then when I thought about it, she had genuine feelings for Fred—and that was the first time I saw that she was really hurt."

During this same period, while so many of her contemporaries were being consumed in the fever of commitment and protests against United States policies in Vietnam, Jean was leading the Girl Scouts every year in the local Westport Memorial Day parade. A friend recalls the contempt with which she refused the suggestion that they attend a major antiwar march and rally in New York City in the late sixties. The whole idea of a concerned, dissident citizenry was one that she dismissed as "dumb" and "unproductive," if not outright treacherous. One of her riding-school friends recalls how distant from their concerns was the national debate over Vietnam. "The war didn't affect people here as much as maybe other people, because guys here beat the draft. I mean, I don't know anybody in my circle of friends, and in my husband's circle of friends, that went, that ever had to go to Vietnam. They got student deferments, they got medical discharges—they'd find some way and they didn't go. So it didn't touch home. . . . People protesting the war were— they wore the jeans and the flowers in their hair and all that kind of stuff—they were unproductive people. For Jean, that would be the main thing."

After 1968 Richard Nixon was in the White House, and Jean's parents, and the parents of most of the people she knew, liked, trusted and supported him. Her parents, and the majority of their friends nourished their world view in the pages of the *Reader's Digest,* the *National Geographic,* and *Time* magazine. It was a traditional view that depended on an unshakable belief in the correct and ethical behavior of all those who held high public office in the service of the nation, most particularly if they belonged to the Republican party. The enemy was "international communism," and while this hydraheaded monster might appear in a hundred guises and disguises, there was never any doubt about its consistently malevolent intentions. In fact, doubt of any kind was not encouraged inside the white middle-class stockade that was Westport in 1970.

Within this oasis of calm, uniformity and prosperity— where everyone had money, property and prospects; where the draft board posed no threat to the members of the graduating class at Staples High School; where almost everyone went to church on Sunday and voted Republican at election time—Jean and Michael grew up in a time capsule, a cultural womb, within whose homogenous ethic the value system of the 1950s prevailed largely unchallenged.

Suddenly, with the onset of college, all of this changed. Michael had left two years earlier to attend the University of Pennsylvania in Philadelphia. Now, in the fall of 1971, at the age of eighteen, it was Jean's turn to leave home for the first time. Her father had long since tired of the daily commute to his job at the Sikorsky factory in Stratford, and no sooner were both of the children out of high school than he and Pat sold their Westport house and moved to a condominium in Stratford that was equally convenient to Ray's office and the Stratford golf club. Thus, after a lifetime in one relatively small town, Jean's future now lay open before her full of questions, possibilities and uncertainties. At eighteen she had no idea what she wanted to do with her life. Her choice of schools had more to do with access to horses and riding than to the pursuit of intellectual stimulation. Mary Washington College is situated at Fredericksburg in the heart of Virginia hunting country, and the campus had its own riding school where Jean quickly found herself a job helping out with the beginners. But the lack of direction in her life bothered her. She talked vaguely to some of her friends about studying preveterinary medicine, an idea that had been floating around in the back of her head ever since she was a very small child and had first fallen in love with the family dog. But she took no steps to pursue it.

Then, two years later, Michael's ability to nail down a highly paid job as an accountant immediately upon graduating made a big impression on Jean, and she decided to follow his example and major in economics. At this point in her life, creating a successful business career for herself became synonymous with acquiring the independence that she craved. Competing in a largely male profession, and acquiring status and financial security in the corporate world, appeared to her to offer the fastest, most concrete method of establishing her credentials as a liberated, self-directed woman in control of her own destiny and life-style.

CHAPTER III

The Road to Salvador:

1972-1979

*There was no way she could foresee the kind
of calling which was hers. And there's no other
word for it. I think she had heard some kind of
calling, an idealism in her own life that she had
to live out. That's why she said about South
America, the only crime here in Salvador is
being young. What she meant by being young
was having a young view of the way life could
be if we only had the courage to make it so.
She was an idealist, she believed in justice, she
believed in her Christianity, and she amazed
herself when she tried to live it and lived it to
the full.*
—Father Michael Crowley

DURING THE CHRISTMAS SEASON OF 1977–78, THE CLEVE-
land branch of the national accounting firm of Arthur
Anderson and Son held an office party in a downtown hotel.
It was the usual rowdy affair, and the climax of the evening
turned out to be the drawing of a lottery in which the first
prize consisted of a trip for two to Spain. When the winning
ticket was announced, the flushed young woman who leaped
to her feet to claim the prize was one of the youngest and
newest executives in the company. It was Jean Donovan,
and she had joined Arthur Anderson as a management
consultant just three months before.

In that New Year of 1977, Jean was twenty-four years
old. She had a master's in economics from Case Western
Reserve University; an executive position at $20,000 a year
with the largest accounting firm in the nation; her own
automobile parked in the garage of her own apartment,
overlooking the lake on Cleveland's "Gold Coast"; and—
her greatest joy and prize possession—her own Harley
Davidson motorcycle on which she dearly loved to shock
and impress friends and acquaintances as she raced the
traffic on Cleveland's fly-overs, or weaved in and out of the
rush-hour morass on her way to and from her downtown
office. In short, Jean Donovan seemed to have achieved the
good life at a very young age, and her gregarious, fun-
loving personality gave every indication that she was enjoying to the hilt the rewards that went with her success.

Yet now, on this night of official good cheer and personal triumph, as she stood amid the catcalls and the
whistles, the streamers and the funny hats, gazing out from
the raised dais across the ballroom of the Sheraton Hotel,
she was struck with a secret impulse. The following day she
made arrangements with her boss to take an immediate two-
week vacation, cashed in the ticket to Spain and booked a
flight to Ireland.

Later, when Jean's family and friends looked back
over her life, trying to find clues that might help them

understand why she had decided to go to El Salvador in the first place, their search always led back to Ireland. She was twenty years old and in her junior year at Mary Washington College when she went the first time to attend the University of the City of Cork as a foreign exchange student. She arrived in Cork determined to live it up in the style to which she was accustomed. A fellow student vividly remembers her first sight of Jean at Shannon Airport, an English saddle slung across one shoulder and her golf bags on the other, yelling for a taxi to drive the eighty odd miles from the airport to Cork City.

Cork didn't turn out to be anything she had expected. In fact, at first the culture shock was disorienting. "I can't help complaining but they just don't seem to do anything over here as well as they do at home," she wrote in dismay to her parents, after the local cleaners had virtually wrecked her fur coat. The university administration had made arrangements for the American students to live in digs in lower-middle-class homes situated in one of the new real estate developments on the outskirts of the city. The typical Irish household consisted of the parents and their four to six children, and the typical house was a two-story building with two bedrooms, one bathroom, a front parlor normally reserved only for entertaining on special occasions (first communions, wakes, anniversaries) and a living-dining room in the rear. Because these houses were new, some form of electrical heating had been built in but was seldom used.

Riverview Estates, as this particular development was called, had no view of the legendary River Lee, on whose estuary the beautiful, eighteenth-century city of Cork is built; the houses, which clung together in semiattached pairs, had been built at the farthermost southwestern edge of the suburbs, where they overlooked a bleak expanse of once-rich farmland that now lies fallow, patiently awaiting the next inevitable surge of development. Across this wasteland the houses of Riverview had no protection from the prevailing southwesterly wind which, with the onset of the equatorial storms in October, came howling in off the Atlantic, laden with mist and driving rain.

Into these already overcrowded and isolated houses came Jean and her companions to be squeezed three to a room (plus the saddle, golf clubs, trunks), fed traditional Irish meals served by shy, monosyllabic Irish children, who had been put to sleep on camp beds in the garage or the front parlor to make room for the paying guests. "They don't have any diet foods here," wailed Jean, who was always struggling with a weight problem. "Everything is bread, potatoes, sweets, fat meats, and creamy milk." Most distressing of all, they were stranded—far from the university, the pubs, the movies, the social life—without any private means of transportation.

It was a rough landing, from the land of horses and golf courses to the clammy cold reality of Riverview Estates, and some of the Americans never recovered from the initial shock—some went home within the first two weeks, all were often homesick—although Jean only acknowledged that she ever felt lonely or depressed long after she had recouped her good spirits. "Things are settling down here finally," she wrote to her parents. "For a while everything was a real mixup and I was sort of homesick, but I think I'm better now . . . we are starting to do more things (get into clubs/societies) . . . don't worry, I'm fine now."

She had acquired a bicycle and had started to make friends and go to parties, or "socials," as her Irish friends called them. At least the music was good, even if the men all congregated on one end of the room with the women at the other. "Irish boys," she wrote, "are very strange. It's not at all like home." Then one Monday night one of her new Irish friends invited her to a gathering of a student group known as the Legion of Mary at the house of an Irish priest called Michael Crowley. The Legion, Jean's friend Maura Corkery explained, was comprised of a group of students who tried to give some of their time each week doing something for someone who needed help. Father Crowley, Maura explained, always knew where there were people in trouble, and so he had formed this group of students who were willing to pitch in a few hours of their time every week to help out, and every Monday night members of the Legion would meet at his house and have a party. Someone would be assigned to keep the kettle on the boil for the endless pots of tea; someone else would bring cookies; someone a cake, or the thickly buttered Irish raisin bread known as Barm-Brack; by nine or ten o'clock in the evening there might be up to thirty or forty people crammed into the small front parlor of Michael Crowley's modest house on the edge of the university grounds.

The Irish love good talk and good music, and at Crowley's house they were assured of both. The talk would range from world politics to the fine points of the latest Ali-Frazer fight. The music was spontaneous and live, encouraged by the presence of an upright piano. Occasionally, Crowley himself would be prevailed upon to sing and then a spellbound silence would descend, as he sang in Irish a ballad out of the tortured Irish past, unaccompanied, filling the little room with a purity of tone and feeling.

Father Michael Crowley was no ordinary priest. At the time that Jean met him he had recently returned to Ireland after spending ten years living and working as a missionary in the slums of the city of Trujillo on the desert coast of Peru. Before that, during the fifties, he had ministered to the needs of the Latin community—largely Puerto Rican and Cuban—in East Harlem in New York City. Now, as chaplain to the foreign university students in his native city of Cork, he had a new and passionate mission: to share his personal experience of the devastating human tragedy of poverty in Latin America and to pass along to this new generation of students something of his own commitment.

In his ten years as a slum dweller in Peru, Father Crowley had witnessed the daily spectacle of mothers and small children "harvesting" at the city garbage dump for enough rotten pickings to stay alive, while in the neighboring ranches in the fertile foothills, the wealthy lived lives of elegant and extravagant idleness behind high fences and armed guards, and accused anyone who sought to change the living conditions of the poor of being "subversive" and "a Communist." Crowley's message was straightforward and eloquent. "We have to have," he would say, pacing restlessly up and down in front of a group of students, "a far more nuanced understanding of poverty. It is a terrible tragedy to see the world powers reading as communism what is in fact nothing more than the cry of the poor for justice. If the free West really wants to contain communism worldwide, then it must attack injustice. If the West were to declare war on poverty and eliminate poverty, communism would be dead, because no one would believe it. Christ," he continued, "dealt with it in very simple terms. He said, you behave equally to all men for my sake. And he said the truth will make people free." And then Crowley would pause, and as the intense blue eyes traveled from face to listening face, he would smile and add, "But you see, people don't like the truth, especially when it is a demanding truth, when it demands reform and it demands a redistribution of wealth."

He was a sophisticated man of wit and wisdom, compassion and charisma, with a profound and subtle knowledge of the human race and a generous embrace of the diversity of life. He was, finally, a man who enjoyed life and most especially enjoyed the company of young people. Jean had never met anyone remotely like him. "During my first stay in Ireland," she would write later, "I met a priest who has had a strong influence on my life. Father Michael Crowley and I became friends when I was trying to find direction in my life. I spent many long hours talking about different experiences with him. The one experience he related to me the most was concerning his time as a missionary in Peru. I had always wanted to talk to someone about missionary work, but didn't know any missionaries firsthand. Not only did he answer many of my questions concerning the value of missionary work, but additionally he helped me explain the calling I was feeling."

It was a calling and an interest that Jean had kept quite private until she met Crowley; but her encounter with him seems to have legitimized, for the first time, the uncertain, ambiguous sense of alienation that she had never previously been able to define.

"I remember her early days in college here in Cork when she came in '73–'74," Father Michael Crowley, now a parish priest of a large working-class district on the southern end of the city, said, recalling his days as a chaplain at the university. "When I first met Jean, she was like a cross section of American young people, I suppose, confused, searching for a meaning to her life. She was a conventional Catholic, if you will, but took it—you know —tongue-in-cheek, in the same way as so many Christians around the world. She practiced, if you like, but she really didn't have personalized a meaning for her own life."

What she did have was an eager, open and inquiring mind. "When we're young, young people are great," Crowley continues. "They're full of dreams, and they're optimists and idealists. She was herself. I often had bull sessions, as we called them, at the house, where we discussed the world's problems and challenged these young people that when you come out now, with a nice degree and a nice job, don't become a nice comfy capitalist. Feel it as your Christian duty to change the wrong structures around you. Try and improve the world."

It was a provocative, stimulating message, one that any young idealist would find hard to resist, and Jean, so recently shaken loose from the mooring of her own environment, was particularly susceptible. She joined the Legion. She started going with Maura Corkery to visit old people and sick people and young mental patients. They organized Christmas parties in the wards of the public mental health hospital and hot Meals on Wheels for those without the strength or resources to cook decently for themselves. And for the first time in her life her eyes were opened on a whole new world of poverty and need and loneliness. "If you stand with the poor," Crowley had said, "identify with them, feel their insecurity, their rejection, and so on, then you begin to understand the world in a new way." And as she became involved in the lives of the people who needed what she had to give—her spontaneous empathy, her humor and warmth, her energy and generosity—she forgot about the hardships of living without diet foods or the discomforts of an unheated house.

Years later she would write of this period of her life in Ireland that her time spent there had taught her that "while many of the conveniences Americans say they can't live without are nonexistent in Ireland, soon you realize they are not that important after all." What was important, what would stay with her for the rest of her life, was the discovery that, in a very different culture, a culture where material success was not yet the number one priority, other values were freer to predominate.

She also discovered in herself a rare gift: she truly cared about the trouble in other people's lives. "Jean was always very aware that there were people who suffered," says her friend Maura Corkery. "Sick people, hungry people, people who were poor. The more she found out about this reality the more uneasy she became. Even as a student she was always committed to doing something about it." Jean's empathy was so direct, so genuine, that she found she was capable of offering help; she had the ability to provide solace and joy. It was a heady and marvelous discovery. "Living in a foreign country can expand you beyond bounds imaginable," she wrote. She had stumbled across much that was new in this Irish life and yet it was also astonishingly familiar. It was as though, reaching back across three generations, she had uncovered the roots of her Irish heritage and found them still vigorous. "She often laughed and said that she had two homes," Maura Corkery recalls, "—the United States and Ireland."

During the first months after her arrival she wrote

constantly, sometimes daily, to her parents. These letters were full of questions and uncertainties, as she grappled with the anxiety created by her unaccustomed separation from their guidance. Then as she became more comfortable with this new transatlantic freedom, the intervals between her letters grew longer. Eventually, the letters became post-cards. In Ireland Jean began to grow up.

She was also starting to have a good time. "She laughed a lot," Maura remembers. "She loved life, she loved people. She was happy." Her friendship with Maura deepened into a true intimacy that would last for the rest of her life. Then, in spite of the lack of initiative of Irishmen, she fell head over heels in love with a medical student. Jean liked and needed to take the lead in her relationships with men. It was less scary that way, it kept her in control. Edward Fenton had the kind of dark good looks and the easygoing flirtatious charm that are not unusual among the "black Irish" of the southwest. Unfortunately for Jean he was also "taken." At the time that she met and developed a passion for him, his girlfriend was away studying in England, and Jean, always a risk-taker, ignored all warning signals and plunged into a relationship that was destined in the long run to bring her nothing but frustration and hurt. Nevertheless, her attraction to Fenton provided a heightened intensity to life and drew her into closer contact with local activities. Very quickly she became an integral part of a group of Irish students.

Ed Fenton and Maura Corkery and their friends accepted her as one of them. "She was a born extrovert," Ed Fenton explains, "she found it easy to relate to people. She was very intelligent, very fresh and very full of life—very interested in others and in different kinds of people; so she spent all her time with Irish people and partook of all their activities in and around town: visiting pubs, and going to the various places that played music—she used to go to the Opera House, and go on trips around. She played a very full part and enjoyed whatever was different here to what she was used to in the States."

By the New Year she and her roommates had abandoned the restrictive living arrangements in the Riverview Estates and moved to a little house of their own in the heart of the city, which they rented for seventy-five dollars a month. Number 47 Bandon Road was situated just up the street from a public house called the Silver Goblet, which quickly became a home away from home for the wandering Americans. A favorite feature of life at the Goblet was the live Irish music played there every weekend. When last drinks were called at eleven-thirty, the party would simply move up the road to Number 47 where it continued into the early hours. Many times, on a Sunday morning, Jean would quietly walk out on a party still in progress to catch the first mass, Father Crowley's mass, at the university chapel. Her religion was never something she made a big deal about, but she never missed Sunday mass, and no matter what shape she was in she would take herself off, hangover and all, to church. Sometimes Crowley would have compassion on the bedraggled blond head, struggling to stay awake through his sermon, and would invite her back to his house to share breakfast with him when the mass was over.

She continued to see a great deal of him on an easygoing, informal basis, and they had a good time in each other's company. He had one of the few television sets around, and she would drop by regularly to watch some sporting event and stay on for supper and long talks that would continue late into the night. He was also a frequent guest at Bandon Road, where Jean loved to entertain and show off her cooking skills. Very early in their relationship something about Michael Crowley inspired Jean to trust him—utterly. Unlike any other authority figure she had ever known, he was too secure and too wise to be shocked by any excessive behavior on her part.

For "do by self" Jean, who in spite of her determination to achieve control over her destiny had not yet managed to cut loose emotionally from the world of her family, Michael Crowley's expansive, tolerant approach to life bolstered her emerging sense of self and offered her the room she needed to grow. To listen to him, to watch him live, was inspiring. At the precise moment when she needed it, Jean had found a spiritual and intellectual mentor, a role model and a close friend, who took seriously her gropings in search of meaning in her life. When she needed to pour out her heart and soul, he listened with genuine interest. Nor did he come back with pat answers. He asked questions, probing, provocative questions that set up a dialogue both between the two of them and also inside herself. His definition of what it meant to live a truly Christian life was exciting and challenging—and also a bit scary. It offered an appealingly rigorous and compassionate view of the world, yet it ran counter to the self-involved, isolating and strictly individualistic ethic toward which the social influences of her upbringing and education to date had been directed. It implied a whole series of demands. At the logical end of the road it asked for a giving of herself.

Jean left Ireland reluctantly at the end of the school year in that summer of 1974 and came home to continue her studies, first at Mary Washington College, where upon graduation she was awarded an alumni scholarship for further study, then in Cleveland, her father's hometown, where she won a second scholarship from Case Western Reserve to study economics for an extra year. In 1976, armed with her master's, she began to look for work and that fall got the dream job for which her education and family history had prepared her. Her parents were proud and happy; her contemporaries were envious and impressed; she herself was enchanted. She had proven her competence; not for nothing was she Jay Murphy's granddaughter. Her father was even talking about setting her up in a business of her own. She was on top, in control, and on her way to a stellar career in business.

"We both liked to laugh a lot. We both liked to argue. We both liked to be right. We loved to argue with each other about anything, everything—books, religion, movies, music . . ." Colleen Kelly was Jean's first cousin and most intimate friend in Cleveland. When Jean got the job at Arthur Anderson and rented her fancy apartment in the ritziest complex on the shores of Lake Erie, Colleen moved in and shared it with her.

Jean and Colleen both liked to drink; they liked to go to bars together and celebrate their freedom and their brand-new sophistication. But Cleveland is a "no one under twenty-one" state and Colleen had no identification and looked about seventeen. Jean herself, big-shot executive in a major company and not yet twenty-four, didn't look much over eighteen, but she loved nothing better than to sweep into one of the smarter bars in Cleveland, take a seat at the counter and request—in slightly too loud a voice—"A Tanqueray martini with a twist please, very dry." Colleen recalls Jean's strategy for getting past the bouncer at the door. "I used to get terrified before we'd go into a bar and she'd say, 'No problem,' and we'd walk up and there'd be a bouncer at the door and he'd say, 'Can I see your I.D. please?' and she'd open up her wallet and hand him her MasterCharge and say, 'Does anyone you know under twenty-one carry one of these?' and they'd let us in. She'd say, 'She's with me.' And that was it. We never were barred out of anyplace, ever. She always could take control of a situation."

Being in control, projecting an aura of self-confidence and assurance was essential to Jean. The reality, however, was somewhat different. Throughout this period of her life she was actually painfully shy and lacking in confidence in her relationships with her peers, most especially with men. The sharp contrast between her sense of assurance as a professional and her personal insecurities regarding her appearance and her desirability as a woman was intensely troubling to her and resulted, most of the time, in a high level of overcompensation. "It used to drive me crazy," Colleen says, "because I knew if she'd just tone down her act a little she would have made it. She would have been accepted as herself. You don't have to be Farrah Fawcett or some gorgeous beauty to have somebody love you, but I think she did feel that. I don't think she thought she was pretty enough, or feminine enough. I don't think she felt desirable. But she would never say so."

At twenty-three she had not yet discovered that she was lovable for herself; but as always, there was no way she could admit these fears and the vulnerability they exposed. Her friends saw it, and knew it, but would not be allowed to help. "Jean was so vulnerable," Colleen recalls, "but you couldn't tell her that she was vulnerable because she'd go out of her way to prove you wrong."

Debbie Miller was another close friend who had been a roommate of Jean's at Case Western Reserve. She remembers her as someone who "came on real strong a lot of the time. She liked to talk too much; she liked to brag and pull the conversation back to herself; and I knew, we all knew, it was just Jean feeling insecure. Kind of like a little kid: Look at me. Look at me! Jean had a real strong sense of who and what she was professionally, in terms of what she could do with the world on a large scale. She could take on large systems; but interpersonally she was extremely vulnerable. She needed to be competent in all respects; she needed for people to see her as more success-ful than she felt, and she was not comfortable unless she was the focus of attention."

When Debbie would take Jean to visit her parents she recalls that "more times than not when she would leave, my father would say, 'That woman! When is she coming back again?' She just had that ability to antagonize, to make people angry, and at the same time to make them wonder when they were going to see her again because she was just so charming."

All three friends had strong opinions on most things, but Colleen and Debbie held more liberal political and economic views than Jean, and since there were few things that Jean enjoyed more than taking the opposite side in an argument, they often had heated discussions. "It got to the point that I stopped arguing with her," says Debbie, "be-cause there was no winning. I'm not exactly sure what her political beliefs were; she claimed to believe that there was no reason for Richard Nixon to be impeached; in economics she just couldn't understand why John Kenneth Galbraith thought the way he did. She maintained conservative Republican beliefs all the way down the line, but her friendships were with people who did not share her viewpoint. Jean liked extremes. In her friendships and in her political and economic beliefs."

Colleen agrees. "Jean didn't like being with the crowd," she says. "The loners appealed to her. She liked the people who didn't go along with what everybody else said. In politics and in her religion too, I don't think she was ever a group person."

Debbie and Colleen were Jean's closest friends during the first two years of her life in Cleveland. The three of them shared interests, possessions, families and houses and a carefree life-style. Debbie and Colleen shared their problems with each other and with Jean. Colleen recalls that "when you were low, Jean was a great person to tell your troubles to. She needed people that she could take care of, that she could nurture. And when I was in trouble, or hurting, when I was at my most fragile, Jean was there. There was nobody better to turn to. She was at her kindest and her best then."

It was a different story when her friends were successful. Then their success stirred up her own insecurities, causing the old competitive spirit to flare up, and Jean would withhold her warmth and support. "She wouldn't share your joy with you," says Colleen. "If I was having a great time, and three or four guys were calling me, Jean was almost nasty to me. Or at least cold. She kept away from me when I was in good shape. It annoyed her if you were on top. That's hard for me to deal with even now, because you get angry with her for trying to cut you down when you were feeling on top of the world." Hard for her friends, hard on Jean too; and since there was no way that she could ever admit to her fragilities and conflicts, since Jean was never able to share her own troubles with her friends, this pattern of competitive behavior in her relationships with her peers remained unchanged.

In that summer of '76 there was one thing missing to round out the image of success that Jean needed so desperately to project—a boyfriend. She had kept up a correspondence with Ed Fenton, and now she saw the chance to reestablish their student relationship on her terms and grabbed it. Fenton, as a medical student, had been to the States once before to take a summer course in Boston. He liked life in America, and when Jean discovered that he wanted to spend his summer working in an American hospital, she set about organizing things to bring him to Cleveland: "All of a sudden," says Fenton, "I got a letter saying that people in the Lutheran Medical Center in Cleveland, in Ohio, wanted me to write to them to make formal application for a summer internship that she had arranged with them." Colleen and Debbie watched with dismay as Jean put herself out on a limb in pursuit of an elaborate fantasy. "It used to drive me crazy," says Colleen, "because I didn't know how to—how do you talk to somebody about something like that? She bent over backward. She made arrangements for his internship at Lutheran Medical Center, she made lots of long distance phone calls to make sure he got his visa to get here, she paid for his plane ticket over, she made arrangements for him to stay with us. It was an elaborate crush and when she talked to me about it, I remember before she introduced me to Ed she said, 'Don't try to steal him away from me or I'll break your arm.' She'd tell me they were in love, that he'd proposed to her and she wasn't sure what she was going to do about it. . . . And I knew that was all made up in her mind."

The whole episode ended, as it had to, painfully for both, with Ed Fenton confronting the fact at summer's end that he'd got in over his head, and extracting himself and reasserting control over his own life. Jean's style never faltered. She'd been crazy about Ed for two years—she'd taken the risk of making herself look ridiculous and lost—

and she took her knocks and sailed right on, flaunting her professional success, her sophistication and independence.

But the Jean Donovan–Superwoman legend that she was at such pains to construct for the benefit of friends, family and peers was showing menacing cracks on the inside. And like an echo that lingers, reverberating in the memory long after the original sound has vanished, the calling to a radically different life had resurfaced to sap her confidence and undermine the conventional professional future that seemed to lie ahead. Had she really intended to slam the door shut on that larger, more meaningful world whose existence she had discovered during her talks with Crowley and in her work with Maura? Did she really want to devote her mind and energy to the task of helping Arthur Anderson's clients become richer?

She was in this troubled state of mind on the night of the Arthur Anderson office party. Perhaps it was the tinsel atmosphere in the ballroom of the Sheraton Hotel, with its strained mixture of organized good cheer and illusory solidarity; perhaps it was the luck of the draw that she took as a signal; or maybe it was the defection of Ed Fenton. Whatever the impetus, by the time she left the party she had made up her mind. She was feeling lost, stuck in a groove of her own making. She needed help.

It was a cold, wet, January morning some weeks later when Father Michael Crowley answered the doorbell in Cork City and found Jean, unannounced, on his doorstep. Her manner was flip, almost defiant. "Don't laugh too loud, Mike," she said, "I've come to talk to you because I think I have to change my life."

Her visit was no great surprise to Michael Crowley. "I think," he says, "what was happening then, was a gut discontent with the so-called twentieth-century utopia. You know she had money. She had everything that money could buy. And she didn't give a damn about money. In fact, she was reckless and she had no regard for money. She'd spend it like a drunken sailor, as we say. She knew quite well what she was doing when she came to Europe that time, when she was tossing over the idea of becoming a missionary; she was basically saying—life as I live it isn't fulfilling me deep down."

Now again it was like the old student days, only better. In the evenings they sat by the small turf fire with a bottle of Irish whiskey between them and discussed Ireland, the world, the church and missionary life, the state of Jean's soul and the fate of Latin America. Two weeks later she was back in Cleveland with a whole new itinerary.

The people in the offices of the Cleveland diocese youth ministry were far from sure whether the opinionated young woman, who appeared from nowhere one afternoon wearing a T-shirt and a leather jacket and carrying a motorcycle helmet, was a volunteer to be welcomed or a menace to be avoided. But if their first reaction was to discourage this abrupt and pushy newcomer who refused to take no for an answer, they never had a chance. Before they had time to recover from the initial shock, Jean had settled in and become part of a group working with inner-city kids.

Mary Frances Ehlinger, a member of the youth ministry team, recalls her first encounter with Jean. "It was a pep rally for young kids in Akron—there was rock music and things like that—I think that appealed to Jean, it wasn't pie-in-the-sky, it wasn't some priest telling you how you should feel—and up comes this motorcycle and this creature gets off with this leather jacket and T-shirt and takes off the helmet, and this is Jean Donovan. I thought—Oh God, we've got a live one here. So then she's got this camera around her neck—she traveled in style—and she's taking pictures, and I really didn't think too much of her. Then the motorcycle broke down, and she fixes it herself. The guys were offering to help her, but Jean's going to do this herself—she got it all taken care of and then she raced us home. She won, as I recall."

Mary Fran and her close friend, Rita Mikolajczyk, fell totally under the spell of Jean's charm. "She intimidated people," says Rita, "not deliberately, but people were intimidated because she appeared so competent and confident, and because she was so unique. Here's this woman with this degree, and working at this outrageous job for all this money, driving a motorcycle, apparently unconcerned about the way she looks, not trying to fit into any particular fashion, and yet completely expecting people will love her and adore her and just go along with whatever she says; she sees things so clearly, why don't they go along with her? That was just her attitude."

Next, in the staid, conservative parish house of St. Luke's in Lakewood, it was the elegant, good-looking young curate, Ralph Wiatowski, whose turn had come to be involved in Jean's destiny. Recalling the day when Jean roared into his life, scattering loose gravel in every direction across the rectory parking lot, Ralph smiles and says, "I just thought to myself, oh, boy! here comes trouble." When he opened the door, she lost no time. "I'm Jean Donovan," she announced. "I've decided it's time I learned something about this God and I've decided that you're the one to teach me."

Soon, Ralph too had fallen victim to the charm. "She was just so honest and so open with the things that she said that she was a delightful person to talk with and discuss things, because she had no qualms about saying, 'Ah, that's crazy,' you know. And it wasn't like you could just provide something for her and expect her to go off happy with that. She really had a very questioning mind and very alert mentality. While she was working in the youth ministry office, if she got on the elevator, and there was a priest on the elevator, by the time he got to whatever floor he was going to, he would be signed up to help out, and he really wouldn't have much choice. Because she had just a delightful way of being able to do that, where you really didn't mind and really couldn't say no. Yes, I was very fond of her."

That spring and summer of 1977 in Cleveland was a period of testing for Jean, a rehearsal for the radical break with her past life that still lay ahead. Her volunteer work with the diocesan youth ministry had brought her into contact with a whole new circle of socially committed community activists, and as she pursued these friendships with people from a more diverse social background, she started withdrawing from her previous friends, Debbie and Colleen, leaving hurt feelings and confusion in her wake. The new friendships she was forming were with people who tended to be more mature than she was, more secure of their sense of values and of the direction in which their lives were headed. In stepping outside the close circle of her own peers she abandoned the competitiveness that had always plagued her in those relationships, and for the first time she found it possible to open up and admit to the soul-searching and the quest for meaning and satisfaction to which she was now committed.

In her weekly sessions with Father Ralph, she was exploring for the first time the theological premises behind the faith in which she had grown up and which she had taken for granted; and the more familiar she became with the basic Gospel texts the more her conviction grew that the answer she was searching for would be found in some form of religiously oriented involvement. Then, one fall day, in response to her desire to pursue additional volunteer work, Father Ralph brought along to their weekly meeting some literature from the main diocesan office listing the range of their social programs. Stuck inside the envelope as an afterthought was a small brochure describing the work of the diocesan's mission in El Salvador. The moment Jean picked it up she realized that her search was over. This was precisely the kind of work that Michael Crowley had told her about during their long conversations in Cork. She may not have been all that sure where El Salvador was; she certainly had very little idea of that country's tragic historical and political legacy. But one thing she did know with utter certitude: here in her hand she held her future, and now that she knew where she was headed, she no longer had any doubts about how to get there. With complete assurance she set about gaining acceptance as a lay volunteer member of the Cleveland mission team.

Sometime between Thanksgiving and Christmas of 1977 Jean told her parents that she was going to quit her job and spend two years as a lay missionary in El Salvador. Pat Donovan called her son Michael, who was newly married and living in Danbury, Connecticut, where he worked as a financial analyst and CPA for a small research organization. At first he refused to believe it. "I thought it was a prank or something, and then Jeannie showed up in Ossining, New York, to take the training course, and she said, 'Oh, by the way, I'm going to go to El Salvador.' And she explained that the group she was going to be involved with was teaching nutrition and child care and that sort of thing. My first question to her was, 'Well, who is going to teach you?' "

Michael Donovan laughs to hide his pain. He was the only person who systematically opposed Jean's decision. "My mother didn't know why Jeannie was going to El Salvador either. We did start to discuss it and she said, 'I don't know why she's going, but she's going.' And I said, 'To do what?' And she said, 'It's some sort of nutrition program.' And I said, 'Why is she doing this?' And she said, 'I don't know.' And I just filed it away in my mind as an adventure. It would be something to do, and it would be exciting. I also filed it away as something a little bit irresponsible—but what the heck—she had no responsibilities, so why not? But then as I became more and more familiar with what was happening in El Salvador, the less and less I thought it was a good idea."

So Michael tried to stop her. "I knew it was dangerous," he says now, "I knew something just like what happened could happen and I told her so, but she wouldn't listen to me." Night after night they would sit around the kitchen table of his Danbury home while Michael, appalled by the results of his research and haunted by a premonition of tragedy, would hammer away at her resolve. "I don't think," he says now, "I could have tried harder." Jean did listen. "She was very stubborn and determined in most things. On any other subject she would always argue vociferously. But this was totally different. With regard to El Salvador she'd be very still, very quiet. She'd just listen to what everybody had to say—she never really got argumentative about it at all."

Michael's tone still reflects some of the bewilderment and frustration that those sessions in the kitchen used to evoke. That, and the painful memory of having lived for two years fighting his premonitions alone. "At least," he says, "I think now that I understand why she went and that she went for the right reasons."

The Cleveland diocese had placed one condition upon their acceptance of Jean as a volunteer: first she must spend four months at the headquarters of the Maryknoll Order, in Ossining, New York, which ran the only existing program in the country designed to give lay people a thorough preparation for working in Third World–country missions. The whole concept of the involvement of lay people in missionary work is a relatively new one for the Catholic Church. Initiated in the early sixties to fill the need created by an alarming drop in the number of vocations, the lay movement was subsequently promoted and developed under the liberal influence of Pope John XXIII and the Second Vatican Council. Among their missionary colleagues, the Maryknoll Sisters and Fathers represent an elite. Theirs is the first American religious order founded, in the second decade of this century, to serve exclusively as foreign missionaries, and as such, they are the only American professionals in the field, with well over fifty years of experience on a worldwide scale. Over the years, their collaboration with lay people has resulted in the development of a rigorous training program for volunteers, and it was to this program that Jean was directed by the Cleveland diocese to apply.

Attached to Jean's application is an autobiographical

essay in which she tries to explain her background and her
reasons for applying:

> At times I'm sure my parents both wonder
> where I got the mission calling [she writes]. To
> me it's obvious after having two people such as
> my parents to grow up with. My father is a
> gentle man. He has never been afraid to show
> love. I think I admire this about him best.
> Many men feel that openly expressing love is
> unmanly. I think my father is a living example
> that, on the contrary, showing love is very
> human. My mother is a very get up and go
> person who always seems to have the energy
> to do something for someone else.

Then she refers to the impact that Michael's illness had
made on her as a teenager:

> The family experience which has most affected
> my life was when my brother got Hodgkins
> disease. He is fine now and just celebrated his
> first wedding anniversary, but at the time, it
> made me realize how unsure our existence is,
> and how precious life is to each of us. Many
> of the values people exalt are not so important
> after all.

She concludes her application with these words:

> I have been thinking about this vocation for
> many years. Actually I think, that for a number
> of years, Christ has been sending various people
> into my life, that through their example and
> actions I saw a calling to missionary work. I
> have a gut feeling that my main motivation to
> be a missionary is a true calling from God.

She was accepted and went to Ossining with the usual mass of baggage. She spent four months there in the fall and winter of 1978 with a select group of eight other volunteers, studying to prepare herself for her new life.

"I think of her bedroom," Pat de Angelis, one of her colleagues at Ossining, recalls. "It was a disaster area: dirty clothes, open books piled on the bed—I used to wonder how she ever found room to sleep. I remember when she was getting ready to leave and had to pack all this junk, and we went in to help her. I noticed she had a couple of pieces of Waterford crystal in there, and I said, 'Oh, how neat— you carry this with you.' Because usually, you know, you leave it on the shelf and save it for company coming—and I think that's what Jean did with her life—she didn't save it for when company comes; it was meant to be used; you didn't get too cautious with it; it had to be filled to the brim, not saved for later on, or for special company." Pat watched Jean's struggles to make sense of the commitment upon which she was embarked. "Do you think this call is really a call?" Jean would ask. "Do you think God's really calling me? Why? Why me? Doesn't he know what kind of person I am?"

Maryknoll was her first exposure to the life of a religious community. As a pupil of Westport's public schools, she had never come into contact with nuns as teachers before. She was very much the "new student," and as usual, determined not to be intimidated, with the predictable result that her passage through the program was often controversial. Her insecurity fueled her argumentative temperament and she managed to tread on a number of toes. She was loud and provocative; she turned cartwheels, in class and out, to grab attention; and she spent a lot of time in Izzy's—the Ossining local bar—drinking beer with the seminarians. Gwen Vendley, herself an ex-lay missionary who taught a course for the new recruits, got to know Jean very well during this period and always championed her cause, yet she admits that Jean's behavior was unorthodox. "She was a bit threatening for some. She wasn't one to compromise her beliefs, even if she felt that being outspoken might jeopardize her being here. She would challenge some of the institutional understandings of what the Church means. She would question women's role in the Church, laity's role, what does priesthood mean—and if you're in a seminary setting that's a little awkward at times." She would also get into hassles with the administration on behalf of some of her colleagues. "If she felt that a person was misjudged, she would not only take it to the director of the program, she would go right ahead to members of the council. She would fight for a person; that was probably what was most lovable about Jeannie. She really loved others and would go out on a limb for them."

When the time came for graduation, some of the staff would have preferred to flunk her; others, going beyond her adolescent behavior saw someone so driven, so determined to find something worthwhile to commit herself to, that they felt disarmed and almost humbled. If going to El Salvador to work with that nation's trampled, hungry poor was necessary for the salvation of Jean Donovan's soul, who are we, they said, to stand in her way?

In fact, those months in Maryknoll, the people she met there, the friends she made, her growing awareness of both the scope and the limitations of the task she had set herself, all had a lasting effect on Jean. For the rest of her life she regarded the Maryknoll community as her personal, adoptive alma mater, and the people she met through Maryknoll were destined to become among her most important role models.

When the time came to tell her friends that she was going to El Salvador for two years as a lay missionary, Jean had a lot of trouble explaining her decision. Essentially, she didn't even try and took the easy way out by telling people what she thought they wanted to hear. This was especially true where her old friends, Colleen and Debbie, were concerned, both of whom were already upset and angered by the fact that in Jean's enthusiasm for the new friends she had found through her activities with the youth ministry, they had been left out in the cold. Loyalty was extremely important to Jean, and she felt defensive about the charge, for it was indeed true that the changes she had undergone, and which were now culminating in her departure for El Salvador, had created a chasm between two very different aspects of her life. Since throughout this period she had never attempted to level with her former friends, she now felt incapable of explaining the true motives for her decision to an overtly skeptical, critical audience.

Looking back with sorrow a year after Jean's death, Colleen and Debbie revealed just how raw the hurt inflicted by Jean's unwillingness to take them into her confidence still was. "I thought she was nuts," Colleen admits. "She said she was bored here. She said there was really nothing doing . . . and I said, you've got a beautiful apartment; you've got a car and a motorcycle and a job that half the people I know would love to have. And she said that she needed more . . . and she made up some stuff about being a Maryknoll jet-setter and that they had great golf courses in South America. Good opportunities to travel, cute priests . . . and I knew she was kidding, but I don't know—the golf courses—she sounded pretty serious about the golf courses.

"She never really put it on a religious level. It was more like, well, they'll be flying me to Ireland when I want, and I can come home when I want, and I'll learn Spanish all over again, and it'll be a great experience. . . . She didn't emphasize the religious part of it at all. It was more like an extended vacation."

Debbie remembers that in their conversation on the subject, Jean pretended that the arrangements she had made with the Cleveland diocese were based on her ability to raise funds for the mission in El Salvador. "The way she explained herself as being valuable to the diocesan program was that she would go down there and gain experience as a missionary so that she could come back here and attract the business community to contribute donations. Through her experience with Arthur Anderson she would be able to speak their language, so she could encourage business people to donate funds."

Debbie did not buy this explanation for a moment. "I was angry," she says. "I felt that Jean was at a loss for what she wanted to do, she was looking for a change, and it was going to be a radical change that she went for. She was looking for adventure. A romantic escapade. The diocese had sent her down for a ten-day period to see if she would be suited, and when she came back she had spent a total of two days in the missions and that was it. The rest of the time she had been in the capital city of San Salvador; had been staying in a plush hotel; had played a lot of golf and acquired a great tan. And she loved missionary life."

Her sister-in-law, Ellen, to whom she gave the explanation that she clearly thought or hoped would most appeal to her brother, Michael, remembers that Jean explained her activities in terms of business opportunities. "She said that after she was bilingual she thought she could get a really good job in South America with an American firm as a CPA. She always presented it to me as though this was something she was doing to attain her dream, which was to be a CPA with an American firm in South America."

As for her former boyfriends, Fred Taylor and Ed Fenton, neither of them could make the least sense of what she was up to. Fred was sure he knew her better. "That didn't seem Jeannie's style at all—to go down to a backward country. That was not Jean. Jean was the kind of person that would truck through a swamp all day to get to her mobile home so that she could take a hot bath and lounge around watching her color TV. She liked her luxuries. I could see Jean doing something like that, but not in Salvador. I could see her doing it in Cleveland, or New York, Los Angeles or San Francisco . . . but not El Salvador."

Ed Fenton, to whom in fact Jean tried to explain the truth, was too shocked by the image of Jean as a near-nun to comprehend what she was trying to tell him. "I was really taken for six when I heard that she was joining the Mary-knoll Sisters. I thought she was going to become a nun at one stage, and I just couldn't figure it out at all. It was only later, when I met her and she explained that it wasn't a nun, it was a lay missionary status she was in, and even that I found pretty strange. . . . She said that there was something going on down there that was always going wrong. And that she wanted to go down there and give what she could give down there . . . and even that I didn't understand."

The people she did take into her confidence, her friends in the Kaleidoscope youth ministry group, Rita Mikolajczyk and Mary Fran Ehlinger, remember that they talked a lot during that year about the choices people make and about what it means to do something that feels right. What does it mean to say: this is something I have to do; this is something that I believe God wants me to do. And why. "Why me?" Jean would ask. "Why do I want to do this? Why don't you or Rita want to go to Salvador? Why is this something that I have to do?"

There was one other person in Cleveland who sympathized with what she was trying to do. During the summer of 1977 a young doctor from a wealthy midwestern Protestant family moved into an apartment in Debbie Miller's house in Cleveland Heights. His name was Douglas Cable, and from the moment she first laid eyes on him Jean decided that here was someone she wanted to get close to. Doug has a vivid memory of their first meeting. "It was probably the most humid day of the year—hot, humid, Cleveland summer—and I had been moving a whole library, carrying boxes of books down from a fourth-floor walkup, and I was in the living room, collapsed, and someone knocked at the door, and I opened it up, and there was this short blond girl with a bottle of whiskey in her hand—and she said, 'Hi, thought you might need a drink.' "

In the course of the next year they saw a lot of each other. "From the very beginning we just fit together. It wasn't love at first sight but we just were friends. We were just immediately good friends. And then as it became clear she was leaving, that she was going to Salvador, I began to miss her, and that's when it became more serious. When she went to Maryknoll, to New York, that was when I realized that I loved her. I realized that with her gone I wasn't happy, so I went to New York. There was one month I went to see her every weekend in the month and we had a marvelous time."

In that spring of '79, when the training program at Maryknoll ended and Jean prepared to leave for three months of intensive language school in Guatemala, Doug was not overly concerned. "We didn't make any lasting pact or long-term commitment at that time, but I didn't really see it as a problem. She was going to go for a couple of years, we were going to be in touch. I would come down and visit. She was obviously deeply committed and I wasn't going to try and discourage her. That would have been wrong, so I accepted it."

Doug also respected her seriousness of purpose and was confident of her ability to look after herself. "She wasn't running off for high adventure. She was an accountant in Cleveland who was going down to Salvador to be an accountant down there. She was going to balance the mission's books and that seemed like a reasonable thing to do, like it was perfectly safe. She wasn't getting out in the jungle, risking her life. There was some violence in El Salvador at that time and she had said, 'Well, when the first shot is fired I'll be on the next plane.' And we all believed her. I thought I knew her well enough by then that she would have sense enough to get out when things got serious. Because she was above all a very practical person. At least so she seemed in Cleveland, when she was an accountant."

It had been a long and twisty road from those first conversations with Michael Crowley, five years earlier, to the graduation ceremony in the Maryknoll chapel, and sometimes it was far from clear to Jean how she had reached the point where she now stood, poised on the brink of a new life. It was spring 1979. Soon, she would be leaving to go to the Maryknoll Center in Huehuetenango, Guatemala for three months intensive language training. She was twenty-six years old, happy, scared and very excited. Within three months she would be arriving in El Salvador.

Patricia and Raymond Donovan leaving the church for their wedding reception, October 18, 1947

Baby Jean with Michael, summer of 1953

Jean, Westport, 1955

Jean and Michael with their dog, Satan. Westport, 1958

Family group, Westport, 1960

Competing on Apple. Fiddle Horse Farm, Westport, 1969

Jean at twenty-one. Ireland, spring 1974

Young executive. Jean on her motorcycle in Cleveland, summer 1978

Father Michael Crowley, Cork City, Ireland

Archbishop Oscar Romero with refugees. San Salvador, February 1980

Refugees in the camp on the grounds of the Archdiocesan Seminary established by Archbishop Romero in January 1980

The Cleveland Mission Team in La Libertad/Zaragoza, winter 1979. *Left to right*: Sister Christine Rody, Sister Dorothy Kazel, Father Ken Myers, Jean Donovan, Father Paul Schindler

Jean holding her kitten, Twerp. Zaragoza, Christmas 1979

Doing the books for the Mission Team. Zaragoza, February 1980

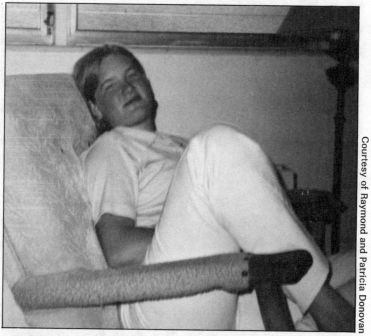

Jean relaxing in her apartment in La Libertad

Douglas Cable vacationing in El Salvador, February 1980.
Photograph by Jean Donovan

Dorothy Kazel with refugee children in Zaragoza, fall 1980

Ita Ford, Chalatenango, fall 1980

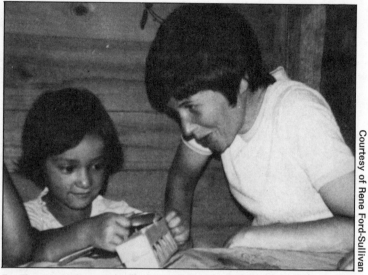

Ita Ford helping refugee child. Chalatenango, fall 1980

Maura Clarke with refugee. Chalatenango, November 1980

Jean preparing to load up the white Toyota van

Jean at the wheel of the Toyota van

The burned-out Toyota van at the roadside between the airport and La Libertad, December 3, 1980

Ambassador White at the gravesite, December 4, 1980, waiting for permission to uncover the bodies

Memorial for Jean and Dorothy, Ita and Maura, on the site of their clandestine grave, San Pedro Nonualco, El Salvador. The inscription reads: "Catholic Missionaries Dorothy Kazel, Maura Clarke, Jean Donovan and Ita Ford gave their lives December 2nd, 1980. Receive Them Lord Into Your Kingdom."

CHAPTER IV

*This Ghost
of South America*

*I think for her, from earliest day in Cork, there
was a growing curiosity about this ghost of
South America. She felt that as an American
what goes on in South America is her responsibility, and the responsibility of every American, and as she gradually educated herself to
what was happening down there, she responded
to it.*
—*Father Michael Crowley*

*We have no concern with South America: we
have no sympathy, we can have no political
sympathy with them. We are sprung from
different stocks, we speak different languages,
we have been brought up in different social and
moral schools, we have been governed by different codes of law, we profess radically different forms of religion. Should we espouse their
cause, they would borrow our money . . . and
possibly extend some privileges to our trade.
. . . But they would not act in our spirit, they
would not follow our advice, they could not
imitate our example. . . . How can our thrifty
merchants sympathize with a people who send
the letter post down the river on the back of a*

swimmer? How can our industrious frugal yeo-
men sympathize with a people that sit and fish
on horseback?"
   —Edward Everett, Secretary
      of State in the administration
      of President James Buchanan

   Arms

You have a gun
And I am hungry

You have a gun
Because
I am hungry

You have a gun
Therefore
I am hungry

You can have a gun
You can have one thousand bullets and even
      another thousand
You can waste them all on my poor body
You can kill me one, two, three, two thousand,
      seven thousand times

But in the long run
I will always be better armed than you

If you have a gun
And I
Have only hunger
                  —Guatemalan poet Manuel Arce

WHEN JEAN TOLD HER PARENTS THAT SHE WAS GOING TO A
place called El Salvador her father candidly admits that he
and her mother "went out to buy a map to find out where
El Salvador was. We knew it was down there someplace, but

just exactly where, we didn't know—and what the political situation was—we didn't know very much about that either."

In 1977 few Americans probably knew "just exactly where" El Salvador was. Fewer still probably had any knowledge of its tortured past or any notion that time was running out on a system of government designed in the earliest years of the country's independence to serve the exclusive interests of a few score landowners and immigrant merchants whose absolute power and extravagant wealth had always been maintained through the coercion and exploitation of a terrorized, submissive population of landless peasants.

In 1976 the United Nations issued a report identifying El Salvador as the country with the lowest caloric intake of any country on the Latin American continent with the exception of Haiti. That same year the International Labor Office of the United Nations cited El Salvador as having the highest rate (50 percent) of unemployment-underemployment in the hemisphere. Seventy-three percent of all children under the age of five were undernourished. Eighty percent of rural families lived in inadequate housing. Between 1971 and 1975, as the coffee growers expanded their holdings to include large tracts of coastal lands to devote to cotton growing, the proportion of rural families without land increased from 29 percent to 41 percent of the total rural population.

In the seventies, El Salvador began visibly splitting apart. While the landowners still refused to contemplate the most minimal change in their standard of living; while they debated among themselves which general, or colonel or even major was sufficiently macho to keep the Indian population in line; while they organized and armed a rural civilian vigilant group known as ORDEN, with cells in every hamlet, village and community to provide the "ears" and the "fingers" for the National Guard, the police and the army, on the other side, organized left-wing terrorism now made its first appearance on the Salvadoran scene. Two small groups of armed, middle-class urban guerrillas initiated a campaign of kidnappings among the wealthy native families and the foreign business community through which they succeeded in driving away foreign investment and amassed many millions of dollars.

In '73 and again in '76 the landowners succeeded in blocking even the most moderate proposals for agrarian reform. In '72, '74 and '77 the military effectively demolished all possibility of the development of a democratic opposition of the center through systematic electoral fraud. They closed the university, silenced the only opposition newspaper, banished or drove underground the moderate opposition leaders. Then, into the vacuum that the military themselves had created, there burst a new phenomenon—a grass-roots coalition movement of organized students and teachers, peasants and slum dwellers, urban and rural workers. The poor, the young, the angry and the desperate poured into the streets of the capital in massive protest demonstrations. They held sit-ins; they occupied foreign embassies, government buildings, banks and churches.

The government and the press—both local and foreign —called them all terrorists and extremists, and the police fired on their marches and arrested their leaders or simply caused them to disappear. But the organizations represented the overwhelming majority of the population, and their demands—for a living wage for workers; for a better price for fertilizer and seed for small farmers; for sanitation and running water in the slums; for land reform and free elections; for education and a free press; and above all, for an end to the random terror of ORDEN and the National Guard in the countryside—were neither extremist nor revolutionary. Nevertheless, within the context of the history of El Salvador, the very existence of the popular organizations, their unity and their strength, represented a threatening challenge to the authority of the military rulers.

In a country like El Salvador, where so little has really ever changed, contemporary history begins on the day that the Spaniards arrived four centuries ago. The combination of rural despair and vengeful hatred that corrupts the relationship between the Salvadoran landowner and the Salvadoran peasant today has roots that reach all the way back to the Spanish conquest of an Indian land. Only in light of that history do the cruelty, the rapacious greed, the lawlessness, the racism, and the disregard for human life that have infected the ruling classes of this small country become comprehensible.

When Simón Bolívar, the great nineteenth-century liberator of the continent, the George Washington of Latin America, sat down in 1815 to draft his political blueprint for independence, he had few illusions:

> We suffer [he wrote] the domination of those vices which are the legacy of a country such as Spain, which has only dominated through savagery, ambition, vengeance and greed.

Fifteen years later, as he lay dying of tuberculosis, and broken by treachery, he wrote:

> Whosoever serves the revolution is ploughing in the sea. This country will fall inevitably into the hands, first of the uncontrolled multitudes, then to be taken over by tyrants of every race and color who will scarcely be distinguishable one from the other. They will say of me that I have liberated the New World. But they will never say that I have achieved the stability or the happiness of its nations.

Two days later, at the age of thirty-seven, he died, leaving his contemporaries and their heirs to fulfill all too literally the bleak and tragic vision he had prophesied.

By the end of the sixteenth century the Spanish colonialists in El Salvador had built a society based on the exploitation of the natural resources of the country and the coercion of the native inhabitants. After the liberation in the first decades of the nineteenth century those Spanish families who owned the land they had taken from the Indians composed an elite. They had established for themselves and their heirs the status of a landed gentry, and there was no one around to challenge their dominance. In due course they became the new rulers of the fledgling republic, with a contempt for the Indian that extended to anyone who performed manual labor. Alfaro, Palomo, Regalado, Orellana, Escalon, Prado, Meléndez, Quiñónez, Araújo—their names figure prominently as signatories to early legislation. They owned the land then, and they own it today.

In the midnineteenth century other European and North American adventurers were attracted to this New World. They came from Germany and England, from Belgium and Holland and France. Some bought land; others made their fortunes as bankers and merchants and processors of the nation's newest source of wealth, coffee. By the end of the century they, too, had been elevated to join the ranks of the native elite: Hill, Parker, Sol-Millet, Schonenburg, De Sola, Deininger and Duke. The oligarchy, the famous fourteen families, was in place.

To consolidate their control over the nation's resources, the new rulers abolished the centuries-old system of communal lands, established by the Spanish Crown under the stewardship of the Indian villages, on which the Indian population was dependent for subsistence farming. For the landowners, every acre of land not dedicated to raising export crops, and specifically coffee, was land wastefully employed. For the Indians, growing crops for export was not only fundamentally alien to their way of life, it was also beyond their resources.

The new pattern of land use and land ownership, established by the first national government over one hundred years ago by men whose heirs still own and exploit the land, remains fundamentally unchanged today—including the presence of a National Guard created in 1921 to provide the landowners with a rural police force charged with control, coercion and oppression of rural workers.

In 1932 the descendants of the conquered native population finally revolted. The rebellion centered in the Indian towns and villages of the northwestern highlands, precisely those areas where entire communities had been dispossessed fifty years earlier by the expansion of the large coffee estates and the abolition of extensive communal landholdings. The original plan for a nationwide uprising, to be led from the capital city by the Salvadoran Communist party under the leadership of Farabundo Martí, was discovered by government agents two days before, and Martí and his coconspirators sat out the uprising in jail. But word of Martí's arrest never reached the Indians. Disorganized, badly led, desperate Indians armed with machetes poured out of the mountains to attack the landowners' representatives—the estate managers and local government representatives in the nearest white towns of the fertile valleys. Their rampage lasted two days. By the time they were overcome by the army they had killed some thirty-five civilians, and one hundred soldiers had lost their lives in the fighting.

To the white population this desperate sortie represented the realization of their worst nightmares. Newspapers of the period reported calls for "the extermination of this race of the plague." A February headline in the leading newspaper *La Prensa* read, "The Indian has been, is, and will be the enemy of the Ladino [white]," and the author went on to explain that "there is not an Indian who is not afflicted with devastating communism." In the course of the next three weeks, the army slaughtered tens of thousands of unarmed Indian peasants. Hundreds were arbitrarily and horribly tortured. Bodies littered the roadsides for pigs and vultures to feed on.

In El Salvador among ordinary people the uprising and its aftermath is known as *la Matanza*—the Massacre. Among the landowners it is referred to as the Communist Rebellion. By whatever name, the awful legacy of those days and weeks of slaughter has remained branded into the collective memory of the nation.

Forty years later, when a potent new grass-roots coalition of militant peasants, students, teachers and workers, supported by the Salvadoran Catholic Church, had emerged to compaign for basic social and economic reforms, Alan Riding of the *New York Times,* reported from El Salvador in May 1978 that "the deepest fear of the country's rulers is that the peasant uprising of 1932 that was put down with the loss of over 20,000 lives will be repeated." Riding quoted a conservative Salvadoran lawyer who explained: "Whenever the peasants make the least demand, people begin talking about 1932 again, so the reaction is always to put down the peasants before they get out of control. The discussion among the rich families now is whether 20,000 or 50,000 or 100,000 peasants should be killed to restore peace."

The ability of the protesting groups to mobilize tens of thousands of people to partake in acts of civil disobedience represented the first revolutionary movement to cut across ethnic, class, rural and urban divisions in El Salvador's history. But it was a revolution without guerrillas or guns— and it had the support of a surprising and powerful new ally: the Catholic Church.

In the seventies throughout Latin America the Church was changing. It began in 1968 at a hemispheric conference of all the Latin bishops in Medellín, Colombia. At that conference the Latin-American Church, bastion of the status quo and ideological force behind the conquest and enslavement of the Indians, dramatically switched its allegiance from the oppressor to the oppressed.

Arriving in Colombia in August 1968 to preside over the opening of the conference, Pope Paul VI struck the first note of warning. In his arrival address to the prominent citizens of Bogotá who had assembled to honor this first visit of a pope to the New World, Paul VI challenged his elegant audience to mend their ways:

> What can I say to you, men of the ruling class? What is required of you is generosity. This means the ability to detach yourselves from the stability of your position, which is a position of privilege, in order to serve those who need your worth, your culture, your authority . . .

You, Lords of this world and Sons of the Church, you must have the genius for virtue that society requires. Your ears and your hearts must be sensitive to the voices crying out for bread, concern, justice, and a more active participation in the direction of society.

Through the eyes of its theologians and bishops, the Catholic Church looked at the societies of Latin America—societies in which the Catholic religion was still the single strongest social influence—and found them to be profoundly un-Christian. They looked at their partners in power —the generals, the landowners, the ruling classes—and they had to admit that after generations of education in Catholic schools, the values by which they lived, and the social and economic structures by which they maintained themselves in power, were repressive, corrupt and murderous. And finally, they scrutinized their own role in this moral morass and realized that this same Church now had the opportunity to become a force for the liberation of the very people whose enslavement it had helped to create. By the time the conference ended the bishops had signed a series of documents that would provide a Magna Carta for a new, socially active "Church of the Poor," committed to the transformation of the Latin societies. In their final communiqué the bishops stated:

> In many places in Latin America there exists a situation of injustice that must be recognized as institutional violence, because the existing structures violate people's basic rights: [it is] a situation which calls for far-reaching, daring, urgent and profoundly innovative change.

Medellín gave birth to a new theology—a "Theology of Liberation"—liberation from sin, but also from the consequences of sin, which the bishops defined in terms of the social evils all around them: hunger, infant mortality, injustice, torture, arbitrary arrest, and the absence of any political rights for the vast majority.

The changed role of the Church implied basic and far-reaching changes in its approach to pastoral work. In El Salvador after Medellín, the priests abandoned their comfortable residences in the cities and penetrated the countryside to live with the poor, share in their struggles for survival, support and legitimize their most basic human needs for housing, land, a living wage, health care, and schools for their children. They brought with them a radical new message of hope, for seen from the perspective of a Latin American coffee picker whose baby has just died from hunger, the words of the prophets of the Old Testament and the social teachings of the man from Nazareth are far more accessible and meaningful than any communist manifesto, and, gradually, as trust developed, as hope and the possibility of change began to grow and spread, small communities of peasants and rural workers began to form cooperatives; for generations they had been told that they were lazy, stupid, useless—but the cooperatives worked well, life was improving. Then they began organizing their own union—the Christian Federation of Salvadoran Peasants. But rural unions had been prohibited in El Salvador ever since the *Matanza,* and the landowners were not about to tolerate them now. As the government directed ORDEN and the National Guard to "defend democracy and stamp out communism," the priests also became targets of the oppression.

The first shots in the war against the Church were fired on a country road at about five o'clock in the evening of Saturday March 12, 1977, just two years prior to Jean Donovan's arrival in the country. The killers had been waiting along the side of the road for the jeep carrying the priest on his way to celebrate evening mass. When the vehicle approached, one man stepped out to flag it down, the others opened fire, and within seconds Father Rutilio Grande and two lay friends traveling with him were dead, their bodies riddled with 9mm dum-dum bullets, the standard ammunition issued to the police and the guard.

Rutilio Grande, a Salvadoran Jesuit, was probably the most highly regarded priest among the Salvadoran clergy. Grande had been the first after the Conference of Medellín to abandon the life of an intellectual, the prestige and comfort of his position as a professor at the seminary, to go out into the country and share the lives of the peasants. These were the people behind the economists' statistics—60 percent of Salvadorans living on less than $150 a year; the people who never knew what it meant not to be hungry. They were the same people whom, a few years later, Jean Donovan would come to Salvador to help.

In 1970, when Grande had begun his pastoral mission in the valley of Aguilares the idea that a priest would converse with a peasant on equal terms, would visit his shack, get to know his children, want to understand his problems and care enough to try to help change his life for the better was in itself revolutionary. Any criticism of authority or tradition implied a sinful questioning of the divine plan. Only God and his intermediaries, the saints and their companion spirits who still lingered in the plants and animals from the days of the old Indian religions, could determine the destiny of man.

The techniques for consciousness-raising that Grande and his group of Jesuit colleagues brought with them to the hillside communities of Aguilares, a fertile valley some thirty miles north of the capital where a handful of wealthy landowners grew and processed sugar cane for export, and some thirty thousand peasants struggled to survive on minute plots of rocky, barren soil clinging to the surrounding mountains, had been developed over the previous decade by a small group of priests working in the poverty-stricken wastelands of northeastern Brazil, where the Church had pioneered the development of adult literacy courses that would become a classic tool in the battle to liberate the poor from their isolation and passivity. Together with these courses came the formation of Basic Christian Communities—small groups of twelve or fourteen people that were also people's councils, linking the reading of selected Bible texts with civic action, education with concepts of responsibility, and class solidarity with Christ's plan for a more just, more ethical and more humane society.

The Basic Christian Communities are, in effect, the building blocks of the transformed society sought by liberation churchmen; and it is not hard to understand how their introduction into the feudal, stagnant structures of Salvadoran rural society would enrage and threaten the landowners. The work pioneered in Aguilares by Rutilio Grande began to catch fire in villages and communities throughout the diocese of San Salvador and beyond. Membership in the Basic Christian Communities was arming the largest, poorest, and most oppressed group in the nation with knowledge and understanding of the world around them. Once they were able to make the connection between the death of their children and the economic structures and priorities that perpetuated the wealth and privileges of the landowners, the manner in which the farmworkers experienced the world and their own place in it was irrevocably altered. From an appreciation of the social causes of hunger, unemployment, infant mortality, it was only a short step to the realization of the need, indeed the responsibility, to organize and mobilize for change.

Before long, the religious lay leaders, or Delegates of the Word, as those who led the discussion groups in the Basic Communities were called, would also become organizers for the Christian Federation of Salvadoran Peasants; and for the first time the rural workers had a union of their own. They also had something else they never had before—the sense that change was possible and that the future could be better.

Although there was violent opposition to Rutilio Grande and his Jesuit colleagues among the ruling class, it was not so simple for men brought up in the Catholic Church to have the blood of a priest on their hands. The persecution of the Church had to be launched in defense of the "authentic" religion and the salvation of the "Patria."

So Jesuits and other foreign, "Third World" priests, became the selected targets. From the landowners' perspective, it was the Jesuits who were not only leading the subversive elements in the countryside, but were also teaching "communism" to their sons and daughters in the classrooms of the school and the university, and publishing papers on subjects such as agrarian reform, which the landowners regarded as nothing less than Marxist-Leninist tracts.

In December 1976, a group of over seventy prominent parishioners in the diocese of Santa Ana, a large rural town in the heart of the coffee-growing region of the northwest, sent a letter of appeal directly to the Pope's personal representative in El Salvador, Monsignor Emmanuele Gerado, Papal Nuncio:

> We entreat your most reverend Excellency to define clearly the position of El Salvador's Apostolic Roman Catholic Church. We would like to know if the Vatican has established the political directives which our priests are presently following. More precisely, are their interpretations of the encyclicals and documents of the Second Vatican Council authentic or arbitrarily subjective?
>
> Also we would like to know if the so-called Theology of Liberation is grounded in Sacred Scriptures and in the millennial tradition of the Church, or whether it is simply an expression of stereotype ideological Marxist-Leninist patterns? Are social mobilization, the organizing of working people, the creation of a political army of revolution, etc., etc., legitimate and significant objectives of what used to be a society of practicing Catholics?
>
> It would seem, your most reverend Excellency, that our Church has gradually tried to change

the correlation of forces between the existing order and Communist subversion by making use of the dialectic of class struggle.

It is fitting to note in conclusion, that in our country the Catholic Church, making use of its religious authority, has created a Campesino-Worker Alliance and implemented its revolutionary orientation. *The Church has taken over from professional revolutionaries the leadership of the subversive movement.* [Emphasis in the original letter.]

In the pages of the government-controlled newspapers, the landowners and their supporters in the business community initiated a press campaign alerting the faithful to the evil in their midst. Exhortations such as "Mothers! Terrorism threatens your children! Unite to defend them!" "Communism threatens our future! Don't let it be enthroned in our Nation!" were followed by double-page spreads taken out by the major organizations of the landowners, the industrialists and the National Association of Private Enterprise, specifically accusing the Jesuits and other foreign priests of "inciting, directing and supporting the vandalous hordes in a plan to create a climate of terror and violence." The Salvadoran Women's Front purchased a full page to denounce "Well-known Third World priests, foreigners and native-born, who instead of teaching the authentic Gospel of Our Lord Jesus Christ have dedicated themselves to teaching class warfare, violence, pillage and crime."

After his assassination, Salvadorans would always remember one of Rutilio Grande's last sermons. Delivered at an open-air mass in a neighboring parish, his words convey a sense of the historical inevitability of the persecution yet to come:

> Soon, the Bible and the Gospel won't be
> allowed to cross our borders. We will get only

the bindings, because all of the pages are subversive. And I think that if Jesus himself came across the border at Chalatenango, they would not let him in. They would accuse the Man-God, the prototype of man, of being a rabble-rouser, a foreign Jew, one who confused the people with exotic and foreign ideas, ideas against democracy—that is, against the wealthy minority. . . . Brothers and sisters, there is no doubt, they would crucify him again.

All spring the campaign against the Church continued to gather momentum. The first of the organized professional death squads began to emerge, anonymous groupings of former and present members of the security forces with names like "the White Warriors Union" or "the Maximilian Hernandez Brigade" who took their orders and their money from some of the best-known names in the land; they published their death lists and took credit for their victims with grisly relish. In May, some days after the assassination of a second priest, printed flyers and bumper stickers appeared in San Salvador bearing the message: "BE A PATRIOT —KILL A PRIEST"; and in June, the most active of the death squads, the White Warriors Union, published a communiqué threatening "the immediate and systematic execution" of all Jesuits who failed to leave the country "forever" within thirty days. By this time international public opinion was aroused, and the alarm raised by the American Church put sufficient pressure on the Salvadoran government to restrain the killers—for a time.

During this period, the second most powerful and surprising source of hope originated in Washington. When in 1976 a new American president announced an American foreign policy based on respect for human rights, a great surge of hope swept through the battered populations of the southern hemisphere. In March of 1977, immediately following the most recent instance of electoral fraud in El Salvador, the U.S. Congress held hearings on human rights abuses. José Antonio Morales Ehrlich, the defeated Christian Democratic vice-presidential candidate, came from his exile in Venezuela to testify and articulated the question that was being asked by ordinary people on the streets and in the cafés throughout the southern continent:

> President Carter's statement on Human Rights and Hearings such as this on a people's right to vote has had a tremendously powerful impact on the average Latin American. In my country the people are asking themselves the following questions: Is it really true that the United States is now going to demand that our governments respect human rights, especially when such rights are violated daily? Can it be that our military governments will no longer be able to rely on U.S. backing, nor be able to continue their abuses?*

The year 1977 was a watershed year. In a bloody prelude to eventual civil war, government violence reached epidemic proportions; political assassinations increased tenfold, prosecution of "subversives" trebled, the number of those who had "disappeared" doubled. Following a short lull in the bloodletting in July and August, President Carter met with the Salvadoran president, Colonel Romero, at the ceremony to mark the signing of the Panama Canal Treaty, and the short-lived hopes that Carter's human rights campaign would spell a new beginning for the relations between the two countries were disappointed. In September, Carter spoke of "great progress in the last two months in human rights in El Salvador." In November, over the protests of Human Rights Commissioner Patt Derian, the American representative of the Inter-American Development bank voted to approve a $90 million loan to El Salvador that had

---

* José Antonio Morales Ehrlich, testifying before the Inter-American Committee, House of Representatives, March 29, 1977.

been pending for several months. Three weeks later a new, drastic public order law was instituted in San Salvador which, among other things, made it a crime to "spread verbally, in writing or otherwise, within the country, or send to other countries, slanted or false news and information, aimed at disturbing the lawfully constituted order, the peace and security of the country, the economic and monetary system, or the stability of stocks and government bonds." In a speech to the American Chamber of Commerce in San Salvador on the day following the promulgation of this law of public order, Frank Devine, the new American ambassador, signaled Washington's approval. "We believe," said the ambassador, "that any government has the full right and obligation to use all legal means at its disposal to combat terrorism."

For Salvadoran democrats, the answer to the haunting question posed by Ehrlich just eight months earlier, "Can it be that our military governments will no longer be able to rely on United States support to continue their abuses?" had been received. It was no. Now the dynamic of repression and revolt moved in ever faster cycles toward more desperate explosions of defiance, despair, rage, hatred and fear.

For the Church, the persecution had only just begun, and yet, the battle lines were clearly drawn and the lives of the churchworkers were already inextricably enmeshed in an unyielding political tragedy. Soon, filled with optimism, idealism, energy and a sense of adventure, Jean Donovan would arrive to join them.

CHAPTER V

A Perfect Time to Be Here

Jean's going to El Salvador was not a lark. It was a very well thought out commitment to something she felt strongly about.

She lived her life and talked and behaved in kind of a casual, offhand way. It was almost . . . a studied cool. But underneath this casual, nonchalant, happy personality was a serious, committed person, with a deep religious conviction, which explained her madness. I mean by any standards of the twentieth century, going down to Salvador and risking your life is a form of madness. But she knew what she was doing and it fitted totally into her life's meaning, which was a commitment, I think, to her Christianity.
—Father Michael Crowley

THE CROWD OF YOUNGSTERS DEMONSTRATING ON THE steps of the cathedral in downtown San Salvador on that sunny Friday afternoon in early May 1979 were mostly young, and all were very determined. They belonged to the largest of the popular organizations, known simply as *El Bloque*—the Popular Revolutionary Bloc. In recent weeks the security forces had arrested a large number of their members, and the tortured, mutilated remains of several bodies had turned up along the sides of the roads outside the capital.

When five of the *Bloque's* leaders, including the secretary general, were picked up at the end of April, the organization decided it was time to fight back. On May 4 they occupied the French and Costa Rican embassies to attract international attention to their demands for the release of their leaders. Their actions brought the foreign press to El Salvador. When the government admitted to holding only two of the missing five, the *Bloque* called for protest demonstrations at five different locations around the city.

It was about four o'clock, and some three hundred demonstrators had congregated on the cathedral steps, when two truckloads of police, armed with automatic rifles, drove into the square. Defiantly, the demonstrators raised the volume of their slogans as some thirty police and National Guardsmen dismounted from the trucks. Suddenly, the sound of a police whistle cut through the yelling on the steps and the police opened fire.

An observer recalled later watching transfixed as a guardsman, preparing to shoot into the dense crowd trapped within the confines of the steps by a high exterior railing separating the cathedral from the pavement, calmly dropped onto one knee in the middle of the street and took careful aim. It was, he said later, as though the guard was practicing for a routine target exercise within the privacy and safety of the barracks courtyard.

Following that first volley a terrible silence filled the

square. For one moment, as the traumatized crowd on the steps froze, each individual confronted the probability of his or her own death. Then mayhem broke loose. The firing lasted for two full minutes. The hollow metallic sounds of automatic rifle fire reverberated through the cathedral square, cutting through the cries of the wounded and the screams of the living, as the crowd fought frantically to reach the safety of the interior of the church. People were tripping and falling over the bodies of the dead; a heroic few struggled to carry the wounded in their arms, or on their backs, while bullets that hadn't found their mark in human flesh ricocheted off the stone pillars, and the steps became slippery with blood.

When the shooting stopped twenty-three people were dead, seventy had been wounded, and a cool-headed, courageous, Mexican free-lance cameraman, working for CBS News, had filmed a record of the entire event. For the first time evidence of the behavior of government security forces in El Salvador penetrated into American living rooms on the national weekend news.

During the first week of May 1979, Jean had flown to Florida to spend a week with her parents prior to her departure for Central America. While she was there El Salvador suddenly hit the headlines. Later, once she had arrived and settled into the routine of intensive language instruction at the Maryknoll Center in Huehuetenango in Guatemala, she made a tape for her friend, Maryknoll priest Fern Gosslin. Fern had several years' experience as a missionary in Central America, and he and Jean had met and become good friends in Ossining the previous winter.

Huehuetenango. May 23, 1979: "How are you? I realize that my visits up to see you probably either speeded up your recovery or set you back for months, I don't know which—but you must be better now, I hope. Now that you got that mustache back you must be sexier than ever . . . (Laughter). So what's the news on Salvador in New York? I guess there's some news coming through here, but it's all in Spanish so I feel like I'm cut off from the world at the moment. I did hear that they shot fourteen more people there yesterday. I bought *Newsweek*—you should look at it—they had a whole front section devoted to Central America, the problems they're having in Guatemala and Honduras and Nicaragua. And they have an interview with the former president of Venezuela—it's kind of interesting what he's saying how the position the U.S. is taking is really poor. His one comment was that Somoza has more friends in Congress than Jimmy Carter does, which could be very true. I don't know. When I was in Miami, I arrived there with my parents, and the first thing that happened was they splashed El Salvador all over the National News every night. They had the CBS clip of the shooting at the cathedral, so my parents, as you can imagine, are hysterical. It was kind of frustrating talking to them though, because well, we stopped talking after a while, because they don't seem to be aware that there's any problem in Central America at all. They're very surprised that any of this is happening, and their solution to the problem is that the revolutionaries should stop; that there shouldn't be any violence, and they just don't understand the kind of governments and stuff that are there. When I wanted to talk to them about it, they weren't interested. They just didn't want me to go; and so we got into a bit of a fight about that. Not a fight—I just refused to talk to them because they were just, to me they weren't making any sense, and I guess I wasn't making any sense. It's the old story . . . you're having a conversation with somebody but you are talking about two different things. So I've been trying to think about it a bit, and if I can get a handle on what I want to say to them I guess I'll write them a letter."

May 1979 was a tragic and bloody month in El Salvador. Two weeks after the killings at the cathedral, members of the *Bloque* tried to march to the Venezuelan embassy to bring food and water to a group who had occupied the building. Again the police fired, and this time they killed fourteen teenagers. By the end of the month the toll was 123 dead, 30 disappeared, 92 wounded, 55 arrested, 64 vehicles and 20 buildings burned by rioting. In Guatemala, Jean began to worry that she might never get to El Salvador: "The way things are going at the moment, I heard rumors they're not going to let anyone in if things continue to blow up, so I'm going to try and go down there in five weeks. . . . There's one thing I know, that I'm supposed to be down here, right now. Not that I'm going to be able to do anything, or contribute to anything, but it's just a feeling I have. And maybe—maybe I *will* be able to. . . . I read a very interesting article before I left in one of the Maryknoll magazines. It was about Tom Dooley hospital—and two of the things that really hit me in it were: first, that you can contribute a lot and make a big difference in the world if you realize that the world you're talking about might be very small—maybe one person, or two people. And the other thing it said was that if you can find a place to serve, you can be happy. I think, they're both really true."

In late June Jean took a break from her studies and went to Salvador to visit her future colleagues in the mission at La Libertad. She arrived to find the Church mourning the assassination of one of its priests by a right-wing death squad. Father Rafael Palacios, a young country curate, had been shot to death in the street of Santa Tecla, a town some forty miles north of La Libertad, on the afternoon of June 20, and the archbishop, Monsignor Oscar Romero, had ordered that all the bells of all the churches should toll in his memory for nine days following his funeral.

Each night, at precisely eight o'clock, the mournful, defiant clashing of the bells rang out in cities, hamlets and towns, carrying a haunting message of grief, anger and solidarity from one end of the country to the other. Jean was impressed and a little awed. "Going to El Salvador, Ralph, was a great experience," she wrote to her friend and teacher, Ralph Wiatowski, in Cleveland. "I guess even ten days changed me a little. I can't quite put my finger on it, but something inside me is different. . . ."

Then it was back to Guatemala and the lonely struggles with a language for which she had no facility. From

Huehuetenango she wrote to her friend Rita at the Cleveland youth ministry: "Since I got here I've had some real ups and downs. I think everybody gets depressed a bit in language school. You have all that theory up in your head but it doesn't seem to hit you in the mouth. So the depression at times really makes you look at all sorts of things.

"I have gone through the 'why am I here' syndrome. I miss Doug and everyone, etc. And the best one is: 'Why would God want me? I'm so inadequate, no good, etc.' But then you have a good day at school and it goes away. I guess I still have some of those feelings. I look and see if I had chosen one or two different paths how I might not even believe in God let alone be a missionary. Actually, I have been having a sort of spiritual renewal—because I have been looking at my life to see what values I really have. Not always good. I have tried to write them down and then decide how and if I would like them to change. Actually I was very interested how hard it is to even be honest with yourself. I'm not at the point yet where I could share them with anyone, because they are still a bit of a surprise to me. I don't think anything earth-shattering, but . . . Jean-shattering. Now I have to have God help me grow. . . . I still have "our" problem of being an extrovert, doing everything and being scared shitless. It's great how fragile we really are; but we repair easily also. I'm off to Salvador in two weeks [August 10]."

Throughout that summer of 1979, as the killings in El Salvador continued, the country drifted deeper into chaos, and in Guatemala City, Jean's friends at the Maryknoll Center offered her the use of their home as a sanctuary in case the persecution in El Salvador became too dangerous. She wrote: "I certainly hope I don't have to hide out. I don't know, the way things sound, maybe I will. I think though, as opposed to what a lot of people have said, in some ways, with all the trouble, this is when you should be here. Because it's not when things are going really well and everybody is happy, that's not when they need support, or whatever. Maybe that's all you can give them, support, when you can't contribute anything else. And now—it seems to me like its a perfect time to be there."

When Jean returned to El Salvador on August 10, she found the church bells tolling once again for the assassination of yet another priest. Father Alirio Macias, pastor of the Church of St. Esteban, had been shot to death on the altar of his church by three civilians whom the congregation recognized as members of the local police force. In a letter to Cleveland after the funeral mass Jean remarked: "It's sad to go to that type of mass—particularly when you know why he was killed and that others will follow."

La Libertad is a small, dusty, tropical port town of some 15,000 people on El Salvador's Pacific coast. It is situated at the exact apex of a triangle, fifteen miles due west of the capital city of San Salvador and north of the International Airport. Like most small towns in the region, La Libertad sprawls outward from a large, central square, dominated by the church and flanked on either side by the barracks of the National Police and the National Guard. In La Libertad the presence of heavily armed security forces is all-pervasive, for in addition to the police and the National Guard, the Salvadoran Navy maintains a base down by the docks, as does the Treasury Police. Green, blue, brown and khaki uniforms, toting rifles and submachine guns, vigilantly patrol the square and the narrow streets at all hours of the day and night.

In happier times La Libertad could offer the delightful, relaxed way of life of an uncommercial fishing town, with some of the finest white sand beaches and the best surfing along the entire coast. Standing in the square outside the church, among the peasant women who come from the surrounding villages to sit all day in the shade of the palm trees, surrounded by small, brightly painted pieces of pottery lined in neat rows on the pavement at their feet, you can hear the waves crashing at the end of the street and sometimes even catch a glimpse of a cresting wave hanging in the western light. But La Libertad today is no resort town. It is a small community of quiet, fearful people, trapped in the seething tensions of a nation governed by the indiscriminate and barbarous use of violence.

It was not easy for Jean at first. Nothing in her training, nothing in the long, groping search that led from Westport through Cork and Cleveland to this tropical armed camp could have prepared her for the atmosphere of crisis and turmoil into which she was plunged from the very first moment of her arrival. Later, by the time the apprehensions of that Salvadoran fall had evolved into the concrete realities of civil war, she would have mastered her personal insecurities and confusion. But in the beginning, the impatient, driven young woman, who had plunged so resolutely, so obstinately and inarticulately down the road that her "gut feeling" told her was a "calling," had a lot of trouble bringing the vagueness of her expectations into line with the harsh reality of Salvadoran mission life.

"I keep getting very frustrated and wonder what I am doing here as opposed to being married and living at lollipop acres . . ." she wrote to a friend back in the States in September. "Sometimes I look back—I don't usually do this —but sometimes I'll think: Oh, my God, I'm twenty-six years old, I should be married; I shouldn't be running around the way I am. And then I think, well that's true, but I've got so many things that I want to do. . . . Besides, I haven't gotten to the point yet that I've found someone that I want to marry. But it is hard when my friends are getting married, my friends that have gotten married are having babies, my friends that haven't gotten married are having babies . . . I mean that's something too. Am I ever going to have any kids? And then I sit there, and I talk to the Lord, and I say, 'Why are you doing this to me? Why can't I just be your little suburban housewife?' And you know, he hasn't answered me yet. I don't know. Sometimes I get mad at him. Sometimes I tell him I'm going to chuck the whole thing. I've had it."

At the time that Jean arrived in La Libertad the Cleveland team in the port consisted of two priests and two nuns: Father Paul Schindler, parish priest of the town of La

Libertad and in-country director of all the Cleveland personnel, lived and worked out of the parish house in town. Father Ken Myers, Sister Dorothy Kazel and Sister Christine Rody, lived two miles away in the hillside village of Zaragoza. Farther down the coast, in the small town of Chirilagua near the Honduran border, Cleveland maintained a second smaller mission consisting of one young priest and a lay worker. The Cleveland diocese had sixteen years' experience in El Salvador, and as the persecution of the past three years had driven many of the Salvadoran priests out of their parishes, the Americans, with the support of the administration of the archdiocese of San Salvador, had reached out to adopt the abandoned communities throughout the region.

There were also two American Maryknoll Sisters working within a fifty-mile radius of La Libertad, with whom the Cleveland team maintained close contact. Sister Madeleine Dorsey lived and worked to the northwest in Santa Ana, the second largest city in the country, where singlehanded she ran a health clinic and ministered to the needs of some four thousand slum dwellers. Sister Joan Petrik ran a small rural parish in the hills to the northeast, in a village known as Tamonique which had been without a priest for sometime; in fact, her parish was one of the areas that Paul Schindler tried to visit on a monthly basis to say mass.

Whereas initially the parish of La Libertad and its outlying districts had accounted for some 35,000 people, by the summer of '79 the Cleveland team was attempting to take care of five additional rural parishes with an aggregate of around 140,000 people. A team member who had returned to the States shortly before Jean's arrival explained, "Ours was a Band-Aid operation. We would go to pass out food to keep the hunger away for a while—when what needed changing was at a much deeper level: you don't pass out food—you need to find out how to help people to grow their own food."

Paul Schindler and his team knew they could minister

only superficially to the areas where the local priests were no longer able to work, but they had little choice. There were areas that they were lucky to get to once a month, sometimes once every two months. They focused their efforts on training local leaders to administer the health programs, the nutrition programs, the dried milk programs that served over 10,000 children from one to six years old, together with their pregnant mothers. They trained leaders who would organize communities in their areas to distribute the food, to pass along basic health instructions, and also catechists who would hold liturgies and celebrations in the church without the priest. It was frustrating work on many levels: first because they simply did not have enough men and women to serve the needs of the people adequately, but also because the people whom they were training to help out were the very ones destined to become the most vulnerable when the "authorities" came around looking for "subversives." When Paul went to see the local commander of the National Guard to ask him why he was telling the people to stay away from the church, why he was spreading the word that he, Padre Pablo, was a Communist, the commander told him: "I know you're not a Communist, Father, but you are training leaders, and when the Communists come, they will take them over."

When Jean arrived, Paul was only too happy to hand over to her the mission's books. However, it was Dorothy Kazel who became her guide as she began getting to know the parish and its people. Jean was lucky, for it would be hard to find a more delightful, wise or compatible companion, and in the pressure-cooker atmosphere of El Salvador, the two women quickly developed an enriching friendship. They were alike in many ways: both cared deeply about people and saw their role principally in terms of the help and support they could provide; both had unlimited energy and an apparently fearless, spontaneous openness to new challenges; both shared a straightforward no-nonsense approach to the world, and an absolute commitment to stand and fight for their convictions—for justice, for people, for

their own beliefs. Unlike Jean, however, for whom her public personality was still all too frequently a mask for imma-
turity and a cover for much inner confusion and insecurity,
at thirty-nine, Dorothy had acquired a hard-earned maturity
along with a rare and solid grasp on reality. Slim, athletic
and very pretty, her youthful appearance belied her age and
the fact that she had spent nineteen years as an Ursuline
nun—eight of them working in El Salvador—where her
midwestern common sense had helped to dispel any illusions inherent in their work: "We know that we are sort of
Band-Aid instruments," she had written home to her parents
in Cleveland. "We are not able to participate fully, completely, in the culture and politics and everything that is
going on around here. We touch on things. But we can only
touch on things in a hopeful way and in a loving way, and
in this way bring Jesus Christ to the people." As Jean struggled, during those first difficult months to get onto her own
two feet and carve a niche for herself in the understaffed,
overextended mission, Dorothy provided a one-woman support system—she became the older sister Jean had never
had.

Paul had decided that Jean should take over the administration of the Caritas food program for a community
of some 6,000 harvest workers, who lived in an area known
as Santa Cruz near the airport. The community had no
electricity, no running water or sanitation. Right beside it
there was a plentiful supply of fresh water on the ranch of
the neighboring landlord, but that water was exclusively
for the use of the landlord's cattle. The inhabitants of Santa
Cruz were prevented from using it by the landlord's guards.
So each day they made the trek to the river, over a mile
away. There was a minuscule wooden shed that served as
a church and sometime meeting hall, but no school, and no
medical facilities. Not that the children would have been
able to attend classes even if they had been available. At
least not during the harvest season from October to March.
Small children, as young as seven or eight, many of whom
didn't even know their own age, spent their childhood pick-

ing cotton from daybreak to sundown for twenty-five or thirty cents a day.

Over the next sixteen months, Jean would spend a lot of her time with the people of Santa Cruz. She had brought a motorcycle with her—not the monster Harley Davidson that she had used in Cleveland, but a lightweight Honda—and when she was not transporting cases of dried milk or sacks of corn, she went everywhere on her bike. It was perfect for navigating the narrow dirt tracks around Santa Cruz. It was also a source of endless excitement and joy to the children, whom she would take for rides around the open field at the edge of the community where the older boys and young men played football on Sundays. She had also brought her guitar. She was a terrible musician, but she worked at it, practicing the same songs for hours on end, so that finally her enthusiasm was catching. Before long, while she played Irish folk ballads for them, the young Salvadorans were trying hard to teach her their rhythms and their songs. So, from the very beginning, she mixed in and made friends. And in the evenings, when the cotton pickers returned from their long day in the fields, she was there to sit down with their families and find out about their problems.

Because of their parishioners' work hours, most of the missionaries' activities took place at night—and of course on Sundays. Then it was up to Jean to coordinate with the local lay preachers—the Delegates of the Word—and set up Bible readings and what were known as Celebrations of the Word. Straggling home exhausted from a twelve-hour day in the fields under the blazing sun, the cotton pickers and their families would find Jean waiting for them, masking her nervousness as she kidded around with the children who had come to love and trust this funny, large, blond *gringa*. Jean would wait patiently until the workers had eaten their supper of beans and a couple of dry tortillas and then, opening up the small wooden shack that served as the community church, she would light the candles. While one of her helpers rang the bell to announce the coming service, she knelt quietly in the empty church and prayed for calm and strength and the capacity to make of the liturgy a source of hope and solidarity to her congregation.

It was Jean's responsibility to select the scriptural texts for these celebrations. First she would read a passage. Then one of the parishioners would repeat it. Then they would discuss the meaning of what had been said. The words were two thousand years old, and it was Jean's job to make them come alive for her congregation of exhausted, neglected peasants struggling to feed their families and to stay out of trouble with the authorities. The message did not vary much. It brought the Good News of a Christ who had a commitment to the poor and the discarded of this world, who spoke of justice, of the individual dignity of every man, woman and child, and of their responsibility to each other in a brotherhood of love.

In earlier times, in the days of Rutilio Grande, the missionaries had concentrated their efforts on adult literacy courses, consciousness-raising and the development of Basic Christian Communities—those cells of Church-educated and inspired activists that had proven so potent an element in the battle against apathy. By the time Jean arrived, however, the Basic Christian Communities were already an established and embattled feature of rural life in certain areas, and the relations between the Church and the landlords had become so violent that the major task of the missionaries was now directed to the next step: protection, support and sustenance for an already awakened population.

In preparing for these celebrations Jean took her cue from Dorothy, who had written of the goal of this work: "The whole Gospel of John is about love, and the whole reason for living is love, and if we can just breathe a little bit of love, a little bit of warmth and a little bit of concern —extend the whole idea of universality—extend this to the people here, then, I think that's all we can really do."

Since Paul could not get out to Santa Cruz more than once a month, these liturgies and celebrations took the place of mass, and Jean took the responsibility very seriously. She would return to La Libertad afterward and give a blow-by-blow description to Dorothy of what had gone on. Sometimes it would take three or four readings of the same passage before the people would really listen to the words, hear what was being said, and begin to respond in terms of its relationship to their own experience. It was all very new and quite scary. "Here I am a missionary—and I'm almost even still scared at times to admit it to people. It's obvious that I am, now that I have my official position, but, well I'm never sure if I've got enough to share with people. And then I realize that I do, and it's God that helps us, he sort of carries us, because I couldn't do this by myself. . . ."

The words sounded reassuring, but there was a lack of conviction that she was too honest not to recognize: to her confidante, Rita, back in Cleveland she confessed: "My spirituality is not doing too well right now. I've not been spending a lot of time praying. I'm not exactly sure what I have been spending a lot of time doing. I seem to struggle so much with—I see so many people doing so much good all the time—and it comes so easy for them. And you know, I think that sin comes so easy to me, and being good is the hard part. . . . I do believe, and I want to make a lot of sense of things. But I just don't have that spontaneous spirituality. I believe a lot of things very deeply, and they're always at the back of my mind, but I have many, many doubts, and I can't seem to put myself in that childlike relationship with God. It's like my personality in some ways. I'm too independent, and I'm afraid to be dependent, even on God. . . . Now let me see. I certainly go on, don't I? And then I never think I make any sense. . . ."

She wrote a lot, when she could find the time. In response to a letter from her friend Maura Corkery, in Cork, she wrote: "How about me? Well, I'm very happy. Happy and exhilarated. Depressed. Glad, sad, lonely, on top of the world, etc." She really didn't feel much like a missionary—whatever that was. Many missionaries, she had discovered, especially priests, never overcame a paternalistic, patronizing attitude toward their parishioners. They talked among themselves about "my people," and "my groups," and whereas it had always shocked her, in an abstract sort of way, now it made her angry. She wanted no part of the prestige that she perceived was attached to the position of an American missionary. She wanted, if possible, no part of the Church as an institution of power and influence. But she did want to be needed. And as she struggled with her doubts and fears of inadequacy, something rather unexpected started to happen. She became aware that the very people she had come all this way to help—the illiterate farm workers and their families, surviving from day to day in their bone-poor, uncluttered houses—had something that she wanted. What they had to teach her about life and suffering, about courage and human dignity, about friendship and solidarity, just might provide some answers to the mysterious, elusive calling that had brought her here.

She began to discover that life as it was lived by the Salvadoran poor was more real, more humane, than any she had known to date. The people of Santa Cruz and La Libertad depended for their very existence upon each other. There was no room, no motivation for any pretense at being other than who one was. Their tolerant acceptance of each other and the warmth and generosity among people who had so very little dazzled her. For the first time she saw and understood the meaning of community. For the Salvadoran poor a neighbor was someone with whom one shared whatever small possessions one had—an extra chair or dishes, a shirt or a fresh laundered dress. A neighbor was someone who cooked for the family next door if the mother was taken ill; minded the smallest children of the family down the hill when both parents and older children were working in the fields; walked several miles to fetch the priest for someone in trouble. Everyone was one other's neighbor and was invited to join in family events—births, deaths, marriages.

To Jean the humanity of this mutual dependence was

a revelation. As she immersed herself in this foreign culture of poverty her new surroundings evoked a resonance within her, and slowly she began to shed the competitive pressures of her own background. It was as if this was what she had been looking for all along.

"Dear Gwen," she wrote to her friend and teacher at Maryknoll. "I'm beginning to understand what you meant about spirituality . . . there is so much to know and feel and grow from inside all of us. I guess you start to wonder if you are down here for yourself, other people, God, etc. Everything gets mixed up at times. It seems that you're here to be ministered to, a lot more than to minister."

Almost as an afterthought she added: "There have been lots of problems in the San Salvador diocese lately, as I'm sure you know. I have the feeling we are really going to feel the effects of Nicaragua in coming months."

During August and September, as the implications of the July victory of the Nicaraguan Sandinistas spread something close to panic among the rich and the military, and excited a wild and dangerous optimism among the popular organizations, the repression became progressively more irrational and more brutal. "We've got a new task down here," Paul Schindler wrote back to a former mission colleague, Sister Martha Owens, in Cleveland. "Twice now we've had bodies dumped on the beach down by Mirador." (Mirador—literally, a lookout—a scenic point on the winding coastal road.) "The Guardia refused to do anything about them so I got permission from the judge and I took some of the boys with me and we ended up by burning them—the bodies were so badly decomposed and partly destroyed by vultures—a couple had been decapitated— really terribly chopped up. The second time it happened two of them were women. I took some pictures that I'll send back to have developed—just don't eat any lunch before you look at them."

On roads all over the country, mutilated, unrecognizable bodies were being dumped out of jeeps and trucks. But politically the repression was having diminishing results.

The rhythm of the armed response by the militant groups on the Left continued to accelerate. They stepped up their attacks on members of ORDEN, on rural police stations, and even on barracks of the National Guard; meanwhile, in the capital, striking workers occupied and burned down factories and office buildings; demonstrations by the popular organizations degenerated frequently into street battles, and the charred hulks of burned-out buses littered the streets. In San Salvador, two hundred and forty-eight priests and nuns, representing virtually every religious order and parish in the country, addressed an open letter to the government: "Many of us," they wrote, "are on the verge of political despair. A desperate people can easily turn to civil war. Justice must be the answer to this desperation, but the powers in command do not give this answer."

In Washington, an alarmed State Department appointed a top-level task force to monitor developments and published a travel advisory warning American citizens of the personal dangers of visiting El Salvador. In Cleveland, the bishop dispatched the director of the mission, Father Al Winters, to study the advisability of withdrawing the team. After three days of meetings, Jean wrote a somewhat shaky letter back to Maryknoll: October 2. "Dear Gwen. I have tried to write this letter three times but it just doesn't seem to come out right. I am writing today because Al Winters is here on a visit from the States and he can mail it in the U.S. I want to write about what's happening here but it's so hard to put into words. And you never know what the truth is. All I can say is that things are really heating up and the tension is unbelievable."

Of her colleagues Ursuline Sister Dorothy Kazel and Maryknoll Sisters Madeleine Dorsey and Terri Alexander she wrote: "I am working with a really *great lady* who is an Ursuline nun. We also see two Maryknoll nuns that are really neat women. One of them was in Nicaragua. She is giving Dotty and me ideas on how to run refugee camps. If war does break out I have tentatively decided to try and set up a center in Zaragoza or La Libertad. Who knows?

It's strange—probably when my spiritual life is at an all-time low I know that I need more help from God than I ever had before."

She was depressed and a little scared. She was also evidently feeling frustrated that Paul, or someone, did not see things precisely her way. Jean's problems with male authority figures, particularly with the latent chauvinism of some of her male coworkers—American and Salvadoran—had much to do with her sense of alienation from the institutional discipline of the Church, and during these early months in El Salvador the barometer of her faith—her spiritual life—was particularly volatile and sensitive to the fluctuating status of her relationship to those who were in charge of her activities.

"I am really at times fed up with the Church," she wrote to Gwen Vendley, "and blame God for it. I find myself asking him if I can't cop out of the institution and deal with things myself—which I can—that is my personal relationship with him. But then he expects me to deal with these men running around calling themselves priests. Everything seems so sacramental and no close reaching out to the people. . . . Don't you love my griping? What I am finding my frustrations in go to what is community. In a way, it's equalizing everyone. I find Christ a lot more in a group of lay people joined in prayer, genuinely caring for one another, than in John Paul II and giant masses in Washington or wherever. . . . I guess I just find that when my heart and soul really pour out, someone always wants to put a boundary on it. But I am sure God is calling me to something and presently I am not listening too well."

Dorothy wrote a note to her great friend and former partner, Ursuline Sister Martha Owens. Martha had spent six years with Dorothy in El Salvador and their shared experience made it possible to communicate almost in shorthand.

October 3: "Dear Friend: We had a good meeting today followed by a swim and a beautiful liturgy. We are now getting ready to go out to eat.

"Before I have to give this to Al, I want to say something to you—I think you will understand. We talked quite a bit today about what happens *IF* something begins. Most of us feel we would want to stay here. Now this depends on *WHAT* happens—if there is any way we can help—like run a refugee center or something. We wouldn't want to just run out on the people. Anyway, Al thinks people we love should understand how we feel—in case something happens—so he and the Bishop don't have to yank us out of here unnecessarily. I thought I should say this to you because I don't want to say it to anyone else—because I don't think they would understand. Anyway, my beloved friend, just know how I feel and 'treasure it in your heart.' If a day comes where others will have to understand, please explain it for me. Thanks. Love ya lots. D."

With the signs of approaching civil war clearly visible, the Salvadoran Church was already laying the groundwork for refugee centers in which women, children and old people, fleeing from the violence in their villages, could be housed and fed and given some protection from the assaults of rural security forces and paramilitary groups like ORDEN. In fact, the first such center would not be opened until the following January of 1980, but when the urgent need for such shelters did arise, the prior planning by Church leaders stood the beleaguered rural population in good stead.

In the midst of all the turmoil and anxiety, a remarkable new presence now appeared in Jean's life, whose influence was destined to be pivotal in her development. She had known of him even before she came. Early in September she had written to Ireland: "I work in the La Libertad Parish in the Archdiocese mostly because I wanted to work in the diocese of Archbishop Romero. He is a great guy. He is the leader of Liberation Theology in practice." But all her information had not prepared her for the impact of his personality. "It is so inspiring," she wrote, "when you see and hear a man like Archbishop Romero. He doesn't back down for nothing. He really is the voice of the people. The way they respond to him is great. It is like the Pope when he enters church. They stand on the pews and clap for him. They clap his sermons, and at the recessional, everyone tries to shake his hand. And I think he does manage to shake most people's hands. At the same time he is a very humble person. He has been nominated for the Nobel Peace Prize. I hope he wins."

Not surprisingly, Jean's most constant and most intimate correspondent was Michael Crowley from Ireland. To get around the censorship, she frequently sent him tapes. When she discovered that she could purchase the archbishop's weekly homilies in the diocesan newspaper, *Orientación*, she also found a way to send him those. "She absolutely adored Romero," Crowley says. "In fact, in the very early days in Salvador, she kept sending me his sermons, thinking, I suppose, that I'd maybe improve the people of Cork by using some of them. . . ."

Oscar Arnulfo Romero was a small man; soft-spoken, shy, a man from the rural middle classes (his father had been the telegraph operator in a small country town near the Honduran border). When his appointment to succeed the seventy-five-year-old Archbishop Luis Chávez y González as head of the Salvadoran Church was announced in January of 1977, the military and the landowners, the businessmen and the bankers had been delighted. Chávez y González had been in charge for thirty-eight years before he resigned. It was under his leadership that the new-fangled "liberation theology" had infiltrated and flourished within the Salvadoran Church. It had been feared that Rome might choose as his successor the liberal assistant to Chávez y González, Monsignor Rivera y Damas, auxiliary bishop of San Salvador. Now the oligarchy could congratulate themselves that their influence with the Papal Nuncio was not for nothing, and an era of Church-State tensions would soon be corrected. True, the Jesuits still had to be taken care of, but the military had an agenda for that problem. What mattered most was that now, from the highest pulpit in the land, and above all, in the only media of communication not under their direct control and censorship, the

Church radio station and weekly diocesan newspaper, the voice that spoke to the Salvadoran people would be one that they could trust to spell out the traditional conservative role of the Church.

Archbishop Romero, according to the popular wisdom, was a conservative, a traditionalist and a timid man of somewhat frail health, who could be counted upon to support the existing autocratic structures, crack down on the socially active priests, and return the Salvadoran Church to its rightful place in the historic triple alliance of the rich, the military and the Church. Now it would be like the old times. The bishop would be on hand to bless the inauguration of the bank's latest new office building, or to preside at the military academy on graduation day. There would be photographs in the press of the president, the generals, and the archbishop gravely awarding medals to the National Guard (duly sprinkled first with holy water), and the president's wife would serve tea at the country club for the representatives of the bishop's favorite charity. There would be no more talk about politics, about the rights of peasants and workers to organize trade unions; above all no more discussions about land reform. The military president, Colonel Romero (not related to the archbishop) through the army and the National Guard, the police and their counterparts in the countrywide paramilitary organization, ORDEN, would take care of problems in the countryside, and peace and good times would return to the swimming pools and the gardens, the polo fields and the golf courses; on Sundays, the prominent families would once again be able to enjoy idyllic family reunions on their country estates.

They had made one miscalculation. As one after another of the bishop's priests were killed, Monsignor Romero changed.

On the night of the murder of Rutilio Grande, Oscar Romero went to the rural town of Aguilares to mourn the death of his friend among those for whom he had died. He excommunicated the killers; closed down the school for three days; and sent the students home to reflect on the meaning of Rutilio Grande's life and death. He announced that until such time as the government brought those responsible to justice, no member of the hierarchy or the clergy would attend any civic ceremony; and in open defiance of an existing state of siege, and a government ban on all public gatherings, he ordered that all of the churches should cancel their services on the following Sunday so that the entire country could participate, in person, or by radio, in a unique memorial mass at the Metropolitan Cathedral.

Rutilio Grande's funeral mass represented the first major demonstration of solidarity between the newly awakened peasant population and "their" church. That day, the new Church of the Poor, the Church of Medellín, paid homage to its first Salvadoran martyr, while in the person of the new archbishop it found its first national leader. Soon, in the official press, at the dinner tables of the wealthy, and in the barracks of the army and the police, they had begun to call him a terrorist, a traitor, a dupe of the Communist priests. But to the people of El Salvador he was known quite simply as "Monsignor," and he became the first and only popular leader the nation had ever known.

On November 7, 1978, Romero had written to Pope John Paul II:

From the beginning of my ministry in the Archdiocese, I believed in conscience that God asked of me, and gave me, a pastoral strength that contrasted with my conservative inclinations and temperament. I believe it is my duty to take a stand in defense of my Church, and from the Church, at the side of my oppressed and abused people.

I have not rejected dialogue with the government, but I have placed as a condition for it that an atmosphere of trust be developed by their ceasing to repress and outrage the people, and by giving signs of respect for their rights.

From the beginning, the mild, sixty-year-old man with the warm voice and the shy yet radiant smile, who had inherited the leadership of the Church at the precise moment when its support for the poor and the oppressed had led inexorably to conflict with the government, never wavered in his commitment to the struggle for a more just, compassionate, lawful society.

That struggle evoked an immediate, fervent response from Jean, for Romero's example validated and brought vibrantly alive for her everything that she had thought or felt about the role of the Church, and his personal charisma and accessibility gave renewed strength and purpose to her own daily struggles to help the people of La Libertad and Santa Cruz.

Among Romero's gifts that so enraged his enemies was a way with words and a clarity of thought and expression. The government, even some of his fellow bishops, consistently sought to distort his message and besieged Rome with complaints about this meddlesome priest who had abandoned the teaching of the Scriptures in order to manipulate the politics of the nation. Romero never ducked their accusations. He simply went right on refining his definition of the role of the Church and the meaning of the Christian life:

"Let no one be offended," he preached from the pulpit of the cathedral at his Sunday mass,

> because we use the divine words read at our mass to illuminate the social, political and economic situation of our people. Not to do so would be un-Christian. Christ desires to unite himself with humanity, so that the light he brings from God might become life for nations and individuals. Each week, I go about the country collecting the cries of the people, their pain from so much crime and the ignominy of so much violence. Each week, I ask the Lord to give me the right words to console, to de-

nounce, to call for repentance. And even though I may be a voice crying in the desert, I know the Church is making the effort to fulfill its mission.

As the situation within the country became more acute, Romero's access to an international audience proved especially galling to those who held power in El Salvador. In February of 1980, he was invited to Belgium to accept an honorary doctorate at the University of Louvain, and availed himself of the opportunity to explain the intellectual and spiritual basis for his ministry.

I come from the smallest country in far-away Latin America. I will not try to speak, and you cannot expect me to speak, the way an expert in politics might. Nor will I even speculate, as someone might who was an expert, on the theoretical relationship between the faith and politics. No, I am going to speak simply as a pastor, as one who, together with his people, has been learning the beautiful but harsh truth that the Christian faith does not cut us off from the world, but immerses us in it, that the Church is not a fortress, set apart from the city, but is a follower of that Jesus who lived, worked, battled, and died in the midst of a city, in a "polis."

The essence of the Church lies in its mission of service to the world. The Church exists to act in solidarity with the hopes and with the joys, with the anxieties and with the sorrows of men and women. To put it in one word, the world which the Church ought to serve is for us the world of the poor. It is the poor who tell us what the world is, and what the Church's service to the world is. It is the poor who tell us what the "polis" is, and what the city is, and what it means for the Church really to live in that world.*

When he traveled the country, visiting the shacks made of pieces of tin and cardboard where his people lived, he made no speeches, brought no promises. He observed. Asked questions. Listened. He held in his arms the babies dying of diarrhea and dehydration caused by malnutrition and the absence of medical care. He looked into the anguished faces of widows and orphans whose husbands and fathers had been found by the side of the road, cut up in pieces, beheaded, mutilated, eyes gouged out, hands and limbs chopped off, and then discarded by their killers in the public light of day to spread terror and enforce submission among the living. And what he saw, what he heard on these forays into the heart of the Salvadoran countryside, became the inspiration for his weekly homilies:

> Within this world which lacks a human face, the Church of my Archdiocese has chosen to incarnate itself. The hope which our Church encourages is not naive, nor is it passive—it is rather a summons for the great majority of the people, the poor, that they assume their proper responsibility, that they raise their consciousness, that in a country where it is legally or practically prohibited, they set about organizing themselves. The world of the poor teaches us that liberation will arrive only when the poor are the controllers of, and protagonists in, their own struggle and liberation.

As he traveled through the abandoned communities, he listened to the stories of men, women and children forced to flee from their homes and live for months on end

* Address at the University of Louvain, February 2, 1980.

in the hills, hiding from their persecutors—ORDEN, the National Guard, the army and the police. He learned about what he would call "the sorrowful mystery of the dis-appeared" from their relatives—"mothers, wives and children who have crossed this entire country end to end searching for their loved ones without finding any answers —hoping, only to end their search in some clandestine cemetery...."

He understood all too well the price that would be exacted from the poor and from the Church for any change, yet he never deviated from the course he had set for himself and for his followers:

> The defense of the poor, in a world deep in conflict, has occasioned something which is new in the recent history of our Church: persecution. In less than three years over 50 priests have been attacked, threatened, calumniated. Six are already martyrs—they have been murdered; several have been tortured and others expelled. Nuns have also been the objects of persecution. Several parish communities have been raided.

> If all this has happened to the Church, you can guess what has happened to ordinary Christian people, to the peasants, the catechists, the Delegates of the Word, to the basic ecclesial communities. As always, even in this persecution, it has been the poor among us who have suffered most.

> The persecution of the Church is a result of defending the poor; our persecution is nothing more than sharing in the destiny of the poor.

Every Sunday morning throughout the three years of his ministry, Monsignor Romero mounted the pulpit at the eight o'clock mass in the Metropolitan Cathedral and publicly exposed, for the nation at large and for the world beyond its borders, the reality of Salvadoran life. Week after week he would document the names, the places and the circumstances of deaths, disappearances, tortures and rapes among the heretofore faceless, anonymous poor. And every Sunday, long before eight o'clock, every square foot of space in the cathedral would be jammed. Those who arrived early enough to have seats, leaped onto the benches to see and applaud his entrance the moment he appeared. When he spoke to the people of El Salvador about the reality of their lives, they would interrupt him with prolonged, spontaneous bursts of applause, in sudden, shocked recognition of truths long buried, silenced, denied.

"These days, I have to walk the roads gathering up dead friends, listening to the anguish of widows and orphans and trying to spread hope." Information. Facts. Understanding. Courage and solidarity. These were Romero's only weapons, and every Sunday he armed the people of Salvador with them. In terms that no other public person would dare to use he denounced the crimes and the criminals and attacked the origins of the moral decadence that he perceived to be at the heart of Salvadoran brutality:

> Among us there are those who would sell the just man for money, and the poor man for a pair of sandals; those who, in their mansions, practice violence and accumulate plunder, those who crush the poor, those who bring the kingdom of violence closer while they lie upon their beds of ivory; those who take over house upon house, and field upon field, until they appropriate the whole territory, and remain sole owners of the country.
>
> That is why we have denounced what in our country has become the idolatry of wealth, of the absolute right, within the capitalist system, of private property, of political power in the

national security regimes, in the name of which the insecurity of the individual is itself institutionalized. No matter how tragic it may appear, the Church, through its entrance into the sociopolitical world, has learned how to recognize, how to deepen its understanding of the essence of sin. The fundamental essence of sin in this world of ours is revealed as the death of Salvadorans; and the worst offense against God is to turn the children of God, temples of the Holy Spirit, the body of Christ in history, into victims of oppression and injustice, into slaves to economic greed, into fodder for political repression.

An American missionary, a colleague of Jean's, recalled later, that on any village street, on a Sunday morning, you could hear Romero's voice emerging from houses and shops all over town. Market women abandoned their produce stalls to gather around anyone with a transistor; in downtown San Salvador the cadences of his voice mingled with the traffic, as bus conductors and taxi drives tuned in to the Church station; and in many places individual churches, responding to local requests, set up loudspeakers to broadcast the service from the cathedral to their own parishioners. The government tried to jam his airwaves; there were repeated bombing attacks on the Church radio station and the printing office of the diocesan newspaper which published his homilies weekly; but they could not silence him for long.

"You knew what he was saying had to be said, and you knew he took his life in his hands every time he said it," the American said, and added wistfully, "They were very beautiful times. He was the greatest man I ever met in my life. He took the Gospel story and wove it into everyday life—he made it come alive; you'd listen to him and say to yourself, 'This is what Jesus was talking about' . . ."

Intellectually, Jean's exposure to Romero was the most

exhilarating encounter of her life. She was not one to get up early, but on Sundays, unless Paul needed her urgently in La Libertad, she never missed Romero's mass. He personified and gave substance to a view of the world and to a system of values toward which she had been gravitating ever since her college days in Ireland. It was Crowley's visions of a Christianity unburdened by hierarchy, mysticism or authoritarianism—simple, direct, focused on solidarity with and for ordinary men and women in their daily struggles for survival.

Since La Libertad was within the diocese of San Salvador, Monsignor Romero would visit the port for confirmation ceremonies at least twice a year. In the months and weeks leading up to his visit, the missionaries would spend long hours with the young candidates preparing them for their religious initiation into adulthood. After the ceremony, Romero would stay for lunch with the members of the team and their Salvadoran lay workers. In keeping with his insistence that the Church must share in the poverty of the people, the meal would be a simple one, served in the open courtyard behind Paul's house. On the occasion of his first visit after her arrival, Jean had baked a batch of chocolate-chip cookies in his honor, which, to her vast delight, the archbishop greatly enjoyed. From then on, every week she would bake a fresh supply for him and drop them off in San Salvador with the nuns who ran the convent where he lived.

A change of government did come to El Salvador. On October 15, 1979, a group of junior military officers overthrew the government in a bloodless coup, and promised a program to bring justice, reforms and democracy to the battered nation. Jean's letter back to Maryknoll said much about the growing influence of Archbishop Romero in her development: October 19. "Dear Gwen: Just thought I would write and say that things are fairly calm here—well, as calm as can be expected. On Monday the junior officers ousted the government. They have set up a junta with three civilians and are promising free elections, agrarian reforms, etc. Right now we are in the middle of a state of siege, martial law and everything else you can think of. Most life seems to be going on as usual, with isolated acts of violence. So, I hope everyone is praying for us.

"I was just sorry Bishop Romero did not receive the Nobel Peace Prize, 'cause it may well have been his prophetic preaching and strength that brought about this change. As one Jesuit wrote about him: 'This man, timid, cowardly, became a prophet. He is the miracle God gave us.' To many Romero is a saint here. It's done something for me, in that I had become very hard—in believing for example that change comes only through violence. Maybe now I can believe a bit more in prayer. . . ."

CHAPTER VI

The Last Chance

ON NOVEMBER 5, 1979, JEAN WROTE BACK TO CLEVELAND about the young officers' coup that had taken place on October 15. "We had a coup, three weeks ago, and at the time—it's unbelievable—I missed it. I was in New Orleans for about four or five days to meet my parents and brother and sister-in-law at the American Institute of Certified Public Accountants Convention. The reason I went is because my parents had been upset about all the violence and everything here, and I wanted to talk to them. So, I went up, and they had a coup while I was up there—my one chance—and I missed it. So I came right back. I was the only passenger on the TACA flight to San Salvador the next day."

Michael Donovan recalls the intrusion of Salvadoran politics into what had been a relaxed and happy family reunion. "Jean explained that we shouldn't worry, that the new group taking over the government were the same people as the old group," he says. Having spent three days conning her family into believing that all was well in El Salvador, that there was no violence in Libertad and that most of what they read in the press was exaggerated, the sudden overthrow of the government by a group of young, reform-minded officers put Jean on a bit of a spot. Ironically, her flip explanation regarding the makeup of the new government would prove only too close to the mark.

"The first junta was a risk but we had to take it. It was the last possibility for peaceful change." Guillermo Ungo, the man who spoke these words, lives in exile now, and today he's a leading spokesman for the Democratic Revolutionary Front, the political arm of the guerrilla forces fighting the Salvadoran government. In October 1979, when the young officers invited him to join them as a member of a new "Revolutionary Military-Civilian Junta," he was a professor at the Catholic University and a leader of what was left of the Social Democrats.

On October 15, the young officers had promised "a new era in Salvadoran history under the principles of peace and effective observance of the human rights of all citizens." But a palace coup was one thing, an all-out confrontation with their military superiors quite another. A fundamental restructuring of the security forces that a total rupture with the past would have required—and that the situation and the Salvadoran people were demanding—was something they may never have really contemplated and certainly took no concrete steps to achieve. With hard-liners still in charge of all promotions within the armed forces, the "new" military very quickly became indistinguishable from the old.

In those crucial weeks of October, November and December, decent men on all sides sought desperately to implement the promises of the October 15 proclamation, to isolate the power of the traditional oligarchic minority while building bridges between Salvadorans of all other ideologies, and in the last resort, to avert the catastrophe of civil war. Meanwhile, the traditional military, from the positions it continued to hold in the high command and its control of key garrisons around the country, pursued its own agenda: one dedicated to eliminating their own and their rich patrons' traditional enemies on the Left, and to obstructing any substantive economic or social reforms.

For its part, the organized Left, the committed activists of the popular organizations, excluded from direct participation in the new government, unaware of the crucial generational and ideological divisions within the army, took to the streets to protest what from their perspective was nothing more than a continuation of the old regime with new faces, fancy promises. In so doing, they played straight into the hands of those intent on subverting the original objectives of the coup.

On October 31 Jean wrote to Rita in Cleveland: "Well kid, I got your letter today and it really brightened up my day to hear from you—firstly I appreciate your prayers. We all need them. Yes, we certainly did have a coup. So far everyone is just holding their breath and waiting to see what happens. The leftist groups are making lots of trouble and twenty-three were killed in the capital yesterday. At times I'm really scared for me as well, but mostly I know the Lord is and will protect me, so I'm certainly not looking over my shoulder."

By the end of October, over two hundred civilians had been killed by the security forces, and the issue that would plague and eventually destroy the junta —the government's inability to control those hard-line forces within its own military who were determined to block the participation of the Left in the process of transition from dictatorship to democracy—was out in the open. Meanwhile, from the sidelines, a powerful new force was preparing to enter the scene and throw its prestige and its support behind the hard-liners. In his homily of November 4, with his customary prophetic instinct, Archbishop Romero drew the nation's attention to things to come:

> On at least two occasions this week, the government of the United States has expressed its support for the junta by offering economic and military aid. But it seems that the best way the United States can help El Salvador at this time is by conditioning its aid to a purification of the security forces, a satisfactory resolution of the problem of the disappeared, and the bringing to justice of those responsible.

> If these prerequisites are not set, the assistance the United States might provide in the military field will only be re-enforcing the oppressors of the people.

It was a gentle admonition, and the policymakers in Washington, their gaze firmly riveted on the rearview mirror in which all they saw were images of the recent Sandinista victory in Nicaragua in July, were not in the mood to hear it.

Jean, good Republican conservative that she still was, almost certainly reflected accurately the views of the embassy staff when she wrote to a friend in the first week of November: "What has happened is that the leftist groups— I think they're afraid they missed out on their glorious revolution and all the killings—so they have been making trouble and everything. They have been having demonstrations and taking buildings and taking hostages and all . . . but we have two colonels on the junta and three civilians and they're from varied walks of life in El Salvador and they're three good guys. We'll just have to wait and see what happens."

Given the division between progressives and hardliners in the military, the situation was extremely complex and delicate. While those moderate army officers loyal to junta member Colonel Adolfo Majano, a highly regarded leader of the October conspiracy, shared his and the junior officers' desires to build bridges to the Left and to implement the reforms called for in the October proclamation, they were naive, politically inexperienced and mortally handicapped by their lack of control over the intelligence services of their own forces. Under the direction of Minister of Defense Colonel García and his deputy, Colonel Carranza, the security apparatus of the state remained a bastion of the old order. The October proclamation had called for an end to the repression of the popular organizations and the rural workers; the abolition of the paramilitary organization ORDEN; the establishment of an independent special commission to investigate the fate of the hundreds of the "disappeared," and the inauguration of a series of economic and social measures designed to break the hold of the traditional oligarchy on the levers of wealth and power. But the hard-liners, who ran the intelligence bureaus of the army, the National Police, the National Guard and the Treasury Police, were strategically placed to discredit the moderates within their own forces by exploiting fears of a Communist insurgency, to obstruct any investigation of the crimes of the previous government—crimes in which many had been personally involved—and to recruit and organize volunteers for the burgeoning death squads. Tragically, and fatal to the new government's commitment to democracy, it was these very forces, run by men who considered the popular organizations and the workers to be the enemy, which virtually controlled the government's contacts and relations with them and their followers.

In the first weeks after October 15, the issue of responsibility for their "disappeared" relatives, friends and former comrades became the number one emotional issue among the young activists on the Left. Understanding the crucial importance of the moment, Archbishop Romero, who supported the program of the October movement, addressed the problem head on: "It is urgent," he said, "to impose sanctions on the guilty. Everyone knows who the guilty are. Who committed the murders. Who committed the tortures." Everyone knew—and no one, apparently, had the power to do anything about it. When the civilian members of the junta received a delegation from the Committee of Mothers of the Disappeared it was a sad occasion. Confronted with the suffering on the worn faces of peasant women nervously, hopefully producing much-handled, creased snapshots of their lost sons and daughters, former chancellor of the Catholic University and junta member Ramón Mayorga Quiróz dropped his head in his hands and admitted despairingly, "I am overwhelmed by the problem. I have no idea where your children are. I pray they are still alive. I just don't know."

So the activists led their followers back onto the streets in kamikazelike demonstrations, protests and strikes; they were met with more violence, death, disappearances and torture, and all hope of achieving a policy of reconciliation and collaboration with the Left, upon which the original program of the October coup depended, ebbed away in so much freshly spilt blood.

From the American perspective, the specter of a Communist insurgency sweeping—Sandinista style—into the vacuum of power created by a division in the traditional structures of authority and control represented the real threat. The Carter administration shared the views of the hard-liners that the "extremists" and "subversives"—the hundreds of angry young demonstrators running amok in the streets, seizing offices and churches to protest security force violence, the lack of action regarding any investigation into the recent murderous past, and to demand wage hikes for the workers—had to be put down and "law and order" restored before democracy could begin to function.

It would be a while yet before Jean came fully to realize the difference between an American cop and the killers in policemen's uniforms who patrolled the streets of San Salvador. "When you see the police here," she wrote some weeks later, "it's not like back home. You certainly don't feel they're going to protect you. You feel like they're going to shoot you!" But to the embassy staff, men like junta member Colonel Jaime Abdul Gutiérrez (new co-commander in chief of the Armed Forces, a role he shared with Colonel Adolfo Majano) and Colonel José Guillermo García, the new minister of defense, Colonel Eugenio Vides Casanova, the director of the National Guard, and Colonel Reynaldo López Nuila, the new head of the National Police (all Salvadoran officers trained by American instructors in Panama) were all eminently reasonable men, fully deserving of American support. On November 9, the U.S. government authorized the sale of $205,541 worth of tear gas, gas masks and protective vests to the Salvadoran security forces; three days later, without informing the civilian members of the government, a six-man United States training team arrived in El Salvador to train the security forces in riot control. A new era had begun. It was not the one foreseen by the young officers of the October movement. Rather it was yet another era of government by the traditional military who would henceforth be able to count on the financial support of a new partner—the government of the United States.

In November, with the active support of Archbishop Romero the junta managed to negotiate a truce with the popular organizations; they appointed a high-level commission to investigate the fate of the "disappeared," raised the salaries of some rural workers, passed legislation dissolving the paramilitary ORDEN and froze large land holdings pending agrarian reform legislation. For a few weeks it almost seemed possible that the promises and the programs of the October 15 movement might become a reality, and during the lull that followed, Jean and Dorothy accepted an invitation from their Maryknoll friends in Managua to visit Nicaragua. They decided to drive.

Because El Salvador and Honduras had been technically in a state of war since 1969, the borders between the two countries had been sealed for ten years. Consequently, there was no direct overland route from El Salvador to Nicaragua and the only method of transporting a car was by ferry across the Gulf of Fonseca to the Nicaraguan port of Potosi. Jean and Dorothy set off in high spirits for a four-day vacation, sightseeing in Managua with their friends. It didn't work out exactly as planned.

When they reached Potosi on their return trip to catch the ferry back to El Salvador they discovered that the ferryboat, their one and only route back, had broken down and they were stranded. "If you ever get the opportunity to go to Potosi," Jean wrote, "don't. I think that it is the worst place that I will ever visit in my life. Nothing, absolutely nothing happens in Potosi. There's no water to drink and no johns—and we couldn't leave to go anyplace because we'd lose our place in the line and there's like two hundred truck drivers hanging around to get on the ferry."

Every morning the ferry was supposed to leave "today" and every evening their departure was postponed until "tomorrow." They were sleeping in the minibus, eating beans, tortillas and greasy eggs for breakfast, lunch and dinner at the one greasy spoon in town, and bathing in the river. "Everyone bathes in the river—I mean the horses, the pigs, the cows . . . but it's the only place you can bathe, using the only soap we had which was my perfumed Esteé Lauder cleansing bar—this really tiny bar which costs like $20—very appropriate."

In the evening, exhausted from trying to make conversation with the truck drivers, they'd try to find a quiet place to read. "We found this spot at the back of a building, under a big light—and on the second night, the 'muchachos' found us—they're the twerps that run Nicaragua—they're like fourteen, fifteen years old, the guys in the army. There were three of them aged fifteen, eighteen, and twenty-four —that's old in Nicaragua. And they each had a different kind of gun. Well, we spent the entire evening learning all about guns—how to take the guns apart—how to clean the guns—how to load the guns—how to load the clips that go in the guns—how to fire the guns. I'm all set, I know all there is to know about an M-16 (which is made in Connecticut)."

Five days into this routine they found out that the original damage on the ferry had been fixed, but in the process one of the pistons had given out and a new one had to be sent for from Miami. Dorothy made a decision: "We are going to get through Honduras, and that's all there is to it." And so they did, though no one, least of all Dorothy and Jean, quite understood how they managed it.

Jean's account of Dorothy's trip to the interior to see the commander of the Honduran Armed Forces set the scene. "It's not the easiest thing in the world to see the head of the Honduran Army, as you can imagine," Jean wrote, "but she has now been to see every uniform and every title and they've all been very sympathetic, and they've all explained that there's nothing that they can do for her. So she now has these two little uniforms with her and off they go to this office—they open the door and it's like a movie: big red curtain across the whole back wall; big huge desk;

immense map of Central America on one side; a huge TV set; a drafting board; open offices attached, full of peons on telephones: This is Enrique—the head of the Honduran Army, and somehow Dorothy has got in to see him, and even she doesn't know how she did it."

At seven A.M. the next morning the minibus, without plates and accompanied by a Honduran army escort, whipped through Honduras at one hundred miles an hour and became the first Salvadoran vehicle to cross the border legally between the two countries in ten years.

Jean and Dorothy's adventures in Potosi and Honduras cemented their friendship; they were a team—Jean, Dorothy and the Toyota van. They shared a lot of laughs and a lot of traveling, and perhaps an overly confident sense of their own invincibility.

That Christmas Jean's parents came to spend the holiday with her in El Salvador. "At the time we felt very relieved about the visit," Jean's mother says. "It was a beautiful country. The people were delightful, and we learned later that she kept us away from any hot spots. So we were pretty unaware of what was going on."

As soon as they had celebrated Christmas Eve and Christmas Day in La Libertad, Jean and Dorothy packed Jean's parents into the van and set off with them over the border to Guatemala to spend the holidays visiting the Indian festival and fair at Chichicastenango. "We did have two run-ins with soldiers," Pat Donovan recalls, "but these were things they couldn't avoid having us see, and they didn't amount to anything."

Ray and Pat went home to Florida much relieved. Michael, unbending in his opposition to his sister's involvement in El Salvador, had refused to make the trip and remained unconvinced by his parents' glowing reports on their return. For Jean, too, her parents' visit brought relief. She had never had any intention of giving in to the pressures from her family to come home, but she hated to cause them anxiety, and the success of their trip was comforting. She and Dorothy drove them to the airport to see them off on a lovely, sunny morning early in the new year, and sped back along the road to La Libertad, back to the people and the work and the life to which they were committed.

The date was January 3, 1980, the date of the collapse of the first junta. On that day, the resignation of the civilian members of the junta, the cabinet, the Supreme Court, and the twelve state-appointed heads of government agencies and banks were read over the national radio. A letter signed by the ministers of education and agriculture and the president of the Agricultural Development Bank was specific in its charges.

> We took office with the conviction . . . that an important sector of the Armed Forces was committed to supporting a political project with an authentically popular intent.
>
> Today, events have demonstrated without a trace of doubt, that the opposite has in fact occurred.
>
> Real power is exercised by the Head of the Ministry of Defense and Public Safety, and several military commanders—transcending the authority of the Governing Junta and against the domestic aspirations of our people.
>
> The alliance between the power of the military and the oligarchy, and the reaffirmation of political repression as the chosen option, is setting the entire government against the people.

The week before, in a final attempt to bring the young officers back to center stage and involve them in the process of salvaging and developing the political program they had themselves initiated, the cabinet had addressed an ultimatum to the Permanent Council of the Armed Forces—the advisory board specifically set up to protect the political process. But within days, even as the junta and certain military officers and cabinet ministers were meeting with Archbishop Romero in desperate negotiations to try and save the government, the Armed Forces broadcast their reply over national TV and radio:

> The Council is not a political body, but rather one founded to maintain the unity of the Armed Forces. The vehicle of communication between the Junta and the high command is the Ministry of Defense.

Twenty-four hours later, the only government officials to retain their posts in the junta cabinet were, not surprisingly, Colonel Guillermo García, minister of defense, and his deputy, Colonel Nicolas Carranza.

On January 9, the military announced the formation of a new government: in return for pledges to keep the traditional oligarchy of landowners and businessmen out of government and to press onward with the economic and social reforms promised in October, the Christian Democrats moved in to pick up the abandoned portfolios. They were supported in Washington, where members of the former government were dismissed as idealistic, naive intellectuals, with no appreciation for the compromises necessary to any political endeavor, and basically "quitters." It would take many years, many lives and many millions of dollars before any cracks would show in the official optimism in Washington regarding the nature of their allies in the Salvadoran military, who in January 1980 had been designated "the forces of moderation," the beleaguered center, "beset by violence from both the Left and the Right."

It was a definition that would enjoy public acceptance for a long time. It ignored the reality of right-wing violence directed and carried out by large segments of those same security forces, whose involvement in abductions, murders and massacres in slum and rural areas was obscured behind official and press reports that blamed *desconocidos* for the extensive murder that had become a tragic element of daily life. These "unknowns"—men in civilian clothes, sometimes hooded, who frequently arrived at the scene of the crime in military vehicles, carrying regulation army weapons—filled the role assigned to them of "uncontrollable extremists," unreconstructed fanatics and remnants of the cashiered military officers of the deposed dictatorship; individuals who supposedly had no connection to the present junta's high command.

On the extreme Left, throughout the period immediately following the collapse of the first junta, violence from the guerrilla groups increased measurably in reaction to the official repression of the mass popular organizations and the persecution of rural workers and their families by ORDEN, whose leaders, far from laying down their arms as mandated by the junta, had responded by announcing that henceforth they would operate in clandestinity "to do the work that the junta is unable to do for itself."

The existence of the guerrilla movement in El Salvador dates back to 1970–71. It received its first important impetus in 1972 when the military stole the election from the civilian candidates, Christian Democrat José Napoleón Duarte and his running mate, Guillermo Ungo, and drove both men into exile. By January 1980 the guerrillas consisted of three small groups: The FPL (Popular Liberation Forces); the ERP (Revolutionary Army of the People) and the FARN (Armed Forces of National Resistance). All three groups were Marxist in ideology, and their original leaders came from the ranks of urban, middle-class students. Their goals and their alliances differed. The FPL was an offshoot of the Salvadoran Communist party; it was also the largest, most orthodox and best organized of the groups, dedicated to achieving a revolutionary government and a socialist society through the strategy of a prolonged popular war. The ERP was the most radical and militaristic; it called for a popular and democratic government of peasants and workers to be achieved through guerrilla warfare. FARN, an offshoot of the ERP formed in 1975, was the most visible and effective in its program of kidnapping prominent political and business figures from which it collected large ransoms—a virtual war chest for the first year of the civil war. ERP's program also called for a socialist society which it believed would be brought about through a popular insurrection.

The guerrilla groups remained virtually isolated throughout the seventies, but now all this was to change. As ORDEN, protected by their allies in the rural police and National Guard posts, stepped up their attacks on "subversives" in the rural villages, from their strongholds in the hills and mountains of the northeast the guerrillas fought back, and for the first time their ranks were swelled as increasing numbers of campesinos—workers, day laborers, small tenant farmers—began to abandon their traditional villages to join those in the hills who offered some possibility of protection for themselves and their families. In the cities, as the mass popular organizations were confronted with the unrelenting repression of the security forces, they too began turning for support and protection to the guerrillas, and new alliances were formed between those who, following the lead of the Church, had continued to believe and act in accordance with the principles of nonviolent civil disobedience, and those who had long since given up on any solution short of violence.

Describing the composition and history of the guerrillas during congressional testimony in the spring of 1982, former Ambassador Robert White told the members of the House Subcommittee on Inter-American Affairs:

> The guerrilla groups, the revolutionary groups, almost without exception began as associations of teachers . . . of labor unions, campesino unions or parish organisations . . . organised for the purpose of getting a schoolhouse up on the market road. [While] it is true in my book that the large majority of the leaders of the

Salvadoran guerrillas are Marxist or Marxist
oriented, there is a substantial number who are
not. There are substantial numbers of people
who are fighting only because they have no
choice. . . . The great majority . . . indeed some
of the leaders . . . are fighting because their
towns were attacked and they were driven into
the countryside and they cannot give up, because if they would give up they would be
killed.

During those early weeks of 1980, from their vantage
point within the archdiocese, Paul and Ken, Chris, Dorothy
and Jean watched while the center disintegrated. Meanwhile, they went on about their work: distributing food
supplies from Caritas to hungry mothers and children; holding *charlas*—the colloquial Spanish word meaning literally
"talks"—a term they used to cover everything from planning sessions with the local catechists to seminars with
groups of mothers on the basics of nutrition and hygiene, to
religious instruction groups for children being prepared for
their first communion, and premarital counseling with young
adults. They sought consistently to sustain the appearance
of normality, rejecting any change in the routine of the
parish that might reflect the unspoken fears spreading
through the streets and communities around them.

Jean had made friends with some of the local youngsters in La Libertad. Through a shared love of music she
found a way to involve them in church activities by enlist-
ing their musical talents in the formation of a church choir.
There was nothing that Jean liked better than taking sole
responsibility for a specific project—especially one that she
initiated—and once a week she set aside an entire afternoon
for choir practice. Soon the musical ensemble of guitars and
voices she had organized was considered the premier choir
in the diocese, a status that was confirmed by a personal invitation from Archbishop Romero to sing at his Sunday
mass in the Metropolitan Cathedral.

Uncomfortable with the notion of being perceived publicly as one of the nuns, Jean had established her own living quarters in La Libertad, in a small apartment above the school next door to the church, overlooking the town square. It was extremely noisy, but she enjoyed the independent status it gave her and the freedom to go out in the evening for a beer, or to the movies with some of the Salvadoran lay workers and their friends when the work load permitted. To share these living quarters with her she had adopted a puppy and a kitten ". . . a little dog named Visa and a little cat named Twerp. They're always bothering me and wrestling with each other and they try to get me up at six-thirty in the morning. We disagree on that completely."

The road from La Libertad to San Salvador is new and fast, so that when on a Sunday morning Jean's animal roommates woke her at six-thirty A.M. she could jump in the shower, drive up the hill to Zaragoza to pick up Dorothy and Chris, and be at the cathedral for Romero's eight o'clock mass by seven-thirty A.M.—time enough to slip in through the vestry and get a good position. They listened with particular care to his homilies these days, for amid the cacophony of manifestos and slogans, of charges and countercharges, official repression and opposition violence, they, together with the great majority of the Salvadoran people, shared the illusion that somehow the Archbishop would succeed in deflecting the impending disaster of civil war.

Not everyone agreed with this assessment. Certainly not the Christian Democrats or the American embassy, both of whom had sought and failed to obtain the Church's official approval for the second junta government. "Only the people," Romero said, "can legitimize the government, and it is not the Church's job to do it for them."

Throughout that pivotal winter, Monsignor Romero retained his independence. While he never hesitated to criticize their excesses, he took the program of the popular organizations on behalf of El Salvador's poor seriously and managed to retain his position as the only national figure with any credibility among their leaders. They were, to a large extent, his children; they had grown up in and around the Basic Christian Communities; they shared a great many of his ideals—but they were also the children of the accumulated violence of the last three years. They were young and impatient and were being driven closer day by day to the militants of the guerrilla groups by the violence directed against them by the government security forces.

Although the U.S. State Department resented his influence and complained to the Vatican that he was fostering a revolutionary line of action instead of backing the Christian Democrats of the junta, Romero, in fact, sought to counter the dynamic of accelerating radicalization, and worked to discredit any romantic notions that the leaders of the popular organizations might have about revolutionary violence.

> Making the revolution is not killing others, for
> only God is the master of life. Making the
> revolution is not painting slogans on walls, or
> shouting in the streets. Making the revolution
> is thinking through political designs capable of
> building a people of justice and brotherhood.

He also denounced the recently initiated guerrilla campaign of reprisals against individual members of ORDEN and the security forces.

> The Church cannot stand by and approve the
> violence of these reprisals. Such acts have to be
> called by their proper name: they are, quite
> simply, assassinations.

On January 22 the popular organizations reached the apogee of their public life. On that day, in an extraordinary demonstration of their grass-roots support, the three mass organizations—the BPR (Popular Bloc), FAPU (United

Popular Action Front), LP-28 (Poular Leagues-28th February), together with their political allies—the Social Democratic party, the rural and urban trade unions, and the Associations of Slum Dwellers, Teachers, Students and University Professors—brought more than one hundred thousand people into the streets of San Salvador for an orderly, peaceful march in celebration of their unity and in commemoration of the uprising of 1932. Looking at the newsreels of that event today it is easy to understand how intoxicated the young leaders must have felt. On that sunny morning, as they marched and filled the streets for block after block, it must have seemed historically inevitable that they would topple the old, divided men in the government and win the revolution by the sheer force of their numbers and the strength of their solidarity and conviction.

Until the shots rang out. As the head of the march reached the Metropolitan Cathedral, National Guardsmen, police, and armed civilians fired into the dense crowd from the roof of the National Palace across the street and from windows of government buildings around the square.

The Christian Democratic junta had given the order for all security forces to remain in their barracks throughout the day. Once again, individual commanders, in collusion with right-wing paramilitary forces, had acted on their own initiative against the "Communist demonstrators."

In the immediate aftermath of the attack some fifty people lay dead on the sidewalk, over a hundred were badly wounded, twenty-five thousand marchers sought refuge in the National University, and every church in the archdiocese was overflowing with refugees, as rural families, terrorized by the idea of returning to a "reception committee" of ORDEN and local police forces in their native villages, sought the protection of Romero and his priests.

On the following Sunday Romero's sermon pulled no punches:

> In response to the intransigent violence of the
> Right, I repeat once more the severe admoni-

tion of the Church which declares them guilty
of the anger and despair of the people. It is
they who are the true germ, the real peril of
the Communism that they hypocritically denounce . . . to the government of the junta, I
must say, with my people, that it is urgent to
show that it is able to control the security
forces by stopping the repression.

That week he had established an emergency committee among the nuns of the archdiocese to stockpile medicines and food and open the first refugee center on the
grounds of the archdiocesan seminary. By the end of January, the first three hundred rural refugees had taken up
residence in the center. Although she herself did not as yet
realize the full significance of this development, the work
in which Jean was ultimately to find the answers to her
quest, and for which she would finally give her life, had
already begun.

At that particular moment she was not paying too
much attention to Salvadoran affairs, for she was full of
nervous and happy anticipation, awaiting the imminent
arrival of Doug Cable from the United States. "This was
something we had been planning ever since she left," says
Doug. "You know: 'One day you'll come and visit me in
Salvador!' "

Doug's memories of the twelve days he spent with
Jean are idyllic. "That was the time that we really got
close. Oh, we had wonderful times in New York, but they
were short, they were for weekends, and there was a lot of
activity, and in El Salvador we had whole days, every day,
to ourselves, and we really got to know each other, to communicate more than with words, to get to know each other
as people, and all the complexities of a person that you
don't get from talking, you get from being together and
knowing each other and doing things together, solving
problems together. . . ."

Though Doug Cable is a shy and private person, it is

clear within moments of talking with him that from their first meeting in Cleveland Jean had permanently entered his life and heart. He remembers the twelve days that he and Jean spent together in El Salvador as among the most cherished of his life. Jean had arranged to take the time out from work, and Paul had lent them the mission jeep, so they were free to come and go as they pleased. Mostly they stayed along the coast, enjoying some of the most romantic scenery in the world. "We stayed at this beautiful resort called Atami, that because of the violence was literally empty. So we had this gorgeous resort all to ourselves, on some cliffs overlooking the ocean, and cut into the cliffs were pools, so you would sit in these pools of warm salt water, and the waves would crash up over the rocks, but they wouldn't hit you; they would gently splash into the pool, and you could sit there all day, relaxing. . . ."

When they'd had enough sun and sea they drove inland to explore other abandoned tourist spots, like the splendid and isolated Hotel of the Mountain, situated at the end of a grueling three-hour drive up a dirt-track mountain road on the very summit of the Cerro Verde, overlooking the smoldering peak of the volcano of Izalco. They had trouble with the jeep on some of these trips, but they were much too happy to care. "You can fix the mission jeep with a number 12 llave—that's a wrench," Doug explains. "You can take that jeep apart with a number 12 llave and put it back together—and we did that—we had to fix that jeep almost on a daily basis, and we got to know it like it was part of us, like it was a threesome—Jean and I and the jeep—and she could fix it just as well as I could. We could do anything with that jeep. We changed the belts, we fixed the distributor, we did something to the alignment—you can do it all with a number 12."

Doug saw no violence in El Salvador. During the two weeks he was there the popular organizations occupied the Spanish embassy and the Christian Democratic party offices in downtown San Salvador and were holding several people in both buildings hostage. But Jean made certain they stayed away from the capital.

Elsewhere, the surge of detentions and killings by security forces that had been responsible in January alone for over 250 deaths in rural areas had not abated, but the repression was concentrated chiefly in the hill villages of Chalatenango and Aguilares. Doug bought the official version about left- and right-wing extremists battling each other in isolated, violent incidents and saw no reason to be worried about Jean. Looking back, with the hindsight gained from his own painful loss, he describes how it was possible then to be so unaware. "I was there for two weeks and never heard a gunshot. We were staying in resorts and traveling about on the main roads, and we were not in the areas where there was trouble. So, I didn't see it. And I assumed that Jean was not seeing it either, but I was wrong. Jean was on vacation when I was down there, and so I did not see her day-to-day activities. And I didn't know, I didn't realize it at the time—that she really was coming up against these situations, that she was working in areas· where there was trouble—that she was in danger."

There were a few clues that someone with a more alert political sense might have picked up. When Doug and Jean drove south, she took him to meet the other members of the Cleveland mission who worked in the small coastal town of Chirilagua near the Honduran border. Immediately, he realized how difficult communication was between the various areas. "The missionaries were spread out over three or four different areas and the way they communicated was just to drive back and forth so they would get together and talk. They didn't call on the phone. They were concerned about the phones being tapped, and the letters opened, so how you got your news was that you just drove from place to place and talked to each other."

But Doug was in love for the first time in his life and deliriously happy. "Words don't do it justice, you know. To be together with someone you love for that period of time

—it was like having a honeymoon before you get married. It was just bliss."

He has a lot of pictures of Jean taken during those days. Jean sunbathing on the beach, Jean surrounded by flowering bougainvillea, tinkering with the jeep. Some of his pictures have caught her in a reflective, introspective mood and reveal the gentleness, the vulnerability that she rarely exposed to the world. Doug had always sensed this aspect of her complex personality. "That was why our relationship progressed so slowly. Because she was vulnerable. Why we were basically just very good friends, and progressively better and better friends, until it really became clear that we were in love. I sensed it initially. I really don't know how—I think in some ways I'm similar, so we matched well. That's what's so amazing to me that we matched well in a lot of things like that. I'm fairly good with social interactions, but I'm also a little reticent on close personal relations. This was the first time I had had anything close to that close a relationship. And Jean, for all of the bravado she displayed in social situations, dealing with people, dealing with problems, dealing with work—on a person-to-person level she was often reserved. Many people never sensed this reserve in Jean because she was so very outgoing —and yet, she didn't really open up. To really get to know her, to know the real Jean with all the complexities, was actually very difficult. Few saw the real Jean."

After Doug had left to go back to his work as head of the Department of Infectious Diseases at Los Angeles County Hospital, Jean, still suffering from the pangs of a painful withdrawal, wrote to her friend Rita in Cleveland: "Well, Doug came to visit. It was very good for me to have him come. Built my ego like crazy that he came all the way from Los Angeles to Salvador on his only vacation just to visit me—must be true love! But it was hard on me too. As a matter of fact it was harder on me than I expected it would be. I went into a little bit of depression since he left. I mean the day after he left, I was just on the floor, . . . I was so deeply depressed. It's funny, you can get real excited and not be depressed at all when he's not here but he's coming. But after he's been here, it's much worse.

"We both have plans, so that kind of rules out permanently getting together within the next two years—if that's what we want to do—or one of us would have to give up some of our plans to do that. I don't know if we're at that point. We're close to it, I think, but I have some doubts. I don't know if he does. I think he's closer to it than I am, and I'm just glad he didn't ask me to marry him—he came very close to it—because I don't know what I would have said. . . . Well I know what I would have said—that I wouldn't have gotten married now. And he's someone I really care about—he's a super guy. I might want to get together with him at some point, and I wouldn't have wanted to turn him off now by what he might have considered a rejection. But I see problems that the two of us have. I have the problem that he works as much as he does. Any doctor works ridiculous hours, and he's not just a doctor, he's a very ambitious doctor so he works more than most do. Then I don't believe in long distance relationships. I think it's impossible to carry on a serious relationship at this kind of distance. I will see, but it's just—I've been through long distance relationships before.

"He's asked me to come to Los Angeles, probably next November, and he's coming to Ireland with me, which will be in September. So we will be spending some time together, at least all of our vacations and everything. I don't know. It's so hard to say. I don't know if anything will come of it, but if I ever do get married, which sometimes I have my doubts, I'll let you know."

CHAPTER VII

The Blood-Dimmed Tide

Because the Church has opted for the real, and not for the fictitious poor, because it has opted for those who really are oppressed and repressed, the Church lives in a political world, and it fulfills itself as Church also through politics. It cannot be otherwise if the Church, like Jesus, is to turn itself toward the poor.
—Archbishop Oscar Arnulfo Romero

THE UPS AND DOWNS OF JEAN'S PERSONAL LIFE DID NOT continue at the center of her preoccupations for much longer. In February 1980 the political landscape of El Salvador was continuing to deteriorate, slipping relentlessly toward catastrophe. After Doug left, Jean began to keep a diary. The first entry read:

Feb. 17:
> Monsignor Romero sends Jimmy Carter the letter requesting the United States not send any military aid to Salvador.

February 17 was the Sunday after Doug had left. Members of the Popular Bloc were occupying the cathedral to protest violence in the countryside where troops, tanks and helicopters were engaged in full-scale military operations against harvest workers, striking because the increase in their wage, decreed by the first junta, had been withheld by the landowners. So Monsignor Romero's mass was held in the nearby basilica. He preached for over an hour on the theme of poverty, and at the conclusion of his homily, he addressed himself, as was his custom, to the events of the previous week. On the previous Monday, an agreement worked out by the Christian Democrats and the government for the peaceful withdrawal of members of a popular organization occupying the party's headquarters had been violated by the security forces, who stormed the building, murdered several of the inmates, and dragged away twenty-three others who subsequently "disappeared."

> It has become evident this week [Romero said] that neither the Junta nor the Christian Democrats are governing the country. Who rules the nation is the most repressive sector of the armed forces.

And he proceeded to call on the Christian Democrats to withdraw from the government:

> I ask you to analyze not only your intentions, which are undoubtedly good, but also the concrete effects that your presence in the government is having. Especially at the international level, your presence serves to mask the repressive character of this regime. As an important political force in our nation, you must take note of where your influence may be used most efficaciously on behalf of our poor. Do you wish to remain isolated and impotent in a government dominated by the repressive military forces? Or will you become one of several forces incorporated into a broad, popular government?

Then he read from the pulpit the text of an appeal to President Carter:

> Mr. President:
> In recent days, a report has appeared in the national press which has greatly disturbed me. According to the article your administration is studying the possibility of backing the present government junta and giving it economic and military aid.
>
> Because you are a Christian and have said that you want to defend human rights, I take the liberty of expressing my pastoral point of view on this matter and of making a specific request.
>
> The information that the United States Government is studying ways in which to build up the armaments of El Salvador greatly disturbs me. Reportedly, you plan to send military equipment and consultants to train three Salvadoran

battalions in logistics, communication and intelligence. If in fact this information is correct, the contribution of your government will do nothing to support greater justice and peace in El Salvador. Without doubt, it will intensify injustice and the repression of the organized people who have fought, so many times, for their fundamental rights. . . . As a Salvadoran, and as the Archbishop of the Archdiocese of San Salvador, I have the obligation to see to it that faith and justice reign in my country. Therefore, if you truly want to defend human rights, I urge you:

—To prohibit the sending of military aid to the Salvadoran government.

—To guarantee that your government will not intervene, directly or indirectly, with military, economic, diplomatic or other pressures, to try to determine the destiny of the Salvadoran nation.

It would be a deplorable injustice if, through the introduction of foreign weapons and forces, the development of the Salvadoran nation was frustrated. Foreign intervention would suppress and impede the autonomous decision-making process already begun along appropriate economic and political lines.

Among those in Romero's congregation whose political consciousness had been profoundly altered since the October 15 proclamation was Jean. By the time the archbishop made his appeal to President Carter, Jean agreed totally with his position. She knew, because she had seen, the helpless, paralyzing terror that "the authorities"—the police, army and National Guard—instilled in the communities where she spent her days trying to provide some measure of support for struggling, frightened people. Hunger was still the number one cause of death in El Salvador in the winter of 1980. Distributing supplemental foodstuffs, transporting sick children and exhausted mothers many miles from their country shacks to a hospital or clinic in one of the big towns, listening to desperate, unemployed fathers, she had learned firsthand the causes of the fear and despair that lay heavily over rural community and village life.

She also knew that while most of the people who came in contact with the Church were not guerrillas, many did have friends who had gone off into the hills to join them, and all sympathized with the popular organizations, seeing in them the only hope for change. The lay leaders—the catechists and Delegates of the Word—had become her friends. When they would assemble in Paul's house for meetings and parish councils, they had impressed her as some of the brightest, most idealistic and certainly most courageous people she had ever known. They were marked people—they knew it, and so did she. But they had not yet lost the ability to believe in a better world, and they were part of a process that was providing hope and some small tangible improvements in the lives of their neighbors. They were the very people whose lives would be most in jeopardy if the junta government received arms and support from the United States.

On the day following Monsignor Romero's public appeal, the entry in Jean's diary reads:

Feb. 18.
> *At eleven* P.M. *in the evening a bomb exploded in the YSAX Radio Station—the Archdiocese station—destroying most of the equipment. Responsible was Frente AntiCommunist for the Liberation of Central America.*

To which, in brackets, she added:

> [*And some of the Pharisees from amongst the multitude said to him: Master, rebuke thy*

disciples. To whom He said: I say to you, that
if these shall hold their peace, the very stones
shall cry out. Luke 19:39–40].

For the next eight months the diary, in which she
scrupulously recorded the names of the victims, the hour of
the day, and the precise location of the rural repression
within the archdiocese, is a devastating chronicle of the
political disintegration that finally led to her death.

On February 25 at midnight, the Christian Democratic attorney general, Mario Zamorra, was assassinated by
six masked men bearing army regulation G-3 and M-16
rifles, who broke into his home during a late-night ses-
sion of party officials. Zamorra had been attempting to
get the stalled investigation into the fate of the "disappeared"
moving again. The Christian Democrats blamed the murder on the rising star of the far Right, a young retired army
major named Roberto d'Aubuisson, and vowed to resign
from the government unless Zamorra's killers were brought
to justice. For the second time in eight weeks the government started to come apart.

On March 2 Jean's diary notes:

> *Radio Station in Costa Rica broadcasts Ro-*
> *mero's Mass to Latin America. Able to listen*
> *on shortwave. (Voice of those without a voice,*
> *striving for peace and defending justice.)*

That Sunday Romero had tried one more time to reach
across the gulf separating the two Salvadors:

> Do not consider me, please, an enemy; I am
> simply a pastor, a brother, a friend of this
> Salvadoran people. One who knows their suf-
> ferings, their hunger, their anguish. It is in the
> name of these voices that I raise my voice to
> say: Do not idolize your wealth! Do not horde
> it to let the rest die of hunger! We must learn

how to strip ourselves of our rings so that they won't be cut from our fingers. Those who are unwilling to give, out of love and social justice, make it mandatory that their luxuries be taken from them by violence. Let them not keep killing those of us who are trying to achieve a more just sharing of the wealth and power of our country. I speak in the first person, because this week I received notice that I am on the list of those who are to be eliminated next week. But let it be known that no one can any longer kill the voice of justice.

On March 3, junta member Héctor Dada Hirezi quit the government and the Christian Democratic party and left the country for Mexico. His letter of resignation sounded like a replay of those of the first junta members, eight weeks earlier.

On March 6 the government decreed the first phase of its Agrarian Reform Program, which authorized the expropriation of landed estates 500 hectares and larger, and charged the Salvadoran Institute of Agrarian Transformation (ISTA) with the responsibility for forming agricultural cooperative associations made up of the permanent resident laborers and salaried employees of the former owners. Under phase I, approximately 15 percent of El Salvador's arable land was affected, involving fewer than 250 estates, and representing in large measure land used for cattle grazing or land that had been lying fallow. The second phase of the reform, designed to affect between 1,500 and 2,000 properties falling in the 150 to 500 hectare range and comprising over 30 percent of the country's most lucrative crop —coffee—has yet to be implemented. It was in fact officially suspended in the spring of 1982 by the Salvadoran Constituent Assembly. By then the Salvadoran legislators were able to rely on the support of the Reagan administration for their opposition to any wider implementation of land reform.

On the morning of March 6, 1980, when truckloads of troops, accompanied by ISTA technicians, moved out into the countryside at dawn to seize possession of some thirty estates they met with little resistance from largely absentee landlords. In the days and weeks that followed, however, reports of the murders of peasant leaders began filtering back to the capital, and a pattern linking the reforms to the repression of peasant organizations began to emerge.

Simultaneously, a state of siege was imposed, with a curfew from eight o'clock in the evening until dawn, which gravely disrupted the schedule of the Cleveland missionaries who were accustomed to accomplishing much of their work between the hours of six and ten o'clock at night, the only time when the male population of the villages was available for meetings and church services. Their schedule was complicated at the best of times by many factors: the large distances that had to be traveled on bad roads from La Libertad to the outlying villages; the constant difficulties encountered in communicating from one end of the parish to the other; the intense heat, and the constant eruption of emergency situations that made any daily routine almost impossible to maintain. Consequently, Paul Schindler and his team organized their work according to a monthly schedule in which the responsibility for touching base once a month with every village and community was shared.

The team's work program was always established at a monthly pastoral meeting attended by all of the local catechists and lay leaders who would assemble in Paul's house to discuss their problems, needs and priorities. After these meetings, at which the work load for the coming month was delegated to the individual members of the team, the visiting church workers stayed on for lunch. They then returned to their villages, where it was their responsibility to inform the local people on which day they could expect the missionaries to visit, when the food distribution would take place, and generally to maintain communication between the parishioners and the missionaries while carrying on the main burden of pastoral work on a daily basis and holding weekly Celebrations of the Word on their own.

The routine, day-to-day activities of the members of the Cleveland team reflected their basic areas of concern: providing guidance and classes in religious instruction, nutrition and health care; holding church services—masses, Celebrations of the Word and liturgies; and distributing supplemental food and medicines provided by Caritas, which either Jean or Dorothy collected weekly in the Toyota minibus from the archdiocesan headquarters in San Salvador. Each month they would select one area for an intensive five-day "mission." Working as a team, Jean and Dorothy, or Chris and Elizabeth, would leave La Libertad early in the morning, drive to the selected community and spend the day there. In the morning they would hold a class with the mothers, afternoons would be devoted to the children, and at night they would hold a class with the men followed by a Celebration of the Word. On the fifth and final day either Paul or Ken would join them to say mass, hear confessions and bless the sick. Their schedule never called for more than one major event during daylight hours. A normal day would involve traveling for an hour to reach their destination; hanging around for another half hour or more waiting to begin their work; followed by an hour for class, an hour of socializing, and then another hour on the road back home. This presumed that all went smoothly, that there were no roadblocks, no hassles with the "authorities," and no crises encountered among the people they had gone to see.

During those periods when Jean was not actively engaged in the work of the parish it was her special responsibility to keep the accounts straight and maintain the books for all of the mission's finances.

On March 9, just three days after the introduction of the agrarian reform and the state of siege, the Christian Democratic party held a convention to decide the party's future course of action. Throughout the sixties the party had played a leading role in the development of a centrist democratic opposition to military dictatorship. One of their founder members, José Napoleón Duarte, had been a popular mayor of San Salvador from 1964 to 1970; in 1972 Duarte had made a bid for the presidency—sharing the ticket with Social Democrat Guillermo Ungo—only to be cheated of victory by electoral fraud and forced into exile by the military. In the years between, repression and exile had their demoralizing effects, and through the decade of the seventies the party lost its former base of support among the workers and the peasants to the popular organizations. When the young officers moved in October to change the traditional power structure, the Christian Democrats were disorganized, many of their leaders were absent, and the historic moment passed them by. But with the exit of the Social Democrats from the government in January, they had come once again to the forefront of the political scene. Now the assassination of Attorney General Zamorra, the resignation of junta member Héctor Dada, and Archbishop Romero's call for the party to quit the government amid overwhelming evidence that they were no more able to control their military partners in the junta than their predecessors had precipitated a crisis among their leaders. At their convention on March 9, a majority of the delegates rallied behind José Napoleón Duarte. Voting to remain in the government, they elected Duarte to the vacant place on the junta and to the leadership of the party. Six dissident leaders, however, including the secretary general, the executive secretary and several other cabinet officials resigned, taking some 20 percent of the membership with them. Among the defectors were men who had been among the original founders of the party and for whom, during those early years of struggle, Duarte had represented a much admired mentor and friend. Now, in publishing the reasons for their secession, they cited the interventionist intentions of the United States and deplored a policy that would "transform us into a battlefield for the struggle of the Superpowers, thereby exposing our people to suffer the attendant consequences."

They also pointed to the inability of the reform program to function in a climate of repression. "Regarding the program of structural reforms proposed by the Party: How can the present process succeed if the peasants are repressed on a daily basis merely for organizing themselves?"

On March 13, the Salvadoran Human Rights Commission published a list of 689 political killings since the first of the year. According to their documentation, 70 of these deaths had been committed by guerrilla forces and the remainder corresponded to attacks by the security forces and right-wing paramilitary groups. Later that day, in the aftermath of a bomb attack on the commission's offices, the police invaded the premises and confiscated the commission's files. Individual members of the commission received death threats by phone or mail. Throughout this period the practice of circulating "hit lists" of the government's opponents became general.

On March 15, newly installed American Ambassador Robert E. White called on the archbishop to deliver a reply by Secretary of State Cyrus Vance to Romero's letter to President Carter. "The defense of human rights," wrote Vance, "has been, and continues to be, one of the principal goals of the foreign policy of this administration, and I can assure you that it forms the basis for all aspects of United States policies regarding El Salvador."

In her diary, on March 21, Jean wrote that FAPU, one of the largest of the popular organizations currently occupying the cathedral, had asked Monsignor Romero to bury seventeen bodies in the cathedral because they were afraid to go to the cemetery. That same day, Amnesty International reported 130 cases of killings by security force personnel in the second week of March:

> Initial eye-witness reports affirm that troop movements by Army and National Guard units that were announced as measures for the implementation of the land reform have in fact involved the disappearance and killing of hun-

dreds of rural people in villages supporting labor organizations. Reports obtained from the estimated six hundred campesinos that have fled Cuscatlán to seek refuge in San Salvador say that at least eighty campesinos have been killed in the area since the land reform was decreed, including thirty-eight children.

Typical of the reports reaching Church and human rights officials during the period immediately following the agrarian reform is this account by an anonymous technician employed by the government agency charged with implementing the reforms:

> The troops came and told the workers the land was theirs now. They could elect their own leaders and run it themselves. The peasants could not believe their ears, but they held elections that very night. The next morning, the troops came back, and I watched as they shot every one of the elected leaders.

But in Washington meanwhile, the Congress was hearing a far different version of the land reform process from State Department officials seeking approval of aid for the Salvadoran military. On March 20, the deputy assistant secretary for Inter-American affairs, John Bushnell, testified on behalf of the aid:

> The armed forces launched the October 15th Revolution. They are key to the implementation of the reforms. Land distribution would not be possible were it not for the protection and security provided by the Salvadoran military for the new owners and the civilian technicians and managers helping them. The trucks and trailers we propose to sell to El Salvador will help Army units move themselves and the

reform officials through the countryside. The radios, batteries and antennas we propose to deliver, will enable these units to keep in touch with senior officers and to receive guidance if a situation develops where violence could take place between landowners and peasants, or between Army and leftist insurgents.

From the moment the Christian Democrats had elected to remain in the government, the foreign press had in large measure adopted the image assiduously promoted by the U.S. State Department, of the Salvadoran regime as a centrist government dedicated to reform. The only dissenting voice willing to clarify the confusion was raised by Archbishop Romero. During the March congressional debate on the military aid package for El Salvador, Archbishop Romero spoke to a reporter from the leading Venezuelan newspaper—*El Diario de Caracas*—and was quoted attempting to contradict this misleading myth. "I have heard so many reports from people abroad who do not understand what is happening in this country," he said. "People who say: The Christian Democrats are in the government, they are carrying out reforms, so what do the people want? What are they protesting about? In this respect," he went on, "I must request of you as journalists that you report with clarity and objectivity about what is happening here. However good the intentions of introducing structural reforms, [this government] is responsible for this horrendous repression and the Christian Democrats are becoming accomplices in this aggression against the people."

In the Metropolitan Cathedral, in his weekly homily of Sunday, March 23, Monsignor Romero continued to document the horrors that were taking place across the country in connection with the new land reform. Day by day, village by village, he listed the names, the ages, the sex of the peasant victims of military operations according to the testimonies received from church workers and the growing flood of refugees fleeing into the capital.

> The fundamental question [he said] is how to
> move along a less violent path, and on this
> point the greatest responsibility belongs to the
> civil government and, above all, to the military.

And then, as the congregation held its breath and a deathly hush descended over the packed cathedral, he proceeded to appeal directly to the consciences of the young peasant conscripts who make up the rank and file of the Salvadoran security forces:

> I would like to make a special appeal to the
> members of the army, and specifically to the
> ranks of the National Guard, the police, and
> the military. Brothers, each one of you is one
> of us. We are the same people. The peasants
> you kill are your own brothers and sisters.
> When you hear the voice of a man commanding
> you to kill, remember instead the voice of God:
> "Thou Shalt Not Kill!" God's law must prevail.
> No soldier is obliged to obey an order contrary
> to the law of God. There is still time for you to
> obey your own conscience, even in the face of
> a sinful command to kill.
>
> The Church, defender of the rights of God, of
> the law of God, and of the dignity of each
> human being, cannot remain silent in the pres-
> ence of such abominations.
>
> The government must understand that reforms,
> steeped in so much blood, are worthless. In the
> name of God, in the name of our tormented
> people whose cries rise up to Heaven, I be-
> seech you, I beg you, I command you, STOP
> THE REPRESSION!

On the following morning the high command made an announcement to the press accusing the archbishop of

treason. A former civilian member of the junta cabinet recalls the impact of Romero's words: "The privates of the
army are peasants; a people that has very deep religious
feelings. A young private, seventeen or eighteen years old,
carrying an M-16 in his hand and trying to shoot another
peasant because a captain has given him an order to do it
—and having Archbishop Romero telling him not to obey
the order, that it is against the law of God . . . that created
a tremendous conflict within an authoritarian structure like
the army."

The next day, Jean made this entry in her diary:

March 24:

> *At five-thirty in the evening while celebrating
> Mass in the Convent of the Good Shepherd
> Monsignor Oscar Romero was assassinated.
> Was shot in the heart with one bullet.*

The archbishop was just finishing a memorial mass for
the mother of a friend when a sharpshooter, concealed behind a pillar at the entrance to the chapel, fired the single,
fatal shot. Monsignor Romero was killed instantly.

As information from classified U.S. State Department
documents has gradually leaked into the public domain,
many details of the conspiracy to murder Romero have
come to light. One year later, former Ambassador Robert
White, testifying before the Senate Foreign Relations Committee, produced copies of documents confiscated from
Roberto d'Aubuisson, two months after the archbishop's
death, by troops loyal to Colonel Majano. A diary, with the
date of the assassination heavily circled, included three
pages of notes and a map of the streets leading to the Convent of the Good Shepherd with a large X marking the site
of the church where the murder was committed. On a separate piece of hotel stationery, under the heading "Operation Piña," White described a shopping list: "You'll find,"

White told the senators, "the following items are required: Five large vehicles, a thousand dollars, a landing strip, four men, a bed or stretcher, five radios, a starlight—which is a scope—a .257 Roberts gun, automatic grenades, one driver, one sharpshooter, and four security men."

D'Aubuisson has consistently denied any involvement in the assassination of the archbishop, but the existence of these documents has continued to haunt him, and later reports described how he and about a dozen active-duty security force officers attended a meeting which he organized, at which those present drew lots for the right to plan the assassination of Romero. A State Department official who had read the secret cables explained, "It was seen as a great thing to kill Romero. Like the only fair way of doing it was by lots—the excitement, you know, the honor and privilege of killing Romero."

The man to whom the privilege of organizing the details of the crime apparently fell subsequently confessed to an American intelligence officer in Panama two years later, while the man American officials believe actually pulled the trigger—a young National Guardsman—is dead, the victim of a death-squad killing eighteen months later.

"He was a fantastic person," Jean wrote to Rita in Cleveland. "Patient and kind, always showed love. He had a gift of public speaking but could talk to people one on one. He was fearlessly honest. He lived a simple life of continual forgiveness and love, he was the friend of the weak and the poor—always available to talk to anyone. The campesinos were always outside his door."

Two days later Jean accompanied his body on its last journey through the streets of San Salvador from the Convent of the Good Shepherd to the cathedral. "We were leading the casket," Chris Rody recalls. "First the nuns, then the priests, then Romero, and finally the bishop. It was one of those times that Jean claimed to be a nun so she could be right up front with the rest of us, and the firing started the moment we came out the door of the convent. It took us three attempts to get down the steps."

The entries in Jean's diary for March 26 and 27 are identical:

Guarded the coffin during twelve o'clock Mass.

An American news team filmed the scene. The cameraman focuses on the dead face of Monsignor Romero, then tilts up and pans slowly across the faces of the three friends, Dorothy, Chris and Jean, standing motionless beside the open casket. Their eyes look inward and their faces, drained by exhaustion of all expression, are white and blank.

March 30:
  Thirty people killed during Romero funeral.

The junta blamed "leftist extremists" for the explosions and gunfire that precipitated a stampede among the hundreds of thousands of worshipers jammed into the square in front of the cathedral. From their vantage point on the top of the cathedral steps where the mass was being celebrated, the delegation of foreign bishops and the news teams claimed that the firing originated from the second floor of the National Palace.

"It's a bomb!" an American voice yelled above the tumult on the steps, as a thick column of black smoke hung in the noonday heat at the corner of the palace, marking the spot of the first explosion. Panic swept through the vast crowd trapped in the square as wave upon wave they surged toward the cathedral steps, fighting to clamber over the surrounding railing and into the comparative safety of the building.

Jean had remained inside the cathedral, waiting beside the tomb where Romero's casket was to be buried at the conclusion of the mass. Later she taped a description of the scene for Michael Crowley: "Dorothy, Christine and I were sitting up by the tomb when it all started. The first bomb went off, and I wasn't sure what it was. But boy, when the second one went off—you *knew* what the second one was; and then the gunfire and stuff . . ."

Chris remembers that "when the first wave of people came rushing into the cathedral after the first explosions, it felt unreal—it felt like you were in a mob scene in a movie, and I just remember—the funny part in all that tragedy— we were standing there, and someone told us that if there were bullets flying around we ought to sit down and cover our heads. Dorothy and Jean were sitting next to each other, and everytime someone said, 'Put your heads down,' Doro- thy would reach over and grab Jean's head and put it down on her lap; and then she'd look around to see what was going on, and she'd jump up and take a picture— although none of her pictures came out."

Soon there was no room to sit down. There was scarcely room to stand, or air to breathe. Many of those who died that day were trampled to death. "I went through a complete spectrum of faith," Jean admitted to Crowley, "from: I didn't believe there was a God, to: What am I doing here? I'm much too young to die! to: There has to be a God, so it's going to be much better, because I know I'm going to die today. I was convinced they were going to throw a bomb in the cathedral. But actually, for all that, I was fairly calm about what was happening. I certainly didn't get upset. You know," she added, with customary honesty and evident relief, "I didn't know how I would react to something like that—but now, I know."

"She was totally involved in the whole sad tragedy of Romero's death," Crowley added, two years later. "She saw this as the triumph of evil, silencing the prophet, quenching the light; because Romero was a light and a hope for any- one in Salvador that had a heart and compassion. To shoot him really broke the heart of the people who looked for a better world. Jean, well Christ was her hero, but I would say Romero was her twentieth-century hero. He had a profound influence on her. And her own commitment was, I think, very much a kind of spinoff, a reflection of her admiration for what he stood for."

To a friend who had written in the aftermath of Romero's murder to try and persuade Jean that it was time to come home, she wrote, "I got your letter, and I really appreciate the fact that you said you worry about me. It's nice to know that people care and they'd like to tell me to come home, as you say. There are lots of times I feel like coming home. But I really do feel strongly that God has sent me here, and wants me to be here, and I'm going to try to do my best to live up to that."

Death had come as no surprise to Archbishop Romero. He had said: "My life has been threatened many times. I have to confess that as a Christian I do not believe in death without resurrection. If they kill me, I will rise again in the Salvadoran people."

And he had said: "A bishop will die, but the Church of God, which is the people, will never perish."

Now it was up to his friends and followers to prove him right.

CHAPTER VIII

Diary of a Nightmare

Part I: April–July 1980

Everything was thrown at her. She found herself challenged to be a giant, challenged to do bigger things than she ever dreamed she'd be asked to do. And she grew to meet that challenge.

I think she went through a whole spiritual metamorphosis. To leave that dimension out of her life—to say, here is a naive do-gooder, foolishly messing in a troubled situation politically—that's a most appalling trivialization of someone who, in a most subtle way, knew what was happening around her and still took the risk for what she believed in.
—Father Michael Crowley

IN THE IMMEDIATE AFTERMATH OF ARCHBISHOP ROMERO'S death, there now came to El Salvador two women who were destined to play a crucial role in Jean's future. Some months before his death, the archbishop had appealed to the American Church to send additional experienced missionaries to work with the Church of his archdiocese. Among those whom his call had reached were two Maryknoll Sisters who had been working for many years in Chile. In the first days of April, a letter from Maryknoll Sister Ita Ford, written to her mother in Brooklyn while en route from Chile to El Salvador, expressed her shock and sense of personal loss at having been robbed of the opportunity to know the slain Romero. She spoke also of grieving in solidarity with the poor of El Salvador at their loss of a pastor who, they knew, loved and cared for them. "But we believe that his death will bear fruit," she wrote, "it's part of the Christian mystery we celebrate this week—and in that same Christian tradition, we'll go to El Salvador. . . . Happy Easter. Love to all."

Accompanying Ita to El Salvador was her closest friend and colleague, Sister Carla Piette. Both women were in the prime of their professional lives. For the past eight years they had been living and working in a well-established and sizable mission run by the Maryknoll Sisters in the shanty towns of Santiago de Chile. There they had shared in the hardship and repression following the military coup of General Pinochet in 1973, and had helped to build a strong and self-reliant Christian community amid the physical and emotional rubble caused by that event.

Carla was striking-looking, tall and large-boned. Her strength and vitality masked the sensibility of an artist and the emotional vulnerability and innocence of a child. Ita, on the other hand, who was physically slight and delicate, driven by nervous energy, full of Irish charm, mischief, and humor, was a natural leader and had a sophisticated intellectual grasp of the world around her.

In the course of their work, these two very different women had developed a deep friendship and a strong connection to the country and people whom they served. Yet the most basic ethic of the missionary calling implies a denial of personal priorities, preferences, or the security of a settled existence. When the appeal from Romero came, Ita, on vacation in the States, and Carla, in the *barrios* of Santiago, each unaware of the other's decision, answered his call for help. On April 15 they arrived together in San Salvador. Courageous, intrepid, dedicated and wise, their presence brought a fresh infusion of energy and spirit to the small, beleaguered community of American missionaries. On Jean, who to date had always found her inspiration and guidance in the example of remarkable men, the strength and warmth of their personalities made an immediate impact, and with all the spontaneous openness—which was such a constant and touching facet of her complex personality—she responded eagerly to their influence and their experience. For the first time in her life she turned to other women as her role models.

Inspired by Romero's pastoral letters, Ita and Carla had looked forward to finding a way to serve and accompany the Salvadoran people during hard and difficult times. They had imagined that building on their experience in Chile, they would be able to join a parish and carry out their pastoral duties by forming small Christian communities capable of providing protection and support through the development of trust and solidarity among the members. But they came into a Church traumatized by the loss of its pastor, and a country rapidly becoming paralyzed by fear. Just two weeks after their arrival, the weekly bulletin of the Legal Aid Office of the archdiocese reported the killing of forty people in a period of nine days, the detention and disappearance of twelve people, and six incidents of military intervention by the army and security forces in peasant zones.

Easter, traditionally that most hopeful and joyous of Christian feasts, had been a sad period in El Salvador—a season of mourning, disorientation and unspoken dread. In her diary, Jean noted her daily attendance at the masses being said for Romero. Beset by pressures from all sides, the Vatican postponed the decision of appointing a successor to fill the vacant archbishopric of San Salvador. On April 10 Jean's diary recorded that Romero's assistant and closest friend, Bishop Rivera y Damas, had been named apostolic administrator of the archdiocese. It was a compromise, an interim solution that failed to give the new leader of the Salvadoran Church the official support and authority that the times required. But at least the choice of Bishop Rivera did reflect the preference of Romero's followers, and provided the diocesan workers with a sense of continuity in the commitment to work for justice, peace and human rights.

In these dark times the missionaries in La Libertad clung to their determination to pursue at all costs the example set for them by the slain archbishop, and in early April Jean, with the support of Dorothy and Paul, set out to organize an intensive "mission" among the people of Santa Cruz. She was now spending virtually all of her daylight hours in the small community. Suddenly, under cover of the curfew, the death squad struck. Jean's diary documents the results of their incursion:

April 26:

> *Eleven-fifteen* P.M. *Barrio La Cruz. Army trucks and civilians decapitated catechist Elizio Diaz, twenty-four years, Miguel Hernandez, thirty years old, Teresita Mejia, fifteen years old. Cut off the feet of Antonio Hernandez, nineteen years old, Teodorio Hernandez, twenty-six years old, and killed beyond identification two others.*

April 28:

> *In the early morning in San Martin, armed civilians with military equipment destroyed the altar, violated the tabernacle, and destroyed the house of the pastor.*

"The constant violations of human rights by the State and Security Forces produces, from our observation, a type of state of 'shock' among the Salvadoran pastoral agents," Ita wrote back to Maryknoll. "Since Romero's prophetic voice has been silenced, no other voice of equal credibility has been raised to speak to the situation of a suffering, divided people, the majority of whom regardless of their loyalties, are the victims of hunger, fear and violence."

Initially, the archdiocese had directed the two newcomers to one of the rural areas where there was a pressing need for pastoral workers. The northeastern province of Chalatenango was the most remote and understaffed parish of the archdiocese, and the local vicar of the province welcomed the chance of incorporating Carla and Ita into his staff. But even as they were exploring the available options, the situation in the province changed. "At the same time that we were in this process, the repression in Chalatenango was increasing significantly, especially in several of the areas where we had been offered work. Due to stepped-up military operations to 'pacify' the area, and the vigilance of ORDEN, many campesinos who survived the attacks fled from their homes, leaving all their belongings and food supplies behind. In some areas townspeople left for refuge in safer areas, and their homes were then occupied by people from nearby villages seeking refuge, etc. What we began to find was the phenomenon of displaced people, strangers among strangers, with great fear and suspicion of any unknown people."

The following entry, from the documentation compiled by the legal department of the archdiocese, describes the expanding military nature of the repression in rural areas:

April 24, 1980: At least one thousand members of the National Guard, the army and the paramilitary organization ORDEN, protected by two armed helicopters and tanks, invaded the neighboring peasant communities of El Campanario, San Benito, Angul, Llano Grande, El

Obrajudo, Las Lomas, La Joya, La Pita, and Santa Amilia. Various eyewitnesses stated that grenades were thrown at the houses of the peasants from the helicopters and that the communities were also subject to constant machine-gun fire. In this brutal invasion the following peasants were killed: [There follow the names of twenty-six peasants between the ages of sixty and fourteen].

Thus the needs of the local church were changing almost overnight. Suddenly, they were called upon to respond to the desperation of an ever-growing population of refugees, and in this effort Carla and Ita found themselves taking the lead in drawing up plans for an emergency committee to arrange funding for the purchase of food and medicines and to organize transportation and locate places of refuge.

Without a permanent base in which to live and work they were truly pilgrims during those first months in El Salvador. Writing to her mother at the end of April, Ita tried to explain something of their ambulatory life-style: "This past weekend Carla and I went to a mini-workshop given for rural leaders of liturgy (called Delegates of the Word) and catechists. There were sixty men in all—farmers mostly—with an extraordinary faith and simplicity. It was awe-inspiring listening to them talk of their experiences. From the workshop I came to La Libertad and there were five letters waiting. By the time we finally get settled we'll have had a slew of addresses all over the country. I'll eventually get hold of a good map and mark it up for you so you can visualize our wanderings."

Carla, who was very close to Ita's mother, also wrote: "Greetings from Saviorland! We are all fine, yet this wild place does bring to the fore the value of life and I'd say a certain sadness and anger that life is snuffed out so cheaply by the use of Made in U.S.A. weapons.

"We've had some good conversations with vicars

about possible works. Neither of us are for running into something, and although being a pilgrim for so long gets to me once in a while, I believe I can grow in this long wait. Your earnest missioner [Ita] reads avidly and will probably know more about El Salvador than the Catholic University here." Speaking of herself she added, "I'm into distractions and mental exercises to prevent sense of humor from turning into sense of horror in Salvador."

"We have just come back from the poorest part of Salvador since that is the priority of the diocese. We saw the faith of a valiant people, the dedicated priests, the ruthless repression—and we got one thousand bites of all the species of insects. Needless to say, we'll go back for more, which is the crazy, absurd life we've been chosen for and choose."

They said nothing of the ongoing persecution of the Church which Jean was methodically documenting. Her diary for this period reads:

May 1:
> *One A.M. in the morning. Rosario de Mora*
> *Church and Convent both destroyed.*

May 17:
> *Eleven Thirty. San José Villa Nueva. The*
> *Guardia National captured and held Sister*
> *Teresa Barrios until six P.M. when Uriosti**
> *obtained her release. Stole money for Church*
> *building.*

By mid-May the Salvadoran security forces had initiated a campaign to root out members of the popular organizations and guerrilla groups from their rural bases in the North, and the "clean antisubversive campaign," advocated by the State Department, had evolved in practice into a program of terror, aimed at depopulating the regional villages and burning crops in order to create starvation conditions. A Salvadoran army commander boasted to an

---

* Monsignor Uriosti was the vicar general of the archdiocese.

American journalist: "The subversives like to say that they are the fish and the people are the ocean. What we have done in the North is to dry up the ocean so we can catch the fish easily."

In the process of "drying up the ocean" the military actions were creating thousands of refugees who had begun fleeing across the border in search of sanctuary in neighboring Honduras. On May 15, press reports in the Salvadoran media referred to a massive antiguerrilla operation by combined security forces and army units along the borders of El Salvador, Guatemala and Honduras. These reports failed to mention, however, that in the course of the operation several hundred refugees, bottled up on the bank of the River Sumpul as they attempted to flee across the river border into Honduras, were massacred in a combined operation of Salvadoran and Honduran security forces. Jean, whose work kept her in constant contact with the archdiocesan Legal Office, learned of the Sumpul River disaster in the week that it happened, through the testimonies of survivors as they arrived, seeking refuge in San Salvador, but the outside world received no news of these events until the following month. On June 10, the presbytery of the Copan diocese in Honduras published a communiqué describing the horrors of the scene:

> A minimum of two helicopters, the Salvadoran National Guard, soldiers and the paramilitary organization ORDEN, opened fire on the defense-less people. Women, tortured before the finishing shot, infants thrown into the air for target practice were some of the scenes of the slaughter. The Salvadorans who crossed the river were returned by the Honduran soldiers to the area of the massacre.
>
> In midafternoon the genocide ended, leaving a minimum number of six hundred corpses.*

* From the Congressional Record, vol. 126, Wednesday, September 19, 1980, as entered by Senator Edward Kennedy.

"The focus of our lives," wrote Ita, as she and Carla began working in the Emergency Refugee Committee in Chalatenango, "is to accompany these displaced, fragmented families in their terrific fear and pain. I don't know if it is in spite of, or because of the horror, terror, evil, confusion, lawlessness—but I do know that it is right to be here. That may be the only surety as, with Carla, I start a work that is going to put us in contact with some of the hurting, homeless, hungry and to God knows whom else."

She ended her letter with a scriptural quotation that spoke directly to the lifelong goal these remarkable women had chosen to make their own: "Each of you has received some spiritual gift, use it for the good of all. Activate the different gifts that God has distributed among you."

In Chalatenango, during the early springtime of the civil war, using their gifts of courage, generosity and compassion, Ita and Carla responded to the urgent needs of the moment. It was a far cry from the pastoral work they had known and lived to date—this living one day at a time, sharing the insecurity, the chaos, the fear; keeping step along the dark road traveled by this terrorized civilian population of poor farmers and workers—but they had come to help, and they remained to do just that.

Though supported by their unwavering faith, they were not without questions or uncertainties, chief of which was the inability to assess their effectiveness in the prevailing climate of fear and mistrust. But there was a crying need for someone to organize a rescue operation for the victims of the terror, so they set about creating a network of volunteers to provide shelters, food, medicine, believing "that the answers to the questions will come when they are needed." They believed there was a reason for them to be in El Salvador at that moment, and in all honesty they could say, "It is good for us to be here."

On May 2, Roberto d'Aubuisson led an attempted coup against the junta government. On May 7 D'Aubuisson, a dozen active duty officers and four prominent civilians were arrested on orders of junta member Colonel Adolfo Majano, sole survivor of the young officers who was still in a position of power. For the first time, Majano had gone over the head of the minister of defense; troops loyal to him, and who received their orders directly from him, surprised and surrounded D'Aubuisson and his friends at an isolated country estate not far from San Salvador. The Christian Democrats threatened to withdraw from the junta unless D'Aubuisson and those with him were tried and sentenced. Enraged by the support of Ambassador White for Colonel Majano, a group of D'Aubuisson's most fanatical supporters laid siege to the American embassy residence. For two days respectable middle-class Salvadoran men and women demonstrated in the street for the benefit of the international television crews. They grew hoarse screaming their favorite slogans: "The Communists must be exterminated like rats!" and "Kill the rabid dog to cure the rabies!" and deposited a bloody corpse on the ambassador's doorstep to make their point. They carried placards in English for the cameras that read: "Get Out White." "White is a Communist." And "White Go to Iran!" But when the insults and the screaming were over, according to the chronology of events as compiled by the U.S. embassy:

> 5/13/80: D'Aubuisson released from jail as special prosecutor says there is insufficient evidence to hold him despite the fact that a suitcase full of incriminating evidence reportedly had been taken from him at the time of his arrest.

The army that voted to release D'Aubuisson also proceeded to demote Colonel Majano, removing him from the joint command of the Armed Forces, a position he had shared with Colonel Jaime Gutiérrez since the October coup. For the second time in three months the Christian Democrats backed down from their resolve, and remained in a government in which Colonel Gutiérrez, now sole commander-in-chief of the Salvadoran Armed Forces, had emerged as the new strong man. As for D'Aubuisson, his status was probably most accurately interpreted by the bitter comment of a U.S. embassy official. Asked by an American journalist whether he thought D'Aubuisson had left the country, the official replied, "If you ask me, he's probably off somewhere having a drink with the high command."

In the country at large, the paramilitary death squads, reflecting the determination of the far Right to eliminate all of their adversaries, continued to act with impunity against labor and peasant leaders, teachers, university professors, moderate politicians, Christian Democratic mayors, and, of course, the Church.

In La Libertad, Jean kept the score of the intensifying persecution:

May 20:

> *Nine fifty-five P.M. San Salvador. Attempt to blow up Radio YSAX [Church radio station].*

> *Ilopango. Parroquia San Lucia. Attack on the Church.*

> *Citala, Chalatenango. Community of nuns was threatened to leave.*

May 22:

> *Three people killed in Santa Cruz—Pastors and Julio—two of the* jovenes [*young men*] *that helped me in the celebrations.*

Later that week she made a tape to send to Crowley, the one person whom she kept constantly and intimately informed about what was happening in her life: "Things now are so much worse it's unbelievable. People are being killed daily. We just found out that three people from one of our areas had been taken, tortured and hacked to death. Two were *jovenes* [young men] and one was an older man. The man had been in ORDEN, had a fight with them and quit. So that's probably why they got him. And the other

two—well they really make me sick—because I knew them
both fairly well. We had done a mission out there recently
and they were coming to the celebrations and stuff."

The murder of her two young friends and fellow
workers made the violence personal for Jean, and she began to feel threatened for the first time. It was the second
time in four weeks that the death squads had made a foray
into Santa Cruz, the one area in the whole parish which
more than any other was her territory. "Everything is really
hitting so close now," she told Crowley. Frightened and
confused she reached out for support to Doug. In the week
leading up to the Memorial Day weekend a surprise phone
call from El Salvador tracked him down at work in the
Los Angeles County Hospital.

"It was a Wednesday," he remembers. "She said,
'There's a three-day weekend coming up for you, how'd you
like to go to Mexico City?' And I said, sure. So I got the
tickets, by Thursday I was on the plane. I flew out from
L.A. and she flew in from Salvador. We had a great time.
Went all over Mexico City, went to the Pyramids. It was so
spontaneous. It was just wonderful, living like that. 'Let's
do something outrageous. Why not?' "

"I went to Mexico City to see Doug again," she wrote
to one of her fellow students from Maryknoll. "He's working hard at the hospital in L.A. but we had been separated
for almost two months—so he flew in for the weekend. Had
a really great time. I could fall in love with that fellow."

But her inability to share with him her fears and depression left her feeling lonelier than before. He was the
same—loving, kind, optimistic, playful—but she had
changed, and she could not articulate what was going on
inside her. Her failure to take him into her confidence
struck the first false note in their intimacy.

On her return to Salvador her need to communicate
the turmoil in her spirit was even more urgent, and she
reached out again, this time to her friend, Maryknoll priest
Fern Gosslin, now pastor of an Indian parish in the Peten

area of Guatemala. Fern was a New England conservative from a Vermont farming community and had been a supportive friend to Jean ever since the days of her training in Ossining. He was someone to whom she could admit her sense of loss and disorientation. "I spent a week up in the Peten with Fern Gosslin," she wrote on her return. "He's really good for me. We talked a lot. He thinks I should get out. I talked to him on the phone after I got back and he said the same thing. Maybe I should? I'm not sure yet. I've got to work some things out. Like where I can go. Because I still want to work down here. But maybe in a more peaceful place. I feel helpless to really work because everyone is afraid to do anything. Presently I spend most of my time going to celebrations in our various communities. Because of problems nobody wants to go without me. Today I started at 7:00 A.M. and finished about 8:00 P.M. In the middle I went to a mass celebrated by Bishop Rivera y Damas in a pueblo [village] where the nuns who run the parish next to ours have been threatened. They were captured and questioned for a day. Bishop Rivera came to show his support. Dotty and I were the only outsiders there because every other parish around has been deserted. Either the priest was going to be killed or the catechists. It's really a situation of anarchy.

"A joyful letter, right? The next one will be, I promise."

As the entries in her diary testify, it was hard to find much cause for joy.

June 7:

> *Four men entered the church of San Pedro Nonualco, Diocese of San Vincente, and assassinated Padre Cosme Spezzatto, a Franciscan, while he was praying.*

The following day she wrote to another of her Maryknoll friends, Gary Martinez, a Maryknoll brother in Peru: "Dear Gary: Down here things are getting bad fast. Every day there are so many killings. I don't know if I can face another body. It may be that each day you get worn down a little. We had an Italian priest killed yesterday while he was praying in church. I hope they don't start killing priests again. It may be hard to find them because so many have left."

In the northern town of Chalatenango, meanwhile, where Ita and Carla had finally settled, the counter-insurgency war between the guerrillas and the army, and the civil war between the guerrillas and ORDEN, was spreading. The town of Chalatenango is the provincial capital of the province of the same name. Geographically situated in one of the poorest rural sectors of the country, extending in the east to the frontier with Honduras and on the north to the Guatemalan border, the mountainous terrain has tradition-ally been populated by small farmers, managing to survive and feed their families by growing subsistence crops of corn and beans in the poor and rocky soil of their hillside plots. This terrain, and the surrounding mountains, was also the territory in which the guerrillas, and those among the popular organizations who joined forces with them during that spring of 1980, had established their bases. With their forces fragmented and their leaders riven by personal rival-ries and conflicts over tactics and goals, the guerrilla strat-egy during the early months of the war was confused and frequently characterized by violent reprisals against urban and peasant families with relatives in the ranks of the offi-cial security forces and the paramilitary membership of ORDEN. In the localized civil war between these two camps, as a general rule the land in the valleys and plains belonged to ORDEN, whose members dominated and protected that segment of the rural population living beside the main roads and in the small market towns of the province; the hills belonged to the "groups" and the guerrillas, who, while protecting their rural inhabitants, also brought upon them the counterinsurgency tactics and retaliation of the security forces. Not all had sympathies or commitments with either side; many farmers and many townspeople were simply caught in the middle—trapped without support or protection from anyone.

Writing to Crowley Jean explained the situation by quoting from a recent presentation to the church workers by the vicar of the provincial diocese: "He said the people have three choices in Chalatenango—and eventually in the whole country. They can join the left and be killed by the right. They can join the right and be killed by the left. Or they can leave the country." Few among the penniless refugees, surrounded by largely hostile borders, had anywhere to escape to, and it was among this terrorized, victimized population that Ita and Carla were now living. In a letter to her young sister Rene in Brooklyn, Ita acknowledged something of the personal pain involved in dealing daily with so much tragedy: "Dear Rene," she wrote, "I'm taking a day off today to be alone: I think I'm supersaturated with horror stories and daily body counts—to the point that I thought I'd hit the next person who told me that someone else was killed. I'm not sure how you get "acclimated" to a country that has an undeclared civil war going—but sometimes you just have to take a break.

"Carla and I now have a job. We're the full-time workers of the emergency committee in the Vicariate of Chalatenango. The Church of San Salvador is facing reality and getting ready to help with food, medicines and refugee centers. There are a couple of refugee centers already in operation as people have had to leave their homes because of threats, steady skirmishes between the army and the popular organizations that want to form a new government, as well as family members having been killed and a lot of fear. I don't think we could have dreamed this job up before we came—but we came to help and this is what we are being asked to do. In many ways we hope this job is temporary—in the sense that the situation not be prolonged —but it's hard to look ahead and imagine what will follow.

"There's a lot of bizarre things that go on in this country including the 'help' from Uncle Sam. It's pathetic that there's millions for army equipment—but nothing for humanitarian help—until war is declared. Groups like the International Red Cross cannot or do not respond until the point is catastrophic. Carla keeps asking—'How many dead make a war? What is the magic number?'

"The one thing that seems sure is that there's going to be a food shortage, because a lot of farmers feel caught between the groups who are training in the mountains and need food—so come to ask for it or rob it if it is not given—and the army forces who retaliate because the farmers are collaborating with "extremist" or "subversive" groups. After a while a lot of people just leave their houses, their belongings, their animals, etc., because they just can't take it anymore.

"There's a lot of other aspects—it's really a complex situation—if only it were as simple as good guys versus bad —but it's not, and a lot of the groups don't have their act together and aren't in agreement about what to do and when. I think a lot of lives are lost that way.

"This must seem a bit heavy—sorry about that, but this is my reality right now, and in the midst of it we still try to get hold of the country and culture, etc. It's like forming friendships in a psychiatric hospital. It's real but crazy.

"How are you—now that I dumped? I think of you a lot and ask for you light, peace, happiness. Much love to you. Ita."

There were no guerrillas, no counterinsurgency war, no civil war in La Libertad—as yet; only the traditional repression of the security forces, ORDEN, and the death squads, whose parallel murderous activities were effectively recruiting the guerrillas of the future. But if the situation was less complex, closer to the good guys vs. bad guys scenario, it was no less agonizing or essentially less dangerous, particularly for the churchworkers. "Presently I have a really heavy schedule," Jean wrote, "because everyone is afraid to go out by themselves. So I am either accompanying them, or doing their Celebrations for them, and it takes a lot of preparation. One of our team, actually our oldest member, left the country last week. She thought we all should go and I'm not sure she isn't right. At times our presence hurts the people by making them targets."

It was something they worried about a great deal. Paul Schindler recalls, "We were constantly meeting and discussing among ourselves: What are the criteria that keep us here? What are the signs that tell us we should leave? What if one of us gets shot at, or hurt, or kidnapped? We did a lot of that. We went through all the possibilities. Why are we here? And what keeps us here? And we carried that type of discussion to our parish council meetings. Since in almost all the parishes around us the priests had left, we had to confront what happens if we leave too? So many of those priests that were killed were close to me. Grande was my idol. He taught me everything I know about pastoral work. Alfonso Navarro, Rafael Palacios, these men were my friends. And we had so many of our catechists killed, so we often discussed: Are we actually being the cause of people dying? And our answer was always definitely not, because in a lot of places where there were no priests there were a lot of people dying. Our presence was actually protecting them, because we always had that telephone call to the embassy that we could make. Just by the fact that I was an American and they were worried about losing arms support, and I had contact with the embassy and human rights people, that would sometimes make them back off."

Paul had a system for rescuing parishioners from the local barracks in La Libertad. "Three or four times a week we would get a visit from someone—'So-and-so has disappeared,' or 'they've come at night and arrested so-and-so.' The families are usually afraid to go to the local security forces, and I would tell them, 'Go. Question them. Ask why have they captured so-and-so and where are they?' Because if the kids were guerrillas, then everyone in the family would flee, and sometimes, if the guards would acknowledge that they had them, then usually they were released. But if they didn't acknowledge that they had them, then I would go personally and tell the captain, 'I'm interested in this kid, he's a member of my parish.' I always knew if they had the kid—they could sit there and deny to my face that they had someone, but I always knew if they were in the cells in the back because I knew the lady who cooked in the jail—she'd always tell me who had been brought in. So each day I would show up and ask, 'Have you had any word yet?' Just to let them know that I knew. After a couple of days, if they kept on denying, then I would go to the embassy and I would talk to someone in covert intelligence, and I would say, 'I know they're there, and if they are killed I will make sure that . . .' And the next day they'd be out. In other words, the embassy would make a telephone call to Colonel López Nuila, head of the National Police, or García, or someone—and I would go back to see the captain and the prisoner would be released."

If someone she knew was picked up while Paul was away, Jean never flinched from harassing the guards or the police on their behalf. On such occasions, hiding her fear beneath a facade of brashness and arrogance, she would march into the barracks and demand from the officer in charge the immediate release of the prisoner, threatening to bring the entire U.S. embassy down on his head unless she got her way. She got away with it—but as she walked triumphantly back into the street, together with the victim that her bravado had saved, she left behind her in the barracks a dangerously humiliated enemy. It was the kind of risk that went with the territory.

"The thing that was so ironic," Paul says, "was that Dorothy and Jean and I worked together, and they were always concerned that I would never go out by myself; they were always concerned that I was covered, that they knew where I was. We were constantly getting threats. The people would come and tell us, 'Father, if you go to such and such a pueblo to say mass, you'll be killed.' And I would say to them, 'Who says? Who is the one that's saying I'll be killed?' And they would reply, '*They* say.' And you knew all along of course that it's the *commandantes* in the local barracks of the Guardia, and the police and so on—but the people are afraid to say so. So my response was always, 'Well, if I don't know who the one is who's threatening me, I can't not go just because someone says I might be killed. . . . Those people are expecting me, they need us to be there, and I'm going.' It got to the point where every time I climbed into the jeep to leave the port I'd say, 'Well, here I come Lord. . . .' You get past fear. You have to get past the fear or you'd never step outside the door. You'd become a prisoner inside your own house. So you just say to yourself, 'I'm going to be killed today, and I'm ready to die, but I have to be with these people.' I just did not fear anymore. I figured I'd seen so many people killed that there was no sense in fearing it. I don't see any real rhyme or reason to be afraid of death."

On June 9, Archbishop Rivera y Damas estimated that 2,056 people, exclusive of members of the security forces and the guerrillas, had died from political violence in the first five months of the year. "Week by week," he said, "the violence gets worse. The excessive force, cruelty and indiscrimination of military operations cannot be justified."

Among the American missionaries, the increased aid from Washington for the military, and the presence of American military advisers, fostered fears and rumors of possible American intervention. From the perspective of the Church in El Salvador there was no longer any doubt that a major realignment of the forces in power—one that would include the moderate Social Democrats, the dissident Christian Democrats and the Marxists of the popular organizations—represented the only hope for an end to the carnage and the development of a democratic, pluralistic government committed to social justice for the mass of the population. In April, all of these forces, together with the major trade unions, had united to form the Democratic Revolutionary Front (FDR) under the presidency of Enrique Alvárez Córdova, former agricultural minister of the first junta, for the purpose of providing an alternative to the governing alliance of the military and the Christian Democrats. Interviewed at the time by *Newsweek* magazine, Enrique Alvárez, wealthy son of the oligarchy, educated in this country, and a lifelong, dedicated democrat, explained the background of this new alliance. "We have exhausted all peaceful means," he said. "Many of us who are in the Front tried to win the structural changes that our country so badly needs by working with previous governments. Many of us even cooperated with the current junta. . . . We thought it was the last possibility for peaceful change. It didn't work. We came to the conclusion that a change at the very center of power was necessary."

In May, through the formation of a political-diplomatic commission, led by Social Democrat Guillermo Ungo, the FDR had initiated links with the guerrilla leaders. It was against this background of a broadly based united opposition of the Left that Washington's commitment to a government without any visible base of support among its own people was perceived to be leading to eventual, inevitable American intervention. During this entire period, concerned American churchpeople within El Salvador were writing to their counterparts at home, and it was in large part through their efforts that the early grass-roots opposition to official policy in Central America started gathering support in the United States.

In June, Ita Ford wrote to Maryknoll: "Since the death of Monsignor Romero, the news coverage on Salvador has declined to almost nothing. The [refugee] committee fears that decisive action will be taken by our government in the guise of 'stopping subversives' or 'containing communism'—and that all of Central America will be involved if this happens. . . . It is still the same strong Church at the grass roots that suffers daily persecution and even death, just for being aware, or poor, or young, or associated or sympathetic to the popular organizations. Priests and sisters have had to leave the country, some after having lived for a time as fugitives. People are making choices and are being killed for those choices, as others look on approvingly. Defenders of 'the true religion' get letters of permission from the authorities to go after the apostates."

Jean continued to document the persecution:

June 12:
> *In the evening, soldiers raid the Sisters of the Sagrado Corazón School—destroy the door and rip up pictures of Monsignor Romero.*

June 13:
> *In the evening soldiers break into the Instituto Secula de Zacamel—a community of religious lay people.*

June 20:
> *In the evening, at the High School Sagrada Familia, more than 100 soldiers circled the school. Said they were looking for arms, medical clinics and fugitives. Ripped up pictures of Monsignor Romero. Took copies of* Orientación *because they were dangerous. Captured one religious sister and 5 employees.*

That day she had written to Maryknoll. "Dear Gwen, I hope that if I come to the States in September I can stop in New York. It's just that my life is so iffy presently I can't make plans too far in advance. I'm sure you all hear the news—so, it's very bad. I'm not sure exactly how long one can cope. . . . In my opinion everyone should go on a 3-year assignment to get the feel of things and then come back for more school or whatever. I seem in a year and a half to be just getting into my own now. . . . But I am also seeing what I would like to know more about."

And the repression continued with monotonous predictability:

June 21:
> *The Guardia and one ex-member of the* FPL *[one of the guerrilla groups] accused the Church*

*of helping import arms—Jesuits especially—
and said P. de Sebastian, de Monchi, Hernandez, are part of Fuerzas Populares de Libera-
ción.*

June 22:

> *Two men killed bus driver in Tamonique.
> Dorothy, Paul and I go to bless bodies. Pass by
> armed drunk camp of* ORDEN. *Other organizer
> killed. Two shots fired in cemetery. Leave
> quickly.*

By late June, recovering and burying the mutilated
remains of death-squad victims had become a regular part
of the routine of parish work. The bodies would be dumped
at night—outside the port, along the street, sometimes on
someone's doorstep. At first the people gathered them up
and buried them. Then the death squads began pinning a
notice on the body: "If you bury this body the same will
happen to you." So the people were afraid and they would
go to fetch Paul. Jean and Dorothy did not want Paul to go
alone, so they would accompany him. The catechists did not
want Jean and Dorothy to do the heavy work of digging
the grave, and besides these corpses were their own people.
It was only right that a Salvadoran should be with them to
lay their remains to rest, so they went along too. And
through the windows of the barracks, from the corner of
the street where they lounged behind dark glasses, smoking
Marlboro cigarettes, the members of the paramilitary squads
observed the *gringos* and their Salvadoran friends disobey-
ing their instructions. Watching, they saw the tenderness
with which Paul reassembled the bloody stumps of hacked-
off limbs, returning something resembling the dignity of a
human form to the mangled remains flung out into the
gutter for the dogs and vultures to pick over. They watched
as he took his photographs. "We always took pictures of
the bodies," Paul explains, "because when they kill some-

one, to make it harder for the families to identify them, they don't kill them in their own area. Usually the bodies dumped into our area were from another section of the country—several times we were able to help people identify members of their family through our pictures."

Among the Salvadorans who worked alongside the Cleveland team in La Libertad was a young man who had grown increasingly close to Jean. Armando Avalae was the sacristan of the church and the leader of the choral group that Jean had founded when she first arrived. He had grown up working for the church, and like other young Salvadorans of his small-town background, the exposure throughout his adolescence to the imported value system of the American missionaries, and the subsequent influence of Monsignor Romero, had given him access to an education and a view of the world far beyond the limitations that his environment and the economic status of his family traditionally imposed upon the members of his class.

At the time that Jean and Armando met, he was a remarkably mature and developed young man of twenty-three. Jean, at twenty-seven, was still immature for her age, but if, as she later admitted, they were instantly attracted to one another, both had prior commitments that appeared to rule out an emotional involvement. Armando was resolved to enter the priesthood and had already been accepted into the seminary for the following year, and Jean was deeply attached to Doug. It was a safe situation for both—one that left them free to relax and enjoy a light-hearted, somewhat flirtatious friendship—just the kind of male relationship that Jean was adept at encouraging and enjoying, while carefully preserving control of the situation and holding onto her own freedom. Neither one could have foreseen the desperate need for closeness and intimacy that would be evoked by the surrounding chaos and death. Battered daily by so much cruelty, so much treachery and danger, they increasingly turned to each other for some tenderness and trust.

Sometime after Jean's frenetic visit to Mexico City to touch base with Doug, Armando changed his plans and withdrew his application to the seminary.

Their happiness, inevitably, represented an irresistible target for those watching within the barracks who wanted to strike back at the arrogant *gringa* blond. In her diary for Sunday, July 6, Jean made the following entry:

July 6:

> *Three men, one with a pistol, shot the sacristan and another young man—Armando Avelae and Carlos Hernandez—both in the head at 10:30 P.M. in the evening in front of the Parochial School in Puerto de la Libertad.*

The parochial school was where Jean lived. They had been to the movies—Jean, Armando and Carlos. Carlos was Paul's adopted son, a young delinquent whom he had rescued off the streets seven years earlier and helped to bring up and educate ever since. Paul loved the boy like a father. Armando and Carlos had walked Jean home. Armando took out the dog and they said goodnight. Jean had barely reached her room above the school when she heard two shots outside her window and in that instant, as she stood poised between terror and hope, she heard Armando cry out for help. In the time that it took her to race down the stairs and out onto the pavement, the killer put the gun into Armando's mouth as he lay wounded on the ground and fired twice more.

Paul Schindler can never forget that night. As he describes it, "It was a Sunday night around ten o'clock. The boys were getting ready to go to bed and walking down the street. There were hundreds of people—maybe two hundred people on the street that night—and these three guys walked up and shot them. Right on the corner of Jean's house. It was the hardest time we ever had together."

It would take Jean several weeks before she was able to write to anyone about Armando's death. After the funeral she sent his burial card to Maryknoll, with a small note attached: "I'm not going to write a long letter, 'cause right now I'm not in any shape to. You can see how I'm a bit unhinged. Just everyone pray for us and all the Maryknollers that are here. They are really great people."

The American missionary community understood only too well that the murder of Armando and Carlos signified a very direct message to Paul and the members of the team to back off from their commitment to help and support the people of La Libertad, and in the immediate aftermath of their deaths the sympathy, support and strength of Carla and Ita was crucial to Jean. It may well have saved her from a crack-up.

At some point she made a tape for Michael Crowley. "I think of all her letters and tapes, that killing probably broke her heart more than anything," he says. "She describes it, full of grief and heartbreak, and tells in detail what happened. She describes how she took the sheets from her bed and wrapped their bleeding bodies and so on. . . . It was really, I would say, the lowest point in her whole Salvador experience."

There are two more entries in her diary immediately following Armando's death:

July 7:

> *Red Cross workers who helped with Carlos in*
> *the Port were almost captured and had to flee*
> *from sailors and police.*

> *The guitarist for the choir of La Libertad was*
> *threatened and had to leave the Port.*

July 8:

> *Armando's 24th birthday.*

Then silence for almost three weeks. Finally, on the third Sunday following his death, alone in her apartment in La Libertad, she tried to tell a few close friends about him. "I'm still very numb," she wrote to Cindy O'Donnell, one of her colleagues from the Maryknoll lay program now working in the missions in the Philippines, adding that she did not feel capable of going into any details about her feelings for Armando, other than to say that he was someone she had loved. In his lifetime, because of the disapproval of Paul and Dorothy for the growing affection between their two youngest coworkers—an affection which in their view ran the risk of alienating Armando from the vocation for the priesthood which they still hoped he would follow— Jean had not said much of anything to anyone about their friendship. Now her anguish over his violent loss was all the harder to bear, cut off as she was from the consolation of those like Doug, like her parents, who, had they known, had they understood her loneliness, could have opened up their hearts to comfort her. Now it seemed to Jean to be too late to share her grief with any who had not known Armando alive. In the letters she wrote to three or four friends on that lonely Sunday afternoon, she described his death—the manner of it, the time, the location—with an obsessive repetition of detail, as though all that was left to her was now concentrated in these final desolate scenes she was forced to relive in her mind: the shots, followed by Armando's call for help, brutally cut off by the gun in his mouth.

"I'm not doing real good," she told Gary Martinez. "My best friend in Salvador was assassinated in front of my house three Sundays ago. Yesterday, I understand a deacon and eleven others were killed in Cuscatlán, near a church where he was to be ordained in two weeks. . . . Guatemela as I'm sure you've heard is not good either. Another Spanish priest was killed in Quiché about three weeks ago. I just don't know where all the violence is going to end, but I think this entire country is going to have a nervous breakdown.

"I'm very much torn about leaving for my vacation, but know that I really need it. Every time I think of Armando and Carlos I get sick and cry. By the way, I was there in the house when it happened. . . . Maybe we can get together when I'm home?"

Armando's death left Jean to struggle on in a colder, bleaker, and more frightening world. But there was work to do, and now that she had become just one more grief-stricken woman among the legions of the bereft—now that she had joined the ranks of those walking wounded—the thousands of Salvadoran mothers, wives, sweethearts and children whose lives and hearts were being torn apart every day—her original choice, her desire to accompany the people in their grief and give what support she could had acquired a new dimension. Her private loss and grief gave new urgency to her ever-deepening commitment.

And she was not alone. Dorothy and Chris had left to go back to the States on a brief vacation shortly after the funeral, but Carla and Ita, isolated in the center of the ever-expanding civil war in Chalatenango, needed all the help they could get. By late July, the transportation and protection of refugees had become the single most critical problem for the archdiocese. Jean, yearning to be part of something concrete and physical, pulled herself out of her depression and plunged into the chaotic center of the action.

Part II: July–September 1980

She absolutely hated violence. She identified very much with the Church because she said the only option for the Church was to stay in the middle. That the Church can't belong to either the Right or the Left. As soon as the Right does something evil the Church needs to have the freedom to say: "That's wrong." And if the Left does something evil, the Church needs the freedom to say: "That's wrong." And this was Jean's position.

She often felt deep anger. She said in her final tapes that life was very frightening for her because so many of her closest friends were being killed. And she still could not opt for violence. She was running a terrific risk in all of her activity—coming to the aid of children, wives, and the fall people of the violence, the refugees. And she knew very well—in fact in one of her tapes she talks about the number of times she was asked to go on mercy errands with different people, and agonizes about what will happen when it's her turn.

She also talked about torture. She said she had seen so many appalling mutilations that she hoped and prayed that if she were ever killed, that she would be killed instantly, because she couldn't bear the thought of torture. And then she made a footnote. She said: I am a coward. I don't want to die.

—Father Michael Crowley

"The situation of repression and genocide," wrote Ita in late July, "continues to grow each day in an unbelievable way. However, no war has been declared. Over 2,000 families have had to leave their homes in Chalatenango because of the persecution either by the security forces or by the popular groups. All these displaced families live with terrific fear and this generates an atmosphere of lack of trust everywhere."

The fragmentation and isolation of daily existence was particularly hard on Ita and Carla, who were accustomed to living as members of a community, sharing in the lives of neighbors among whom they could visit and make friends. Now they had no neighbors. "We cannot visit," Ita explained, "because of the very real danger of placing others in danger because of belonging to the Church which is one of the security forces' biggest enemies."

Yet the lack of a home base, the impossibility of maintaining open communications on controlled phones, the constant travel in buses nicknamed "the microwave cookers" by Carla, since the temperature inside was never less than one hundred degrees, and above all, the strain of inventing their jobs daily was beginning to tell. "Neither one of us are emotional or psychological giants in this crazy situation," Ita admitted. More and more of their energies were being consumed in the daily struggle to keep their spirits up, to "keep walking down this dark road without becoming as dark as the situation." Attempting to describe the situation, Ita made a shopping list of their activities:

What do we really do?
1. We continue to seek out dialogue and collaboration with humanitarian groups.
2. We drive priests to outlying country districts.
3. We drive food to contacts who will get it to people hiding from the security forces or the popular groups.

4. We transport refugees and clothes to different hiding places.

In her diary, Jean began recording the changed focus of her activities:

July 26:

> *Two children and a few others shot in Chalatenango. The others died. Got the children out to San Salvador on Monday.*

> *18-year-old killed in the hospital.*

> *Nuns and priests threatened and fired on during Mass in Chalatenango.*

> *Man killed near the church in Santa Cruz.*

August 5:

> *Meeting with the International Red Cross. Say 3,000 people on the river border with 17 weapons keeping* ORDEN *at bay. Have chosen to die because they have arms. 200 people say they want to come down for the Red Cross bus on Friday.*

August 6:

> *Maryknollers here are having an area meeting at the house (Zaragoza) but Carla was very late arriving this night. Was trying to arrange for 300 to come down to Red Cross bus.*

August 7:

> *Chris and I drive up to Chalatenango to stay with Carla for the night because we leave at dawn for Dulce de Maria. Ron has 23 children in his house to be evacuated.*

August 8:

> *No gas in Chalatenango. Change for Ephraim's jeep. Not much gas. Fly to Dulce de Maria. Learn 26 have been killed on Guardia side.*

Pack kids up in jeep and leave. At entrance to Chalate I'm out of gas. Transfer kids and go for gas. Guardia calls to talk to Carla. They are moving 90 families into Ron's church. No one has wheels. International Red Cross takes 31 people (3 women, the rest kids).

August 9:

Ita trying to arrange transportation for a kid shot in Chalatenango hospital. Four families talk to Carla for relocation.

Five bodies found on the road to the airport.

August 13:

Talk to Carla and Ita. Violence bad in Chalatenango. They took food to 50 people in Ron Potter's house.

40 soldiers killed in a truck in San Antonio Abad.

August 14:

Helicopters, trucks and soldiers very active in Chalatenango.

"Chalatenango is absolutely civil war at the moment," Jean told Crowley. "They've got bodies lying all over—no one can bury them because they get shot at if they try. Some nuns were up there. ORDEN just really turned on the nuns. They got a message to leave in six days or you're going to be killed, and they burned their jeep to prove it. So they believed it, and left. People don't have liberty to do anything. They have to take a side. And it's very hard not to take a particular side. It's so much harder to fight for your liberty in a nonviolent way than it is with a gun. It's funny—people very close to me have been killed now, and yet I still think that. So I'm starting to think maybe I really do believe it. At the moment, the only nonviolent voice in the whole country is the Church, and I think they have to remain in a neutral position."

That neutral position was a very lonely one. It was also, inevitably, misunderstood, misinterpreted and fatally lacking in any credibility among the partisans of the Right. Yet they held fast to their commitment to all of the victims of the violence—that desolate population of old men and women, young girls and boys, mere children themselves, carrying the smaller children in their arms as they wandered the roads and mountain paths, dazed with fear and exhaustion and weakened by hunger. Carla and Ita, Jean and Dorothy never stopped to ask which side had driven these shattered people from their homes. They just pitched in and found them food, transport and shelter in one or another of the refugee camps that were expanding daily under the jurisdiction of the archdiocese. And when Ita learned that an eight-year-old boy, wounded in a fire fight between the army and the guerrillas, had been machine-gunned as he lay in his hospital bed early one morning, she and Carla instantly became involved in rescuing two other wounded "guerrillas"—eleven and twelve years old respectively—from the hospital, and made arrangements for them to receive shelter and medical care in a safe house belonging to a middle-class Salvadoran friend in the capital.

The women knew they were vulnerable and defenseless in this no man's land where they had chosen to carry on their work. They understood, only too well, the extent to which they were exposed daily to the hatred and the scrutiny of their enemies. The young priest for whom Carla drove had been personally threatened, and when she would drive him up into the hills to say mass for the fugitive communities in one of the contested areas, they were both perfectly aware of the risks. Carla described how the young priest would ask her to step on the gas on some mountain road that even the commercials for Toyota jeeps did not adequately portray. For even as they drove past some ORDEN lookout post, it never occurred to either of them to turn back. Retreat from the people who needed them and who were counting on their support was never even an option.

In their response to a situation they recognized to be growing daily more insane, more irrationally violent, the women were being drawn always closer to the extreme edge of danger without any safety net in sight. They had no map to guide them, no master plan for the future—only their total trust that this was what they were being called upon to do. Each day they put themselves and their lives on the line in the pursuit of a shared faith in what it meant to live as a true follower of Christ. That was all they had to sustain them—that and their friendship and sense of humor. Like Peter, stranded in the Sea of Galilee, Carla was able to tell her friend that in spite of everything she was glad she had jumped out of the boat in answer to God's call. She described how even as she felt herself sinking, even as a part of her began to scream in terror, she could feel herself being held; she knew she was not alone.

"You say you don't want anything to happen to me," Ita wrote her younger sister Rene. "I'd prefer it that way myself—but I don't see that we have control over the forces of madness, and if you choose to enter into other peoples' suffering, or to love others, you at least have to consent in some way to the possible consequences." Among themselves they had grown accustomed to looking those possible consequences in the face. To her sister Ita explained: "Actually what I've learned here is that death is not the worst evil. We live with these evils, hate, manipulation, selfishness. We look death in the face every day. But the cause of the death is evil. That's what we have to wrestle and fight against.

They had always known that the rejection of death, its exclusion from life, diminished and impoverished life itself. Now that death had invaded their lives, now that its reality faced them daily, they had begun to experience amid all the destruction and evil, the truth of the age-old paradox: acceptance of death, the admission of its inevitability, not only made it easier for them to carry on with their work, it had given their lives new meaning, richness and intensity.

"What I want to say, some of it isn't too jolly birthday talk, but it's real," Ita wrote to a favorite niece about to celebrate her sixteenth birthday. "Yesterday I stood looking down at a sixteen-year-old who had been killed a few hours earlier. I know a lot of kids even younger who are dead. This is a terrible time in El Salvador for youth. A lot of idealism and commitment are getting snuffed out here now.

"The reasons why so many people are being killed are quite complicated—yet there are a few simple strands. One is that many people have found a meaning to live, sacrifice, and even die. And, whether their life-span is sixteen years, sixty, or ninety, for them their life has had a purpose. In many ways, they are fortunate people.

"Brooklyn is not passing through the drama of El Salvador but some things hold true wherever one is—and at whatever age. What I'm saying is I hope you come to find that which gives life a deep meaning for you. Something worth living for—maybe even worth dying for— something that energizes you, enthuses you and enables you to keep moving ahead."

Saying yes to death had enlarged their lives in big and little ways. When nothing could be taken for granted anymore, when all superficiality and trivia had been shed, everything, from the quality of their enjoyment of each other, to the appreciation of a Big Mac at the San Salvador McDonald's, to a rare day off relaxing at the beach, had the freshness, vitality and joy that comes with the ability to live fully in and for the moment.

August 19:

> *Fun day. Carla, Ita and I came down to the Port for the night. Carla read articles in* Glamour *and we finished off a bottle of Chilean wine.*

August 21:

> *Helped Carla move refugees in the morning, then left for Guatemala. Trip took six hours. Met Don* in Guatemala City. He is using a*

---

* Don, a young Irish priest from Belfast, went into hiding shortly after this meeting.

> *new identity because they want to kill all priests*
> *in his area. Tried three times. Three times he*
> *had a magnum under the Bible on the altar.*
> *Very hard for me to play these games.*

August 23:
> *Chris and I ran around getting food for the*
> *Center. Called Carla and Ita. They didn't call*
> *back. Got worried about four-thirty* A.M.
> *Should have called.*

On the evening of August 23 Carla and Ita received an urgent call to pick up a prisoner from the military barracks. The man was a member of ORDEN who needed to be returned to safety in his village in the hills through guerrilla-held territory. To Carla and Ita he was just another refugee, but to the other refugees sheltering in their house that night he was a potentially dangerous informer, so Ita and Carla decided to take him home right away.

They left Chalatenango after dark on a very wet and stormy night. August is the height of the rainy season—a time of washouts and sudden flash floods in the narrow mountain streams that cross and recross the winding dirt roads. They had a choice of routes that could take them to their destination in the hills. One road, though free of river crossings, was extremely susceptible to landslides, and since the local population was reporting many of these, they chose to take the alternate road. They made it safely across the riverbed four times; then, when they reached the fifth crossing, Carla, who was driving, decided they could not make it through. But in the time it took them to return to the previous crossing, the situation had changed dramatically. Not more than five minutes could have elapsed between the time they had crossed the river on their way out and the moment they reached the same crossing on their return. But in the freak weather conditions that prevail in that part of the country during the rainstorms, those few minutes made all the difference. They had barely started across the riverbed, when a wall of water struck the jeep and turned it over on its side. From the driver's seat Carla somehow managed to shove the slight, skinny, little figure of Ita out through the half-open window.

"I just went bobbing down the river," Ita recalled. "I was like a piece of something that was being turned around and upside down, down very very deep, and I just said to myself, 'You won't make it'—so I said, 'Receive me Lord.' I was a little curious about what was going to happen but I really wasn't afraid. I never said 'help,' it never occurred to me to say, 'Save me'—I don't know what that means, but I just said 'Receive me, I'm coming.' "

But she was wrong. The current finally drove her against the root of a tree and she survived.

It was Jean who finally found Carla's body the following morning, washed up on the riverbank nine miles downstream from the crossing. She was buried very simply in the little country cemetery in Chalatenango.

"It was really quite a beautiful mass," Ita wrote, "with the people very touched that Carla was going to be buried in Chalatenango. We had been offered to have the wake in one of the Sisters' chapels in San Salvador, and I said no. She died right here working for these people, and it's like robbing the people now she's dead—she belonged to them and they belonged to her, and this is not the time when you march somebody off to some kind of a solemn church thing."

August 25:
> *Had a beautiful procession to the gravesite.*
> *Held Ita during Mass—she was really great.*
> *Went with her to the hospital.*

Six weeks earlier, at the death of Armando, Ita and Carla had known how to extend their strength and their hearts to comfort and support the shattered Jean. Now it was Jean's turn to try and provide strength and solace for Ita, who was not only struggling with loss, but also on the edge of physical collapse, following her all-night ordeal in the river. In the hospital, when Jean brought her there after the funeral, they found that she was dangerously dehydrated, and she had to stay there and be fed intravenously for five days.

"Of course," Ita admitted to her mother, "it's much more difficult being the survivor. Carla and I had talked lots of times about the possibility of our dying, because of things here, very violent things. I guess we talked about how it would be much more difficult if it wasn't together, for the one who was left behind. So I started thinking about what I am feeling and saw the very, very end of St. John's Gospel—this little scene of Jesus with Peter—John seems to be in the background. Jesus says to Peter, 'Follow me.' Peter turns around and says, 'What about him?' And Jesus says: 'That's really none of your business. I'm telling you to follow me, and he is to wait around—I'll take care of that.' And I guess that's just what it boils down to. I don't feel guilty. Some people feel survivor's guilt but I don't think I have that. I miss Carla dreadfully but there is still a lot of work to do and I want to get better and get back to do it."

The death of Carla, so soon after the death of Armando, had a profound effect on Jean. Once again death, sudden and violent, had reached into their little community and altered irrevocably the texture of their daily lives, bringing new stresses, new demands and different options. Probably for no one was this more true than for Jean, who was undergoing so much inner change so fast. Although she and Carla had only known each other for a few months, Carla's influence had been remarkably healing for Jean. Whether they were working together to rescue orphans and refugees—driving long hours, under terrible conditions, to ferry food to hungry families hiding in the hills who were unwilling to abandon their land and unable to live in safety in their homes—or on those rare occasions when Carla and Ita could take a break and come to La Libertad for the night, and Jean, in the midst of the chaos that was a permanent feature of her apartment, would cook a gourmet dinner, and together with Dorothy and Paul, Ken and Chris, seize the opportunity to turn their visit into the pretext for a party—she and Carla shared a similarity of temperament and outlook on many levels that had made all the crises of their lives seem easier to handle. They were both spontaneous, large-hearted women, always ready, as Ita said of Carla, "to put their bodies where their mouths were." With Carla gone, Jean looked into the void created by her loss and responded with a strength and certainty that were new for her. "Until then," Maryknoll Sister Terri Alexander recalled, "Jean would always talk—sometimes about staying in Salvador—sometimes about looking for some other work." Not anymore. Whatever lingering doubts had survived the murder of Armando, whatever ambivalence she had felt in the past lay buried now with Carla in the Chalatenango cemetery. "I know now," Jean told Terri some days after the funeral, "I know that I want to stay and work in El Salvador because of the work that Carla had begun."

She also knew that she wanted to be transferred from La Libertad to Chalatenango to work with Ita full-time. She had set her heart on taking Carla's place, and lost no time lobbying within the Salvadoran diocese to achieve this. On August 27, two days after the funeral, she recorded in the diary:

> Went to see Uriosti (vicar of the Salvador archdiocese), Fabian (vicar of the Chalatenango parish) and Su Servidor* about Carla, refugees, etc. Had a good meeting about possibilities of work. Needs are great, especially for Norte-Americanas.

However, the Maryknoll Sisters who had come together from the Central American region for Carla's funeral were also holding meetings, and they had their own solu-

---

* The nickname they had given to the young priest Padre Sigfredo for whom Carla had chauffeured.

tions. "You probably know," Ita told her mother, "that Maura Clarke will be coming out to Chalatenango. Maura is a tremendous woman, has a lot of experience in Nicaragua, and has been home for the last three or four years doing Mission Education. She is very Irish and has a huge, loving, warm heart. I think she's going to be fantastic for all these people who come in who are traumatized, or who have been hiding, scared for their lives—I just think Maura's going to be God's gift to them."

Ita's assessment of Maura Clarke was perfect. At forty-nine she was somewhat older than the rest of the group; slight and a little stooped, her physical appearance gave an impression of fragility, or more precisely of a delicacy which did no justice to the strength of her character. Her smile did that. Maura's smile radiated a kind of wondrous, inexhaustible goodness. For most of her life, she had served as a missionary in the Nicaragua of Somoza. She had been scheduled to return to Managua, where all of her friends in the *barrio*, now renamed Cuidad Sandino, were waiting to welcome her back after a three-year absence teaching in the States, when Sister Joan Petrik fell ill in Salvador and had to return home. It was June, and Maura's mother has never forgotten the chill of presentiment that entered their home in Rockaway Park, Queens. "I remember the first time. She got a very long letter from some Sister telling her about the *need* there. And she read that letter, taking a great deal of time reading that particular letter, and I felt then that she was going to go to San Salvador."

All her life, Maura had remained extremely close to her parents. Like many Irish immigrants they had married late and were both now in their mideighties, so it must have been hard for her to resist their pleas that she not go to El Salvador. Her mother has often relived the last weeks they spent together. "The twelfth of July. That was the day she left. I remember the weeks leading up to that—feeling lonesome and sad, somehow. I remember saying to her, 'I wish, Maura, you would just go back to Nicaragua and try building it up. I wouldn't feel so lonesome about you being there, because I've been there, and I sort of feel I know the people.' I could sort of visualize her there, whilst in Salvador I couldn't picture her. I'd no picture in my mind about Salvador. And while we didn't know too much about it, we hadn't heard anything good from it. I had a strange fear about her going there. And . . . well it seemed to me that she just had to go there."

She wrote to them on July 21 from Nicaragua: "My dearest ones, I would really love to stay here in Nicaragua where there is so much to do, but I know I must go to El Salvador to see if it is right for me to be there as one of our Sisters there has been alone for sometime. I'll be leaving Wednesday—the day after tomorrow but I'll call you before I go. Don't worry about me. The Lord takes care of us all. If I see that it isn't the place for me I'll return to work in Nicaragua very soon. We must not be afraid. No matter what happens we are one with God and with one another."

One month to the day after she arrived in El Salvador Carla was dead, and Maura volunteered to take her place. Jean kept her disappointment to herself. On September 1, she noted in her diary the shape of things to come.

September 1:

> *Ita and Maura are going to work in Chala-*
> *tenango. Dorothy and I are going to help out.*
> *Group meeting decided on all our new work.*
> *Was decided that Dotty and I would help out*
> *in Chalatenango, and Ken was going to open a*
> *home for children. Chris will continue in her*
> *center [for refugees].*

Ken Myers' decision to open a refugee center for children in Zaragoza would create an even more direct link between the Libertad and Chalatenango areas where the majority of the refugees were still being generated. With their new, authorized status as the backup team for Ita and

Maura, Jean and Dorothy and their Toyota van would soon acquire their official nickname—The Rescue Squad.

Dorothy was "home." By rights she should not have returned, but she had used her visit to the States to get permission from the bishop of Cleveland to extend her stay in Salvador for one more year. Soon Jean would be leaving for a much needed vacation and Dorothy took the opportunity to write to Martha Owens in Cleveland.

September 5: "Jean is mailing this from Florida as she'll be on vacation as of Tuesday, so I hope to fill you in as much as possible . . .

"Well, we've been doing lots of running around here. . . . The Maryknollers left in stages—the last few this past Thursday. It's still hard to believe all that's happened. Ita is OK—she and the other three here (Maddie, Terri and Maura) will be going to the retreat in Guatemala next week. We decided not to go. First of all, Chris is managing a refugee center at San Roque in San Salvador. Carla got her involved. It's been a good thing for her but is exhausting. She's there Monday–Friday and then comes to Zaragoza on the weekends to help with conferences, meetings, etc.—and to eat and sleep decently. Her bed there is an examining table in the clinic—a very narrow one! So she needs to come back once a week. The place is a church in the process of becoming—not quite done— but it serves the purpose. The people are from Chalatenango. She had one hundred and thirty-four but twenty-nine left to go back to their village—hopefully they will be OK.

"Caritas does a lot of providing for the centers— there are seven of them—we've been helping out too.

"The other thing is that Ken decided to use the Casa Communal for the kids refugee center. It will be called a *Hogar de Niños* [children's home] but really it will be [for] lost and orphaned refugee children. Details are being worked out now—so—should be interesting. It seems like Jean and I will be helping Ita and Maura out in Chalatenango when needed. Maura is a lovely person who came to accompany

Maddie in Santa Ana. Since Carla's death she has volunteered to be with Ita in Chalatenango.

"On Friday, I went out on my motor to advise our catechists about Confirmation *Charlas* [briefings]. Just past Congujera and Chaquiton there were three cadavers. I didn't stop cuz people were there—I thought I'd go to Valle Nuevo first and stop on my way back. Well, as I pulled in to Valle Nuevo—where the health clinic is—there were lots of people, and I saw the candles and the *caja* [coffin]. Here they also shot and killed the father of Margot (the girl catechist who helps us). He was the caretaker of the center. It seems a group of masked men came in about midnight and shot him. A seventeen-year-old son and eight-year-old boy were there, but they hid in a bathroom that doesn't work and luckily weren't found as these guys hung around until four-thirty A.M. There was one other killed from Valle Nuevo, one from Congujera and one from Los Planos—but no one we knew.

"Jean just came back from Zaragoza. The *Escuadron de Muerte* [death squad] is running around up there—tried to get a man out of the catechist's house. Also supposedly the 'boys' (Julio, etc.) are all on their list—so they're all in Ken's house now. The E.M. went into the clinic—seem to still be there.

"[Later] It's now Monday. Zaragoza calmed down after the E.M. left—they seem not to have killed anyone, thank God. We did lots of running around—hope this gives you some idea of what's happening. Hello to all. Love ya, D."

The time for Jean's departure was approaching, but as her diary testified, she kept on working up to the last moment.

September 2:

> *Had priest meeting. Fabian presented condition*
> *of the country. Was very good. People trapped*
> *on both sides.*

Called Ireland last night.

Got news about Majano at priest meeting from Uriosti.

The struggle within the government between the influence of the hard-liners, led by Colonels Gutiérrez and García, and what was left of the reform movement, led by Colonel Majano, had reached a new and decisive stage. Ever since his demotion in May from the post of cocommander-in-chief, Majano had been waging a lonely and losing struggle against the alliance of the high command and the far Right. On September 1, when word leaked that he had been holding talks with representatives of the Left, Defense Minister García, supported by Colonel Gutiérrez, acted swiftly to reassign all of his remaining supporters within the officer corps to minor command positions. The battle order of September 1 marked step two in the move, begun in May, to oust Majano from the junta. It eliminated whatever slender potential remained for putting the brakes on the intensifying militarization of the civil war, and robbed the Church and the moderate opposition of a mediator of last resort within the army.

September 3:

Mass for 9 days for Carla in Chalatenango. It was really beautiful. The seminarians came up to sing. After the Mass they had so much trouble. First their bus was stopped outside Chalate. All people out with hands on their heads. Then later, 25 kilometers out of San Salvador, the groups stopped and burned the bus. Finally they walked with Rafael Urrutia to Apoya, went in the rectory. The army surrounded it with tanks. They told Rafael it was only for the Padres' protection.

September 4:
> *Were in La Libertad most of the day. Finally*
> *went to see* Ice Castles. *Ita called at 2:30.*
> *Checked her out before going.*

Ita was convalescing for a week at the Convent of the Assumption Sisters in San Salvador where she had gone to try to recuperate after Carla's death and deal with her pain in solitude. During these few days of calm and reflection she wrote to her mother. It was a long, thoughtful letter, full of concern for her mother's distress. Ita understood not only how deeply Carla's death would affect her mother: she also realized that the accident that had robbed her of an adopted child must have intensified her fears for Ita's own safety.

"I know this is a very hard time for you," she wrote. "I know that you're concerned and worried about the situation and I don't know really how to alleviate that. I truly believe that I should be here and I can't even tell you why. A couple of weeks ago Carla and I were praying and we both cried because it was so unclear to us why we were here, although we felt strongly we should be. Well, it's now quite clear for Carla, but I still have to keep asking to be shown. I can't tell you not to worry—that would be un-natural—it would be like someone saying to me—don't hurt because Carla died. In fact the last few days have been really hurting ones—probably because the shock of the whole thing—the event and to my system—is wearing off. All I can share with you is that God's palpable presence has never been more real ever since we came to Salvador. He's made a lot of things clear for us—what we should be doing, etc.—and I trust in that and I hope you can too. I'll be in touch. Take good care."

She also wrote, some little while later, to her younger sister, Rene. The two sisters had always been exceptionally close, and now Ita's letter revealed much of her inner turmoil. "Of course I've been angry and I felt it was a stupidity," she wrote Rene. "It's much more than having a friend die—because Carla was friend, coworker and con-

206

structor or shaper of a lot of things because of her personality—and maybe more important at times, sister and sharer of a faith and vision in the midst of so much violence, hate and death.

"I can't answer logically the struggle we have in front of sickness, human limits and mystery. As I said on the tape, it's not our own strength that gets us through but a gift that we're given at the time. Do you really think I'm an acrobat, which I had to be that night? Or a frogman? Maybe we rage against the things/events we can't control because we're scared, and it shows just where our power ends and where we have to hang on in faith or else throw in the towel. Because whether it's a flash flood or a weird virus or whatever—there's a lot of things beyond us.

"It's not a question of being good or bad but human. So I'm mad, sad, confused, and still coping and trying to make sense and meaning of it all—because I need some kind of meaning. In the long run, no life or death is a waste —and I certainly don't think Carla's was. It was rich and full, but for me, too short!!

"Write again. I need to hear from you. I love you. Ita."

Jean, who felt very protective of Ita, made a point of staying in touch and being available if needed.

September 5:
Went to San Salvador to do errands. Buy gifts.
Found 5 bodies Valle Nuevo and Congujera.
Picked up Chris. The people at the Center have
no meat. Twenty left to try and bring in their
crops.

Struggle going on at present in the Junta. Majano says Gutiérrez is acting illegal. Told army
not to obey.

September 6:
Went to Zaragoza. Did the books. Three bodies
found in Zaragoza. Afternoon had confirmation
briefings. Went to movie—Sea Wolves.

September 7:

> *Today in the afternoon a man was taken out of Chus's house [catechist] and beaten up by Death Squad.*
>
> *Supposedly a list came out with almost all* jovenes *on it to be killed.*
>
> *Had Mass in the Port with choir, about 15 young men. Also Mass in Santa Cruz. Was a fairly good crowd. Dottie and I went to sick houses while Paul heard confessions. Blessed houses and gave communion.*

On Tuesday, September 9, Jean flew from Salvador to Miami to spend three days with her parents before continuing to London, where Doug Cable would be waiting for her. She had planned her itinerary with great precision. Miami, London, Ireland, New York/Maryknoll, Connecticut, Cleveland, Miami and back to Salvador. All in six weeks. Three weeks in London and Ireland with Doug, three weeks in the States.

It was almost eleven months to the day since her previous trip to the States to meet her family in New Orleans. Over three months had passed since she had last seen Doug in Mexico City. And something that she couldn't quite put her finger on was making her apprehensive.

"Dear Everybody," she had written cheerfully enough some weeks earlier to Maryknoll. "I can't really write here. But I will have a lot to relate when I arrive. I will probably need debriefing on how to be normal in the States . . . but when was I ever normal. See you soon. Love."

She was going home—to the people and the places that she loved, to the country and the life that she belonged to. For six weeks she would never have to listen to another atrocity story; never hear a gun fired; never notice the watchful eyes of the National Guard following her from the moment she stepped outside the house in the morning. There would be no roadblocks waiting around the next bend; nobody would be monitoring her telephone calls; and she would never need to wonder about the occupants of the strange car parked at the corner. For six weeks she would relax. She was going home to lead a normal life and to have a good time. There would be plenty of Tanqueray martinis on the rocks, steak dinners in good restaurants, and she and Doug would have a great time exploring London. She had so much to relate to Mike Crowley, to the Maryknolls, and they would be impressed and proud of her. Ireland would be full of parties, music and old friends. At home, even Mike had given up trying to run her life, and they would have a fine and carefree reunion in Connecticut, just in time for the Westbury fall fair. It would be like old times.

But what about the faces of those bereaved, hunted wives and mothers whose helplessness haunted her? And what of those long lines of lost and orphaned children who waited in a strange, undemanding silence for someone to hold them? Children whose large, expressionless dark eyes had seen too much. Who shook uncontrollably at the sight of a man in a uniform, and woke alone and screaming in the night. Already, Ken's house was filling up with these disturbingly quiet survivors of massacres and flight, who no longer smiled, or cried, or even asked for help.

These images of Salvador had seared her heart and it was too late for escape.

CHAPTER IX

Last Trip Home

You cannot understand how hard it is for one to be practical who hopes for tenderness behind every face. . . . Others can be impersonal, but not one who believes that he is on an eminently personal adventure. . . . Others can be sensible, but not one who knows in his heart how few things really matter. Others can be sober and restrained, but not one who is mad with the loveliness of life, and almost blind with its beauty.

—Found in Dorothy Kazel's
    prayer book after her death.

ON SATURDAY, SEPTEMBER 13, JEAN FLEW FROM MIAMI
to London to meet Doug. It was a difficult encounter for
both of them, and his memories of their last vacation together are full of bewilderment and pain. "Jean had really
changed," he says. "It was quite clear she was just totally
different. Her letters didn't have a lot of substance because
she was concerned about them being opened and read.
From her letters I could get the news that she was helping
in the refugee camps, and I could hear on the news that
there was trouble in Chalatenango, but it was only later
that I realized, when I met her and talked to her, what real
danger she'd been in. The stories she told, instead of the
little adventures about traveling around Central America,
were really gruesome."

Sadly, in relation to the one story that she needed the
most to talk to him about her courage failed her. "I didn't
even hear about the two boys until later," Doug says. "She
couldn't even bring herself to tell me about that for a week.
She tried a couple of times." But in recounting the story of
the death of Carlos and Armando, she described the scene
as though it had happened to two small boys—the sons of
Paul Schindler's cook, whom Doug had met during his
vacation. Thus Doug could have no real sense of the gravity
of what had happened to Jean.

"We spent a few days in London and went over to
Cork for the wedding of one of her close friends. It was a
beautiful wedding, in an old Irish chapel that was known
all over Europe for its stained-glass windows. The bride was
gorgeous, and the whole ceremony was beautiful.

"The time at the wedding was really the only time that
she was her normal, lively self. It was such a beautiful
wedding, and we had a wonderful time at the reception and
we danced and that was when I was sure we were going to
get married. We knew. And everybody else knew. I think it
was obvious. Everybody was saying, 'You'll be next . . .'
That was when we made arrangements to meet in Costa

Rica. That was when I was going to propose. Her parents were going to come, and it was going to be a big deal. That was going to be for February 1981, which she never made.

"I couldn't get her to stay. I talked to her for two weeks, and Father Crowley was just eloquent, and neither of us could convince her not to go back. He pointed out to her, that even though she was not a revolutionary, was not aiding or abetting the revolutionaries, and neither was the Church, they were perceived to be on the revolutionaries' side by the army—the army saw them as being sympathetic, and that's all that mattered. And because she wasn't a revolutionary she didn't have the advantages that they have. They had no defense. They couldn't arm themselves. They couldn't hide. They discussed this—maybe we should arm ourselves—they couldn't bring themselves to do this. It was against everything that they were down there for. They were down there to heal, and to save lives, save souls. They couldn't carry guns.

"It was so clear that she was in immediate danger, and yet she wouldn't admit it. And Jean was a very bright person, so I knew she could figure these things out." For Jean, who had long since gone beyond the point where she felt capable of sharing the truth about her life in El Salvador, there was no way to explain or justify her stubborn refusal to listen. For Doug, the frustration was intense and painful.

"I was very angry in Ireland. We never had a fight, but it took me a while to realize how committed she was—it took me a while to realize that these little excuses she gave were meaningless. That her denial was a front. And then I backed off. Initially I had told her, 'I'm not going to meet you in Costa Rica if you go back.' And I really meant it. It was just a blatant, blackmail ploy, but she went back anyway, so I knew that wasn't going to change her mind.

"She went back because she knew she was doing some good. She was showing these poor Salvadoran people who were being massacred, whose families were being decimated, that they weren't alone. That she cared, and that we care, that most North Americans care. And I realized

that this was something that was more important than anything she could possibly do in California—that she needed
encouragement, not discouragement; so I wrote her a letter.
I said, I'll still meet you in Costa Rica, which meant I was
still going to marry her. I don't even know if she got it
because I wrote it in late November and I think she was
killed before she got it."

The more people tried to dissuade Jean from returning
to El Salvador, the more stubbornly she resisted the pressure to make her change her mind. For Edward Fenton, her
former boyfriend, her position was inexplicable. "She was
very different, when she came back from what she had ever
been before. I don't think she was at all as enthusiastic—
as full of life—as I had known her before. I spent a long
time talking to her, as did just about everybody else who
met her while she was back for the wedding, and it made no
difference. Nothing would stop her. I said to her, 'What's
the point of going back there? There's enough trouble in
the world besides going looking for it." And her reply was,
'They don't shoot blond, blue-eyed North Americans.' And
I said to her, 'Well, how do you know when they're going
to change?' But she said she was going back, and she was
resolved.

"She had some drive, something inside her that we
didn't know about and certainly couldn't understand—
something inside her was taking her back. And even that it
was pointed out to her, because we said to her, 'Well Jean,
you know, you could be next.' And she said, 'Yeah. Maybe,
maybe not. Who knows?'

"Maybe she didn't care. In the sense that she was
prepared to accept whatever she was going to face, for she
always gave us some reason for doing it. I really don't know.
I don't think I'll ever know, or I'll never understand, because it was totally the opposite to what I would have
expected from somebody like her."

One friend who was not surprised was Maura Corkery,
her closest Irish friend and former companion during their
student days when together they had worked among the

sick and the poor in Father Crowley's Legion of Mary. Maura had always seen the serious side of Jean, and so was not perturbed or bewildered by the distance that her friend had traveled from the rest of her youthful, student friendships. "To me, her ultimate decision was very much in keeping with the person I knew. Once Jean made a friend, or once Jean embarked on work, she was very loyal. And I would see her decision to go back as being her commitment to the people she was working with, and the people she was working for. Nobody was going to be abandoned.

"She was very preoccupied while she was here—I think she was frightened of what might happen if she did go back. On maybe two or three occasions I tried—I asked her not to return. I tried to make her see she could do valuable work elsewhere. And she listened. On the last night I saw her, we went for dinner in town and we met Doug for a drink afterward. As we left and came out onto Patrick Street, all three of us were catching the last bus; they were catching the No. 3 and I was catching the No. 8 and when we came out on the street both buses were there. So we said goodbye, and they hopped on theirs, but I realized mine wasn't going to go for a second or two, so I shouted in the window at her—I just caught her eye and I shouted in, 'Don't go back!' And she smiled, and said, 'OK! OK! But write to me to Salvador anyway.' "

Throughout those two weeks in Ireland, the one person for whose approval of her resolve she fought the hardest was the one man in the world who felt most constrained to withhold it. Not, certainly, from any lack of understanding or appreciation for her position. But Michael Crowley knew both Jean and the situation in El Salvador too well, and he also knew how much she relied upon his judgment. In the circumstances he did the only thing he could. "I did my damndest to dissuade her from going back. Sometime before she came, she made a phone call in the middle of the night, and I never quite clarified why she made it. I suspect myself that she felt threatened, and maybe she felt that a phone call to Ireland would perhaps give her some protection. She felt she was threatened by someone. She felt there was someone out there listening to her, and it might have thrown off people who were following her and watching her movements.

"In my judgment her life was at risk and I told her that in very, very clear terms. I said, 'You're going to get it. You'll be picked, lifted, and tortured and killed. It's going to happen.'

"She came back the last time I suppose for many reasons. She wanted to get out of El Salvador for breathing space. She wanted to rest. She wanted to come here to Cork to meet old friends. She wrote to me and said she wanted to talk over what had happened in her life, and what was happening all around her. She felt a great need to tell this story outside of Salvador, because she was very conscious that it couldn't be told from Salvador—and she came and she stayed with me for the two weeks, with her boyfriend, Doug.

"We had a youth vigil on at the time, here in the church. I don't like asking people coming back from a wedding to give sermons—I mean the situation isn't right —so when she came into the house after Pat's wedding, I said, 'Jean, are you in good shape? Would you have a few cups of black coffee because I would like you to talk to the young people out there in about a half an hour.' So she knocked off a few cups of coffee, and came on up—and just talked. She talked about what was happening around her, in Salvador. She talked about the impact that it was making on herself—her feelings, her frustrations, her loneliness, her anger at seeing innocent friends killed and tortured. It was a kind of catharsis really. She just poured out all the heart, and the sadness and the joy, and the complete mixture of her feelings about what was happening.

"I think she enjoyed her stay. When she left, after two weeks, with her boyfriend, she wrote me something like eight pages—it was written somewhere on the plane to New York—and it was really a defense of her decision. She had already decided to go back, and she said quite simply,

'I know this isn't going to be understood.' It was very important for her that I would understand it. She felt a lot of her friends wouldn't. She felt perhaps her family wouldn't. But I think it was terribly important for her to demonstrate as clearly as she could why she was going back. She said, 'I belong there. Those people need me.' "

In early October Jean arrived back in New York with Doug and went straight to Ossining to stay with her friends, Gwen and Bill Vendley, who administered the Maryknoll Lay Mission Program. Gwen was shocked at the change. "Jeannie was a much different person. She was the same Jeannie, but very alone, kind of desperate. She had seen an awful lot of pain, she had experienced the death of very dear friends, and she was afraid. She was afraid to get close to other people, to know that same kind of pain again.

"She was almost shell-shocked. She would have to speak very fast, and she so needed somebody to listen to her. We talked for hours actually. Some things were very simple—about her . . . simple and ordinary. About her desire to marry, to have a child, to nurse a child, to enjoy what she perhaps thought of as ordinary, living your life. She had been asked to get married and she was trying to make that decision. But she had so many things before her, it was very difficult for her. I honestly think, that as much as she would have liked to get married, she knew she couldn't go back to something that she'd left behind . . . and really she'd left that person behind. That person, meaning herself, more than the one she loved.

"All that she identified as Jeannie she had left behind. That vibrant person who could go down to a bar with a bunch of friends and have some extra beers . . . she knew it wasn't her, that unaware person. Maybe she was becoming the more serious person that she always was but never allowed herself to be. And yet, that same person that she knew wasn't her was the person that so many people, I think, thought was her. And that was her dilemma.

"She was incredibly lonely. I think there were very few people that she could talk to. Very few who could understand what had happened inside of her because of living so closely with life and death. When she visited our home in October, Maryknoll, I think, represented for her people who understood.

"She talked to those of us at Maryknoll for hours on end, trying to explain what the recent events were like; the numbers of deaths; the kinds of oppression. When she found out how little coverage Salvador was getting in the press, and how misrepresented it was, she could not remain silent for any misrepresentation. She contacted different government officials and friends and family.

"She had made her decision to go back. I argued with her quite a bit about it, because there was no question, she couldn't live as she was without being killed. We talked about it a lot. I said, 'What difference does it make if you go down there and you get killed? You're just one other person that's killed down there.' She knew she could go to Los Angeles and work with the refugees—and all the good she would do by doing that. But it wasn't enough. Something more was calling her.

"Death was not so much of a fear as was torture. That was a terror for her. One of the last things she said was, 'I just hope I'm not found on a ditch bank with all the markings of torture . . .' So I don't know . . . the bravery . . . the bravery came in saying yes. She didn't know when it was going to happen, she just knew. We all did. We all knew. Because Jeannie wouldn't run from a situation. She wouldn't leave people who needed her because it was dangerous. She was a person who walked out on a limb. To stay there was to die."

While Jean was at Maryknoll, the Salvadoran government launched a "definitive military operation" against the guerrilla strongholds in the northeastern province of Morazan. Some 5,000 troops of the army and security forces were deployed, and for the first time the Salvadoran Air Force was used in counterinsurgency. As reports of the indiscriminate bombings of villages and the plight of thousands of new refugees reached Jean, she canceled her

planned trip to Cleveland and cut short her vacation by
two weeks. Then she left Ossining to spend the weekend
with her brother in Danbury, Connecticut.

Mike recalls that during her visit the two of them discussed politics for the first time in their lives. "I don't think
we ever discussed politics before she went to El Salvador.
It never came up. But because of what she had seen in
El Salvador she was very frightened of the possibility of a
Republican administration. Although she didn't think the
Democrats had been lily-white, she felt the Republicans
would be worse. I used to be a staunch Republican, and
because of what she said to me, because of what I've learned
since her death, and the things that she said, more I think
in retrospect than at the time she said them, I've changed
my views.

"I think that she answered the question, 'Why did she
stay in Salvador?' in a letter that she wrote to a friend about
two weeks before she died. The letter said: 'Several times I
have decided to leave El Salvador. I almost could except
for the children, the poor, bruised victims of this insanity.
Who would care for them? Whose heart could be so staunch
as to favor the reasonable thing in a sea of their tears and
loneliness? Not mine, dear friend, not mine.' That was the
closing of the letter.

"There can't be any other reason. You don't give your
life for El Salvador any more than I would give my life
for Bangladesh. But you can become that involved with
other human lives that they become that important to you.

"When she left I drove her to meet my uncle who was
taking her to the airport. She said goodbye, and she kissed
me, and she got into my Uncle Jay's car and they drove off.
And I sat there and watched them go, and I can remember
—as clear as can be—thinking, She's not coming back."

Jean's uncle, Jay Murphy, Jr., put her on the plane for
Florida from JFK laden with baseball gear that she'd promised to bring back for the children in Ken's house. "I walked
with her to the security check, and as she was going
through, with this baseball bat over her shoulder, the guard

said. 'You can't take that on board—it's a weapon.' And Jean turned to me with this look of, 'You've got to do something—I've got to take that bat.' So I walked up to the guard, and as I got close enough I saw his name tag was O'Malley. So I took him aside and I said to him, very quietly, 'She's a nun.' And the guy looked at Jean—torn jeans, T-shirt, baseball bat—and he turned back to me and said, 'They sure don't make nuns like they did when I was a kid.' "

The final week of Jean's vacation, at her parents home in Sarasota, Florida, was the happiest of her entire trip. According to her mother, she was her old self, happy and carefree. "As far as we could see, a perfectly normal girl. She had no trouble sleeping, eating. She talked to Doug on the phone every night at eleven o'clock, and everything seemed to be the way it had always been.

"We know since then, [from] other people who had seen her in that month that she was back, that she was mortally afraid of something in El Salvador. I don't think she knew exactly what it was, but she was afraid of the situation, to the point where she was shaking. One priest at Maryknoll said that he advised her to stay home for a month or two to get herself together. A nun at Maryknoll that Jean was very close to said Jean was a basket case. She said she wanted to spend a couple of hours in the chapel. She went into the chapel, and Jean was a great one for talking with God—if she got answers she's the only one that heard them—but when she came out two hours later, Sister Joan said that she was an entirely different woman. She was . . . she was ready to go back.

"I don't think she could have fooled us if she had still been as frightened as she was when she was in Maryknoll, or perhaps in Ireland. She had somehow reconciled herself to what was happening and what she was to do, and she had made her peace with whatever frightening thoughts that she had. She was really the old Jeannie when we put her back on the plane, joking, laughing. . . ." And laden with baseball gear.

Jean had now made the decisive choice of her life. She had made it quite alone, in all freedom, knowing exactly what she was returning to in El Salvador. And for the first time she seemed at peace with the world around her and with herself. She had come of age. She was happy.

CHAPTER X

"The Return"

El Salvador is such a beautiful country. Where else would you find roses blooming in December?
—Jean Donovan

ON FRIDAY, OCTOBER 17, 1980, JEAN RETURNED TO EL Salvador and immediately resumed her work with the refugees. The need for help was more urgent than ever. In San Salvador over eight hundred people were cooped up in the main refugee center on the grounds of the seminary, some of whom had been there since January. Six more centers, able to offer shelter for about two hundred additional people, were now operating in different church locations around the city. Elsewhere, according to reports received from the international relief organizations, Medical Aid International and Children's Aid Latin America, the latest military operations in the eastern province of Morazan had resulted in three thousand civilian casualties and had created thousands—some said twenty thousand—new refugees who had fled across the border to camps in Honduras, Costa Rica, Nicaragua; while in towns and cities throughout the western provinces of El Salvador, temporary shelters, tent cities, had been established to try and cope with a fleeing population of women, children and old men.

Over the weekend Ita called, looking for help to evacuate some children and bring them down to safety in the center that Ken had established in Zaragoza. Jean immediately got out the white van and set off for Chalatenango. "The Rescue Squad" was back in business.

"Much of the work they were doing during their last days was providing protection for refugees," Paul Schindler explains. "There'd be a caravan of trucks and cars, and just the presence of the women, if the soldiers stopped them, would be enough to let them go by and take these people out. Because they were noncombatants, and Jean and Dorothy were there as a protection for the people that they were trying to get out to safety."

While Jean was helping Ita and Maura in Chalatenango, Dorothy was needed urgently in another area of the country. "Tomorrow," she told Martha Owens, "we are going to go up into the mountains above Santa Ana in a big truck because they have fifty-five people they want brought down from the hills (forty-five kids and ten women). They want me to go because it's always good to have a *gringa* face around in case something happens. We're supposed to leave at six o'clock, and get there about nine-thirty. I don't know where we're going, or exactly what's going to happen. I guess they've had fighting and shooting and all kinds of trouble up there, and the people's houses have been burned to the ground. They're sitting there living in the debris, so they want them out as soon as possible. Tomorrow, then, that will be my mission, and we shall see."

At the conclusion of her mission, Dorothy finished dictating her tape. "Well, it was a long, interesting day. Yesterday morning I was at the *Arzobispado*** at six A.M. and from there, Rafael, the priest, Miguel and this girl Blanca drove to Santa Ana. Then we looked for a man who had a big truck so he could take us up into the hills.

"This area is maybe forty kilometers north of Santa Ana. We went in, up this dirt road, very very slowly. The road was all washed out and rocky, and the girl kept saying, 'Oh, it's just a couple of kilometers in. . . .' Well you know how it is, a couple of kilometers turns out to be about twenty kilometers. So we're passing all these little houses along the road and everyone is looking at this huge truck, and this little jeep following behind, and wondering what the hell is going on. It was beautiful—we had a beautiful view from the top of the mountains overlooking all these other gorgeous mountains. Up and up and up—and down, down, down—and finally the guy stopped and said he didn't think he could go any farther. We got to a part where there were rocks in the road—they'd been put across the road on purpose to keep people from coming in—so the driver said maybe it would be better if the jeep went ahead to wherever these people were.

"So Rafael, myself and the girl continued on by ourselves. We got to the part where the girl said the people had

* Archdiocesan headquarters in San Salvador.

lived until about a week ago; eight days ago, she said, the Guardia came in and attacked them and burned their houses and all. So then we left Rafael with the jeep, and she and I go tripping down this road—you know how it is—you never know where you're going or what you're getting into, it's just a riot. It was around ten, ten-thirty in the morning, sunny and bright, thank God it wasn't raining, and going in, it was very, very quiet; there was nobody around; it was very, very still. So we walked for about eight, ten minutes and then we came upon this cluster of a couple of houses, and there were people.

"The first people I saw were these two guys with rifles —and Martha, honestly, they're like Daniel Boone. You know—it's worse than rinky dink Cowboys and Indians— it's like Indians against the United States marines. I don't know how these guys think they're going to win this war. These guys are, they're nothing but campesino guys. I guess the place that we were in is all organized. I don't know what group they belong to—I asked Rafael and he said they could be FPL, but he's not really sure himself. The men all had rifles and pistols, but the rifles are like, you know, overgrown BB guns. You just wonder how this is all going to turn out.

"Anyway we got there, and we were supposed to pick up forty-five kids and ten mothers and of course there were other families coming from down below, and they hadn't got there yet. . . . So we went back up to where Rafael was (now we had an escort from the boys), and when we got there the truck had managed to get down and had backed in, so they were preparing to load people; they had the planks set up for people to walk up. Well, we waited around, we never got out of there until noon or twelve-thirty. The people were really wiped out, poor people; this one young woman must have been in her twenties, her husband had been shot in an earlier encounter in September, and she had three kids and then this six-day-old baby who must have been born premature. Just an itty-bitty skinny little thing—was he ever undernourished—so she rode with us in the jeep.

"And you know, my heart just aches for these people; when I see what they've got to work with. And they're really hoping to win. I just don't know how these guys think they're going to do it, when we're giving money for communication equipment and huge trucks and such so that the military can get up there easier to kill them. It just makes me ill. Anyway, that was my day yesterday.

"Right now, it's about two o'clock at night, and I'm sitting out on our beautiful patio here in La Libertad, looking up at the sky. At least we are in summer—it's nice and clear—so that moon is looking at you, too, wherever you are!"

After her vacation, Jean made no further entries in her diary. Her colleagues noticed other, more profound changes; it was evident to them that since her premature return she had acquired a serenity and a self-confidence that were new. A young American priest who worked for the Cleveland mission farther down the coast in Chirilagua remarked on the change. "She had achieved a degree of peace that we all struggle for. The fear of imminent danger comes in waves, but biblically speaking, the opposite of fear is faith. You can't be so foolish as to think you can do anything to save yourself. This implies a greater dependence on God, greater trust, acceptance of the fears and overcoming them through faith. Jean had made faith decisions that shaped her life and her heart and shaped her relationships with others and her relations with the people in her mission."

In fact, she was probably feeling happier than she had ever been in her whole life. It was hard for her family and friends in the States to understand her love for this impoverished and tormented country—or to comprehend why it was necessary for her to pursue the solutions to her own needs through embracing and alleviating the needs of others —but that was how it was for her. That was how it had always been. And because this was so, El Salvador had become the place where she belonged, the place where she knew her life was worth more than it could ever be worth in the States or in Ireland.

The original impulse that had drawn her to this anguished center of the American hemisphere had been purely instinctive; never anything that she could define or articulate, defend or explain. But her courage, her drive to endure, to persevere along the difficult, unmarked path that she had chosen to travel in her pursuit of some compelling inner truth, had never faltered. Now, since her most recent struggle with doubt and fear, she had emerged at last with a novel, hard-won sense of self.

In the weeks ahead she wrote twice to Doug, who was still hoping against hope that reason and their feelings for each other would prevail; that she'd return before Christmas; hoping to hear that she would come to Los Angeles and settle down to build their future together. But she wrote him instead that he should come to see her in Costa Rica in the first week of February; that she would try to get to Los Angeles to see him by the following May or June. And Doug understood what she was telling him. He realized that in the midst of the torment and danger in El Salvador, she had made a commitment to the people who needed her that she was resolved to keep. "She was telling me who came first in her life and asking me to accept," he says, and adds: "I never got the chance to tell her that I did. It's my greatest regret."

On October 20, just a few days after her return, she wrote to her friend and teacher Ralph Wiatowski (he was studying at the American College in Rome and sometime during her European trip Jean had hoped to go and see him there):

"Dear Ralph: As you may realize by now I didn't make it to Rome. I just felt that I had to get back.

"The situation is bad and believe it or not, at times I'm actually helpful. I also was trying to deal with some very close friends that had been killed the last week in August.

As a matter of fact I was with Carla so much the *National Catholic Reporter* got our photos mixed up for her obituary and had a very fine picture of me. I've already had a couple of calls about that . . .

"We are still plugging along. Sister Christine is running a center, and Dorothy and I are doing anything needed. Mostly driving and watching out for funds we receive.

"Life continues on with many interruptions. I don't know how the poor survive. People in our positions really have to die unto ourselves and our wealth to gain the spirituality of the poor and oppressed. I have a long way to go on that score. They can teach you so much with their patience and their wanting eyes. We are all so inadequate in our help. I am trying now more and more to deal with the social sin of the first world. It's not an easy question. Well, take care, Ralph. Love, Jean."

It is not known what triggered the closing of this letter to Ralph; she never did explain the steps by which she had arrived at the conclusion of First World responsibility for the suffering and poverty in the Third World; only her painful, stark admission reveals the distance she had traveled from the conservative economic beliefs that she still had held when she arrived in El Salvador eighteen months before. The lessons she had begun to learn from the earliest days of her exposure to this "culture of poverty," when she had written home with touching awareness that "it seems you are here to be ministered to far more than to minister," had transformed her view of the world, and had begun to raise questions of the most troubling and far-reaching significance which, with customary honesty, she was not able to evade.

In Chalatenango, in October, where Jean was now spending most of her time, they had something new to worry about. "For the first time in this area the death squads have moved in during the last three weeks," Ita told a visiting reporter.* "There's no place to go to complain

* Free-lance reporter David Helvarg. His interview with Ita Ford was broadcast after her death by WBAI radio, New York City.

about the death squads. They come in, stake out a town, and kill with total impunity." Maura wrote to her parents: "My dearest ones, Father Paul is leaving for the States tomorrow and I will ask him to mail this letter when he gets there. I know that you would like to hear a little bit more of the reality here and what we are doing. Ordinarily, by mail or phone call, one cannot really say the truth because of the extreme vigilance. There is a great deal of tension and violence. The situation is very tragic. People are fleeing from their homes looking for some kind of safety as the so-called death squadron strikes anywhere and everywhere. The squad is made up of the military rightists who are the most ruthless. The cutting up of bodies by machete is one of the tactics to terrorize the organized groups from continuing their efforts. There are crimes on both sides, but the military and the rich oligarchy have committed extreme crimes, and many, many more.

"The effort of the oligarchy is to wipe out the farmers and the workers who have organized for change, and they do this in the name of fighting communism. It is a much more vengeful, confusing and frightening case than that of Nicaragua. The other day, by way of example, a very Christian family in a nearby town was machine-gunned, killing seven members including a five-year-old. The organized groups do not trust or accept the present Revolutionary Junta as it continues to permit such outrageous slaughter of human lives, so they feel they must fight, even with their little, almost toy pistols.

"Each day we trust the Lord to guide our ways as to what he wishes of us. Often there is a lot of frustration and pain involved as one cannot do enough; or anything, at times. At times one wonders if one should remain in such a crazy incredible mess. I only know that I am trying to follow where the Lord leads, and in spite of fear and uncertainty at times, I feel at peace and hopeful.

"Perhaps I should [not] tell you all of this bad news, but often when I write I feel superficial as I cannot say the truth; and the truth is best."

In Chalatenango in the winter of 1980, the war and the climate of terror, which had resulted in the exodus of thousands of small subsistence farmers from their rural holdings, had created a situation in which less than 50 percent of the small plots had been planted with the basic grains, and land where crops waited to be harvested had been abandoned. In November the threat of food scarcity for the coming year was a primary concern. "These days," wrote Ita, "I feel like a Chicago merchant specializing in grain futures—or maybe Joseph in Egypt—storing grain against the coming shortage. There's nothing so absurd as two Brooklynites judging the quality of red beans and corn!"

One Sunday soon after her return, Jean set out on her motorbike for Chalatenango to spend the day with Ita and Maura and coordinate her schedule with them for the week ahead. She arrived just in time to accompany Ita on the kind of mission that had become a habitual part of their daily routine. A woman whose teenage son had disappeared had come to the house to ask Ita for help. There had been a report that the boy had been taken off the bus by the police, and that morning, his mother had heard that the bodies of two young men had been seen by the side of the road at dawn and later removed and buried by a local farmer.

The woman came to Ita to ask whether she would accompany her to the site where the bodies had been found to try and find out whether or not one of them was her son. So Ita and Jean got out the parish jeep and set out with the woman to find the farmer. When they reached his shack, they found the man reluctant to open the grave since his action constituted a clear and dangerous breach of the law. Confronted with the mother's anguished uncertainty over the fate of her son, he finally agreed. Making a small opening in the fresh grave he dug down just far enough to reveal a white cloth with which he had covered the face of the dead boy; when he raised the cloth, the mother looked down onto the face of her son and said very quietly, "Now

I know where my son lies. I know he is with God and now, I just want him to rest here."

Something about the incident, maybe the intimacy of that shared moment of recognition as she stood beside the dead boy's grieving mother, affected Ita deeply. Jean did her best to distract and comfort her, but all day she remained uncharacteristically depressed. The image of that young, dead face, lying surrounded by dirt and abandoned in an empty field by the side of the road, obsessed her. Later that day, when Madeleine Dorsey and Terri Alexander came up from Santa Ana to pay Ita and Maura a visit, they were concerned to find Ita so distraught.

One month later, when Madeleine and Terri stood together again in another field, looking down into another freshly opened grave onto the dirt-covered faces of their friends, they were reminded of that Sunday afternoon in Chalatenango. As the memory of Ita's disturbed state of mind came flooding back they suddenly saw the incident in a new light: They felt then that the sight of that dead, abandoned boy, must have triggered for Ita some deep, intuitive premonition of approaching events. The date, that Sunday, was November 2. Exactly one month to the day of her own death.

Two days later the American elections provided the world with a new American president. In the elegant suburbs and the military barracks of San Salvador, the victory of Ronald Reagan was celebrated with champagne and fireworks around the swimming pools of the private mansions, and there was dancing in the streets.

In Chalatenango, Maura and Ita's parish priest, Father Ephraim Lopez, received a letter signed by one Roberto Fogelbach Perez, coordinator of the Anti-Communist Front —a right-wing paramilitary group. "Esteemed priests," the letter began,

> You and a majority of the Salvadoran people
> know that you have innocently become in-
> volved with subversion since initially you were

thinking in the good of the majority—which is laudable—but the methods which you are now employing are inadequate, in addition to being illegal and contrary to Christian teaching.

You have introduced enough anger into Chalatenango and you have provoked the deaths of many. I do not know why the commanders in charge do not act to eliminate the real leaders. It may be that they are in connivance with you because communism is subtle and intoxicating.

I believe that for the good of the Fatherland we will have to bring our special units [i.e., death squads] into action to protect the Fatherland in this province. Please put an end to your evil activities and dedicate yourselves in some other place to your true apostolic mission or else emigrate to Cuba since you will find that here you will no longer be permitted to remain.

Later that week a sign was posted on the door of the parish house in Chalatenango where Ita lived. Crude but expressive, it depicted a human head in which was embedded a knife: a stream of blood spurted toward the text which read: "This is what will happen to anyone who comes to this house because the priests and nuns are communists."

For many months, relations between the Church and the army in Chalatenango had been steadily deteriorating. Colonel Peña Arbaiza, the commander of the local barracks was, in Ita's words, "an eccentric man." Disgusted years before by the changes in the Catholic Church, he had quit the religion of his forefathers and joined a fundamentalist Protestant sect. When Carla and Ita visited him, as they often did, to discuss specific problems concerning military harassment and abuse of people with whom they were working, he would keep them in his office for hours, lecturing them on the authentic duties of the religious vocation and reading from the Old Testament Bible that he kept permanently on his desk. Colonel Peña Arbaiza was convinced that the role of the Catholic Church in general and of the personnel of the Chalatenango parish in particular was subversive.

Shortly after the appearance of that first overt threat on the parish house door, Arbaiza summoned one of the lawyers from the archdiocesan legal department in San Salvador to attend a meeting with him and his staff in Chalatenango.

During this meeting, the colonel once again accused the Church in Chalatenango of engaging in subversive activities, implied that he was interested in finding out how he could use Ita and Maura to obtain access to the guerrillas, and specifically accused the vicar of Chalatenango, Father Fabian Amaya, of providing the guerrillas with arms. Arbaiza based this charge on the alleged testimony of a twelve-year-old boy whom he had apparently questioned at length in the hospital where he had been brought in wounded after a confrontation between the army and the guerrillas.

As the Church lawyer prepared to leave the barracks, an army captain who had attended the meeting took him aside and told him privately that the colonel had not been speaking the truth about the testimony of the twelve-year-old boy. Nevertheless, ten days later, the child turned up again in an unusual location: Carlos Paredes, former under secretary of economic planning in the junta cabinet was there and reports: "It was a meeting of the Political Committee of the government, our regular Wednesday meeting, fifteen days before the American nuns were shot.

"In that meeting Colonel García [minister of defense] brought in a little ten-year-old boy to tell us about the situation in the northern part of the country—in Chalatenango. There was a discussion because first, the little boy was not on the agenda; second, he was a ten-year-old boy and we didn't think he was a responsible representative to talk to us about the situation. Nevertheless, García brought this little boy in, and the little boy talked for about twenty minutes about the role that religion was having in the northern part of the country, specifically in Chalatenango. He told us that religious people in Chalatenango were inciting the people to fight against the government, to feed and house the guerrilla groups. It was a direct accusation against the role of religious workers in the region.

"After the little boy had talked, Colonel García spoke to us for another twenty-five or thirty minutes, specifically saying that the government should take very energetic measures against that situation, because journalists and religious people were becoming involved with guerrilla activity in El Salvador. He said they were taking advantage of the hospitality of the country, and that they were a threat to the stability of the country and a threat to the activities of the government."

Some of the parish workers left Chalatenango after these events. Ita and Maura did not. Like Jean, for the benefit of their worried colleagues, they continued to sustain publicly the notion that they had nothing to fear from the army because they were protected by their nationality. Privately, however, their last letters provide evidence of a starker, more realistic assessment of the dangers. The "horizon of death" was closing in from all sides on all of them.

"I am beginning to see death in a new way, dearest Katie," Maura wrote to a friend. "We have been meditating a lot on death and the accepting of it, as in the Good Shepherd reading. There are so many deaths everywhere that it is incredible. It is an atmosphere of death. The work is really what Bishop Romero called *'acompañamiento'* (accompanying the people), as well as searching for ways to help. This seems what the Lord is asking of me, I think, at this moment. We are on the road continually, bringing women and children to refugee centers. Keep us in your heart and prayers, especially the poor forsaken people."

A constant source of anxiety was the lack of any official guarantees of protection even for those whom they succeeded in getting to the refugee centers. "The difficulty with the centers," Ita told a visiting American reporter, "is that only when a state of war has been declared can there be formal guarantees of protection. In my estimation there is now a state of war—it's a civil war—but how many people do you need to die, what sort of conditions do you need to say that a war exists? It seems that the government is not going to say that there's a civil war." So neither the International Red Cross nor the United Nations could provide any legal protection for the refugees in centers which were frequently raided by security forces searching for arms and guerrillas.

In November, the main refugee center in the grounds of the archdiocesan seminary suffered one such raid:

> At 4:00 P.M. the Archbishopric was surrounded by armored vehicles, so that, in a combined and perfectly coordinated operation, a number of soldiers not in uniform could enter the premises and carry out a violent search. The premises of one of the ten refugee centers of the Archbishopric, set up for the protection of women and children, was broken into. The medical aid clinic was destroyed.

> The Archbishopric and its environs remained surrounded by policemen of the National Guard for two hours. In the course of their incursion, the soldiers beat up various employees of the Archbishopric.*

On November 20, one week after the raid, Jean wrote a letter to Senator Edward Kennedy:

> Dear Senator Kennedy:
> I was just given a copy of the Congressional Record Proceedings and Debates of the ninety-sixth Congress, second session, volume

* From the documentation of the Legal Aid Office of the archdiocese.

126, Washington, Wednesday, September 24, 1980, number 149. As I am sure you are aware it is your statement about the plight of Salvadoran refugees.

I am a Catholic missionary working in the port of La Libertad, in the archdiocese of San Salvador. I have also been recruited, by necessity, to work in various other locations in the archdiocese, due to the refugees' plight. I would like to applaud you, for recognition of the grave problem here.

As a North American, one of the hardest things to see is how the people are suffering here because of the actions of our government. Archbishop Romero asked in his letter in February 1980, before his assassination, for the U.S.A. not to send any military aid, since it is being used to murder and torture an already oppressed people.

Since the Rio Sumpul river killings, the violence has only increased. The Church has been persecuted since it is the only voice against the oppression. Recently the army and other military forces moved into Morazan for a clean-up operation. We still don't fully know what happened, but the reports from the refugees we have picked up are devastating. Now the confrontation has moved to San Vincente. I picked up a twelve-year-old boy last week who appeared to have been macheted by members of ORDEN, the paramilitary security force. Two days later I helped move him to the *Arzobispado* refugee center. Last week, the *Arzobispado* was searched by military forces. Unfortunately, I arrived fifteen minutes after they had left, because a number of witnesses testified that the men that were running the search spoke and appeared by their faces to be *gringos.* It takes another *gringo* to determine what country they are from. I certainly hope that they are individual mercenaries.

Once again, thank you for your interest in the plight of the refugees.

Sincerely,
Jean Donovan

In the last week of November, Ita and Maura, Maddie and Terri were looking forward to attending a regional conference of the Maryknoll Sisters to be held over a four-day weekend in Nicaragua. In the weeks preceding their departure, things in Chalatenango and the surrounding countryside had grown daily more tense and frightening. The church in Chalatenango itself is situated on a small square directly across from the army garrison, and ever since Colonel Arbaiza's meeting with the archdiocesan lawyer and the cabinet meeting at which Colonel García had presented the testimony of the little boy, the surveillance of the activities of the churchworkers in general, and of Ita and Maura in particular, had stepped up dramatically. At first the soldiers started coming into the church in civilian clothes; soon they entered in their army uniforms; then they took to parking their tanks on the pavement right outside the entrance to the church and conducted daily armed drills on the raised terrace at the top of the church steps. By mid-November it had reached the point where the army had virtually occupied the church, and churchworkers had literally to request permission from the local commander in order to ring the church bell.

Elsewhere in the province, reports of soldiers raiding church premises and desecrating tabernacles in their search for arms, guerrillas, medicine and "subversive" propaganda reached the local vicariate daily.

Meanwhile, the slaughter of families and children, sliced and hacked into pieces by the heavy steel machetes that the guards and soldiers routinely wore on the belts of their uniforms, was on the increase. Maura wrote of passing a small lake in the jeep and seeing a buzzard standing on a floating body. "We did nothing but pray and feel," she wrote sadly. Chalatenango had become a graveyard of unburied bodies and parts of bodies flung out on the side of the road.

Ita and Maura had opened the doors of the ramshackle parish house where they lived to provide temporary shelter for women and children fleeing the violence. The refugees gathered at their door brought with them their personal stories of unimaginable cruelty, hatred, vengeance and despair—and they also brought tales of endurance, courage and amazing faith. Ita and Maura took them in, fed them, sheltered them, and provided a halfway house until Jean or Dorothy could make more permanent arrangements for their transportation and protection. "One cries out: Lord! How long!" wrote Maura. "And then too," she admitted, "what creeps into my mind is the little fear or big, that when it touches me very personally, will I be faithful? And I keep saying to him: I want to trust. I want to believe. Help me."

Maura's last letter to her parents, written in Chalatenango, was mailed from Mexico, en route to Nicaragua, on November 27. "My dearest Mom and Dad: Your wonderful letters cheered me. Ita just brought them to me from the city. She was there doing many errands.

"It was so good to get your letter, Pop, telling me about Mom resting on the couch after supper. I can see you so well with the eyes of my heart and have so many precious memories of you always.

"Here we are all well and trusting very much in the Lord's strength. Tonight we had a lovely time of prayer together with our three Assumption Sisters and a sister and priest from the U.S. who are visiting us. Now it is bedtime and there are six sisters altogether, all over our tiny apartment. Being together makes us feel more secure and peaceful."

Attached to her letter Maura included a quote from
Thomas Merton which, she explained, "has a lot of meaning for me these days."

> My Lord God, I have no idea of where I am
> going. I do not see the road ahead of me. I
> cannot know for certain where it will end. . . .
> But I believe that the desire to please you does
> in fact please you. And I know that if I do this
> you will lead me by the right road though I may
> know nothing about it. Therefore will I trust
> you always. Though I may seem to be lost, and
> in the shadow of death, I will not fear for you
> are ever with me, and you will never leave me
> to face my perils alone.

Her final sign-off was "Good night my dearest ones.
I love you and miss you. Your Maura."

In La Libertad, on Sunday, November 23, Jean and
Dorothy spent the day with Monsignor Uriosti, the vicar of
the archdiocese. Uriosti had been Archbishop Romero's
assistant and he was an old friend. His description of that
day reveals how strongly the Salvadoran Church still believed in the myth of the invincibility of the *gringas*. "Ten
days, I think, before they are dead, I went to La Libertad
where Jean and Dorothy were working, because they invited me to a countryside town by the name of Tamonique.
They were celebrating Our Lady of Peace. I went with my
car to La Libertad, and from La Libertad to the countryside, they took me in their jeep. And when I sat in the jeep,
Jean was driving, and I told her: 'For the first time I feel
secure when I go to the countryside, because with your
face, everyone knows that you are'—a *gringa*, I said—'a
North American. And so we are so secure in your hands.'
And she was laughing, so secure too, that she was driving
me safely to that countryside town. And that was the last
time I saw them, the last time I saw those two magnificent
Christian women."

Monsignor Uriosti's recollections of that day of Fiesta

in Tamonique fade abruptly. A far different memory surfaces, and for one moment, as images of the brutalized bodies of the women flood his memory, Uriosti stands again inside the funeral parlor in San Salvador where Paul Schindler brought the dead Jean and Dorothy, Ita and Maura exactly ten days after their excursion to Tamonique. Recovering, he continues: "When I think of those four women who were here in the passion of our country, I remember them as the wonderful Americans—the ones who are ready to give themselves, give their ideas, in order that the poor may become people, in order that the men who are not men may become men, that those who are not Christians may become Christians. When I think of them, I think too of those courageous women the Gospel tells us about during the passion of Our Lord (you know that the women at that moment were more courageous than the men), and I remember them, all of them, as those courageous women who were working here for the Gospel, for Our Lord, and for the people of El Salvador."

On the following Thursday, November 27, six of the most prominent leaders of the left-wing opposition party—the Democratic Revolutionary Front (FDR)—were eliminated by the Salvadoran security forces in an action so blatant and brutal that it brought the anarchy in El Salvador back onto the front pages of a shocked world press. During the preceding summer, representatives of the FDR led by Enrique Alvárez, Guillermo Ungo, and Ruben Zamorra had traveled extensively in Mexico, Panama, Europe and the United States, visiting foreign governments and speaking out in universities and churches in the search for international understanding and support for their goal of establishing a pluralistic coalition of the Left as a viable alternative to replace the existing Military-Christian-Democratic Junta. Now they had come home, and on that Thursday morning they were meeting in the premises of the Jesuit San José High School in downtown San Salvador, just two blocks from the United States embassy, preparatory to holding a major press conference.

At eleven twenty A.M., plainclothes police, armed with machine guns and G-3 rifles, entered the school, forced everyone to lie face down on the floor, and abducted six of the leaders. Among those who were forced into three waiting vehicles with their hands tied behind their backs by their thumbs (in typical Salvadoran death-squad fashion) were president of the Democratic Revolutionary Front, Enrique Alvárez Córdova; the leader of the *Bloque*, Juan Chacón; the representative of the Social Democrats, Manuel Franco; and three other members of the FDR's executive committee. Within twenty-four hours their mutilated bodies showed up on the main road, fifteen kilometers outside the capital.

The junta government denied any involvement in these murders and blamed "an extreme right-wing group," which lost no time taking responsibility for the action. However, some twenty minutes prior to the raid, over two hundred soldiers and police had surrounded the school building and according to the testimony of the school porter, who was arrested and held on the premises of the Social Security Institute one block away, police within the institute were communicating throughout by radio with those inside the school.

That Thursday was Thanksgiving Day. The American community held an ecumenical service, which Jean and Dorothy, Paul, Ken and Chris all attended. Afterward, during the reception, Jean and Dorothy met the American ambassador, Robert White, for the first time. They got along well and by the end of the evening the Whites had invited the entire team to come to dinner on the following Monday, the first day of December. "We encouraged them to bring their things with them for an overnight stay," Mary Anne White, the ambassador's wife, recalls, "because we did not want them driving back on the very dark and very dangerous road to La Libertad."

The dinner party included the consul, Patricia Lasbury, and White's deputy, Mark Dion. As Mary Anne remembers it, "It was a delightful visit for all of us. We had a very good evening—a combination of serious discussion and just plain enjoyment." Jean, not surprisingly, charmed her hosts. "We were very curious," Mary Anne admits, "so we did go into her previous life-style, compared with her current life. She had left her extremely interesting job in the States to come and work with the poor in El Salvador and did not regret it for a moment. In fact, she seemed to enjoy to the fullest what she was doing, and there was a very fine balance. Before dinner, I think we all had a drink, and she said, 'This is terrific. I haven't had a glass of Scotch in a long time.' "

There was discussion during the evening about politics, local and American. After the murders of the opposition leaders there could no longer be any doubt that the Right in El Salvador was on the rampage. Robert White remembers the tone of their discussions. "A large part of the conversation that night was about what was going on in the United States; Jean was very interested in discussing what were the trends—political, economic, social. I think all of us who have lived a good part of our life outside the United States follow with keen interest what's going on there—and Jean was very well informed, she was a person who obviously had a keen interest in world affairs, national affairs— she was an alive, aware person. There was discussion also about politics in El Salvador, because it would be unrealistic to think that people who were so intimately involved in the life of the people would not have viewpoints on what was going well, what was going badly. . . . I particularly used occasions like this to probe what they were thinking, what evidence they had for their opinions, because this added to my knowledge of the country.

"There's no more radicalizing experience in this world than living among the poor of Central America, because you see daily testimony to oppression and injustice. There's no way out for these people, and I think Jean felt this terrible injustice very much in her own inner being, and identified very much with the need to bring some new deal to the people of El Salvador. However, it's a great disservice to accuse missionaries of being 'political.' That's just a mis-apprehension. What Jean was saying is exactly what Arch-bishop Romero was saying, that things cannot go on the way they are without an explosion."

They had brought their overnight bags, and when the party ended, late, they stayed the night. For Jean and Dorothy it was the last night of their lives.

"The next morning was fun for me," Mary Anne White remembers, "because Bob, as usual, had one of his daily breakfast guests—I think the foreign minister was with him that morning—and so the women and I stayed upstairs, and had breakfast in the study, and we got so carried away discussing what they were doing, and what they would be shopping for before returning to La Libertad, that it was a quarter to eleven when one of them looked at her watch and said, 'Oops, we'd better get going if we're going to get our shopping done and be back in time to go to the airport.' "

They made their farewells, packed their bags and left. "Don't forget," Jean shouted out the window of the van to Paul Schindler, who was going to spend the day in the city, "Get back to Libertad early—we'll have a party tonight with the Maryknollers when they arrive."

They had many errands to accomplish in the city before setting out for the airport to meet Ita and Maura, Maddie and Terri, whose flight from Managua was due to arrive at three o'clock that afternoon. There were purchases to be made for the children's center in Zaragoza, and they wanted to pass by the offices of the archbishopric to pick up any messages from Chalatenango for Ita and Maura.

A tense, menacing quiet lay over the city that morn-ing, as it braced itself for the funeral the next day of the murdered leaders whose coffins were laid out in a long line in front of the altar of the cathedral. Usually Jean and Dorothy never visited the city without stopping by the ca-thedral to say a prayer at Archbishop Romero's tomb, but on this morning it seemed wiser to keep away. They accomplished their errands, grabbed a quick hamburger with Chris at McDonald's, and were on their way.

There had been no messages from Chalatenango and Dorothy and Jean never knew that on the previous evening a second anonymous threat had been slid under the door of the parish house, or that within hours on the street in Chalatenango a death list with Ita's and Maura's names, and the names of every person on the Chalatenango parish staff with the exception of the cook, would be handed to one of the local lay workers with the words "And the killings will begin tonight."

Joking, laughing, they were in good spirits as they sped along the road to the airport. Jean, in particular, couldn't wait for Ita and Maura to arrive so that she could give them a detailed description of the previous evening's entertainment at the embassy residence.

Meanwhile, on that Tuesday morning in Nicaragua, the participants to the Maryknoll conference prepared to return to their individual missions. The conference had brought together one representative from the Ossining headquarters and all fifteen of the Sisters currently assigned to Maryknoll's Central American missions in Nicaragua, Panama and El Salvador. They had met for four days of intensive discussions, during which the members had shared their individual experiences over the past six months and defined their most pressing regional needs and goals. The night before, at the closing liturgy of the conference, Sister Ita Ford had selected and read a passage from one of Archbishop Romero's last homilies that reflected all too well the conditions into which she and Maura, Maddie and Terri were about to return: "Christ invites us not to fear persecution, brothers and sisters," Romero had written, "because believe me, he who is committed to the poor must share the same fate as the poor; and in El Salvador we know what that fate signifies: it is to disappear, to be tortured, to be captive and to be found dead by the side of the road."

Now, as the little community prepared to disband and

take up once more their individual commitments, renewed and refreshed by the mutual support and solidarity that are such a signal characteristic of Maryknoll life, they said farewell to their Nicaraguan hosts and departed for the airport. Maddie and Terri, Ita and Maura had been unable to book return flights to El Salvador on the same plane. As Ita and Maura planned to stay overnight in La Libertad, because they had scheduled an early morning meeting at the Convent of the Sisters of the Assumption in San Salvador for the following day, it was agreed that Maddie and Terri would take the first flight—departing at two o'clock in the afternoon—Ita and Maura would follow on the second plane. They sent Jean and Dorothy a message with Maddie, telling them not to bother returning yet again to the airport to pick them up; rather, they would catch the bus from the airport to San Salvador, which would drop them off at the entrance to La Libertad.

Maddie and Terri's flight arrived on schedule at three o'clock, Jean and Dorothy were there to meet them, and the four of them drove back to La Libertad where the travelers dropped off some packages for Ita and Maura in Jean's apartment, picked up their jeep, which they had left for safekeeping in the patio of the parish house, and set out for their own base in Santa Ana. Jean and Dorothy, who would not hear of Ita and Maura catching the bus, went for a quick cup of coffee in a little café by the water where they sometimes ate, and drove back to the airport in time to meet the COPA flight, due to arrive at around six o'clock.

The airport was particularly busy that night because foreign delegations and news crews from all over Central America, the U.S. and Canada were arriving to attend the public funeral of the six slain opposition leaders on the following day. Ita and Maura's flight was an hour late leaving Managua, and as Jean and Dorothy waited they met and chatted with some of the visiting church and human rights representatives, among whom was an old friend of Ita's, Heather Foote of the Washington Office on Latin America.

Later it would be revealed that Jean and Dorothy were not the only ones waiting that night for Ita and Maura's plane to land. The International Airport in El Salvador is a military installation under the jurisdiction of the National Guard. When Ita and Maura failed to arrive on the first flight, shortly after the plane had landed a National Guardsman entered the office of the Salvadoran airline, TACA, and requested the use of a telephone. An employee of the airline later recalled him saying, "No. She was not on this flight. We'll have to wait for the next one."

Finally, at around seven o'clock, the flight from Managua arrived, and as soon as Ita and Maura had cleared customs, the four women said goodbye to the visitors, piled into the white van, and drove off for La Libertad. It was dark when they left the terminal building. They were not seen alive again.

CHAPTER XI

They Were "Subversives"

Questioned about the accusations made against him, the accused National Guardsman, Joaquin Contreras Palacíos, twenty-five, married, recalled taking part in the murder of four women on the night of December 2, 1980, and stated that the following was what occurred:

On December 2, 1980, he was on guard duty at the International Airport in El Salvador. At about six P.M. his immediate supervisor, Sub-Sergeant Colindres Alemán, the officer in charge of the post, ordered him to put on civilian clothes. Guardsmen Francisco Orlando Contreras, José Roberto Moreno Canjura, Salvador Rivera Franco and Daniel Canales Ramírez were ordered to do the same. Colindres Alemán also put on civilian clothes and told the aforementioned guardsmen that they were going out on assignment, but did not specify where. He also ordered these men to take their G-3 rifles and appropriate ammunition.

At seven P.M. Colindres Alemán accompanied by the witness and other guardsmen in civilian clothes got into a jeep that belonged to the post and started out of the airport. When they got to the control booth, Colindres Alemán got out to give some orders to the guards on duty there. He then got back in the jeep and they continued on.

When they reached the vicinity of the first tollbooth, Colindres ordered the jeep to halt. Everyone got out and took up separate positions on the road. Approximately twenty-five minutes later, a white microbus approached and was given the order to stop. The witness observed that there were four women in the vehicle. The witness and the others got into the microbus and began driving.

When they reached the crossing with the road to San Pedro Nonualco, Colindres Alemán told the driver to take that road. After they had gone about six kilometers they came to a turn off onto a secondary road and Colindres told the driver to go down there. The witness noted that it was a deserted area.

Then Colindres told all of the guardsmen to fire their weapons and kill the four women. The order was obeyed by the witness and the others in the jeep. The witness recalled that Colindres Alemán had to use the rifle of one of the guardsmen because his own rifle had jammed. Before they killed the women the witness and the others abused them sexually.

When it was all over Colindres said he had done it this way because the women were subversives.

—From the confession of the accused, as witnessed, heard in full, read, ratified and signed by the accused at National Guard Headquarters, San Salvador, 8:00 A.M., on February 9, 1982.

IN THE EARLY MORNING HOURS OF THURSDAY, DECEMBER 4, thirty-six hours after the disappearance of the white Toyota van in which Jean, Dorothy, Ita and Maura had left together from the airport to drive to La Libertad, an anonymous rural worker passed the word to his parish priest that in a remote field, by the side of a dirt road leading to a small village called San Pedro Nonualco, fifteen miles to the north and east of the airport, there was a newly dug grave in which the bodies of four foreign women, wearing sandals, had been buried. The priest contacted the archdiocese; the archbishop called the American embassy.

There was trouble on the phones between San Salvador and La Libertad that morning, and the archdiocese was unable to make contact with the parish house, where Paul, Ken, Chris, Maddie and Terri were anxiously awaiting a promised visit from the ambassador. However the news quickly reached the Convent of the Assumption Sisters where Heather Foote was staying, coordinating calls from the Salvadoran Church to their counterparts in the archdiocese in Washington, D.C. Heather called Washington to pass the word to Maryknoll headquarters in Ossining; it was almost noon before the telephone finally rang in Paul's house in La Libertad.

When it did, Father Ken Myers, who picked up the receiver, covered the mouthpiece and said to Sister Christine Rody, "It's a call from Washington!" Chris and the others did not want to believe what they were then told. "We were just sort of stunned," Chris remembers. "We said to each other, 'Now don't get panicked. This could be a hoax, it could be a rumor.' So we tried to call the *Arzobispado*, because we figured if anything was known, they would know it; it would be true whatever they knew. So finally—it took about three tries to reach the *Arzobispado*—and they said yes, it was true, it was not a rumor, and they had been trying all morning to get through to us to tell us."

Ambassador White was at the International Airport,

saying goodbye to the official Canadian delegation who had requested his protection on the road out to the airport, when his deputy, Mark Dion, reached him over the radio in his official limousine. Consul Pat Lasbury was with him. What followed next is indelibly burned into her memory:

"Mark Dion had told White that the gravesite was by this hacienda called San Francisco, about ten miles down the road toward Zacatecoluca and then off the main road toward San Pedro Nonualco. So we got back in the car and went to look for them. At the time, I remember thinking as we turned off the main highway onto those God-forsaken roads in this huge limousine—you wouldn't even call them roads in this country—here's this official Chrysler limo, with a lead car—a jeep, and a follow car, another jeep—and I thought: This is ridiculous. Here we are in this poor under-developed country looking for these women in this limousine over hill and dale—it was unbelievable—they weren't even roads, we were making our own roads, they were little paths. Evidently we went past the site, because we were way back in the hills someplace and we decided we had missed it. So we turned back, and as we were on our way back down, there by the side of the fence was Paul Schindler.

"We parked the cars and went into the field, and there was this campesino who was telling Paul that yes, he lived there on the property, and two nights before he had heard shots, and on the next morning, the milkman who was delivering milk had come along and found these bodies. And then the National Guard had arrived and ordered the people to bury them. The grave was just inside the fence, beside the road, and there was a very rustic cross made of two pieces of twigs that the people had placed over the grave to mark it. So White said, 'Four women, look like *gringas*, this has got to be them. We've got to dig them up.'

"But the campesinos were afraid. They told us that without permission from the justice of the peace they would be breaking the law. So two of the embassy security men went into town to fetch the justice of the peace, and they brought him back, and he showed us the entry in his book where the burial had been reported and gave permission to dig them up.

"By the time we started to open the grave it was twelve or one o'clock, and there were press and people all over the place. . . . They dug quite a way down, and the thought occurred to me that we were on a wild goose chase, that there had to be some reason that the women had not been able to contact us. . . . Well, when they reached a depth of I guess three feet, one of the diggers signaled us over: he had uncovered what turned out to be Jean's hip. All you could see were the blue jeans and just a section of her hip. So then we said to proceed. And we stepped back. And that's when the thing just turned into a total nightmare.

"They kept digging. And the first thing I knew was, they pulled Jean up with ropes. They had a rope around her shoulders and one around her legs, and they pulled her up over the edge of the grave, they pulled her body out, and pulled her with the ropes like they were hauling a sack of alfalfa or something, across the dirt, across the weeds, away from the grave; and the whole time they were pulling her I was thinking to myself, Oh how awful! They're going to scratch her face, you know, they're going to mar her skin. Later I realized—what a dumb thought. She was dead. It didn't hurt her. And they were not doing it out of disrespect, they were just doing a job, unearthing a dead body and pulling it away from the grave.

"So they laid her out. She was the first one. And she was so disfigured, you really couldn't be sure it was Jean because her face was so disfigured. It appears the bullet had collapsed the bone structure of her face and she was unrecognizable.

"Then they proceeded to pull the next body out—I think it was Maura. They pulled her over to the side and some of the people came over and broke branches off the trees and covered the two bodies so that people couldn't stare at them. I remember the stench was terrible. Oh God, it was awful. They pulled up Dorothy. She was dressed in jeans but she had her jeans on backward. Subsequently, the campesinos told us that they found them without their jeans on; they had put their jeans back on but put hers on backward. And then they brought up Ita. Of course Ita was a very tiny person, it was very easy for them to bring her up. It was like practically bringing up a child. But her body was crumbled and broken. Jean and Ita were very badly bruised; the least was Maura. Maura and Dorothy. Then they laid them all out there and the people covered the rest of the bodies with branches.

"I remember, somewhere during the whole time they were digging them up they were throwing things out of the grave, and at one point I walked over and picked up one of these things just to see what it was, and it was one of their panties. And the whole thing just hit me with disgust, what had happened to them. I could not believe I had seen these women, well two of them anyway, just two days before. And they were so alive, and so vibrant . . . and then here was testimony to the fact that they had been through a terrible experience. All the evidence was around to testify to that fact.

"I remember at one point we knelt, I was kneeling beside Maddie, and we said some prayers. I don't know whether we prayed for them or for those who were responsible for this terrible thing.

"And then White. White was fuming. I remember his saying, 'We're going to do this one right. We're not going to let the military get away with this.' He brought the justice of the peace over and he started questioning him: 'Did anybody come to see you about this? Did anyone have any questions about this? Why didn't you report this?' And the poor justice of the peace, he was so intimidated by all these foreigners that, well, I think he told the truth. He said, 'You know this happens all the time. We're always being asked to sign reports to the effect that dead bodies have been found by the side of the road. This is an everyday occurrence in this province, and other than the fact that these women maybe looked like foreigners, there's nothing to make me believe that this was any different from the hundreds, literally hundreds of other cases that we have, that occur in this region. Therefore I thought nothing of signing this and bringing it to its logical conclusion, just as those hundreds of others were brought to their logical conclusion.'

"White decided to bring the justice of the peace to the city. I remember we put him in the limousine and drove him back to San Salvador. We wanted to keep him under protection. We were afraid he might be the target for revenge on the part of the military because he had allowed us to open the grave and uncover the evidence."

The funeral mass in San Salvador was scheduled for four-thirty on the afternoon of Friday, December 5, but when the ambassador and Mrs. White arrived to attend the service there was some delay in opening the church, and White was besieged by the press corps as he waited on the street outside. The fact that the Salvadoran government had failed to provide the embassy with any information regarding either the burial of the bodies (which had been presided over by a detachment of their own security forces) or the existence of the burned-out wreck of the white Toyota van (which Sister Chris Rody had had no trouble locating on the afternoon of December 3, parked on the shoulder of the road leading from the airport to La Libertad) had raised immediate rumors of an official cover-up of military involvement in the murders, and White was in no mood to mask his sense of outrage. In his answers to the press he spelled out the reasons for his own suspicions:

> Q: Which authority told you they had no knowledge? The National Guard?
> WHITE: The people, the Ministry of Defense people told us that they had no knowledge.
> Q: Do you know what the normal chain of command is when something like that happens?
> WHITE: The people who are at the burial would be obligated to report this to the National Guard Center in Zacatecoluca. They should

have communicated immediately. And then,
when I called the Minister of Defense at three
P.M. the day before yesterday, presumably, no,
not presumably, one of the first things he did
was to call this Lt. Colonel Casanova* in
Zacatecoluca.

Q: Mr. Ambassador, do you think there's a
cover-up going on here?

WHITE: I'm not prepared to make any comment
at this point on cover-ups or anything like that.
At this point the authorities have promised us
a thorough investigation and we'll certainly
give them . . . we'll certainly be watching the
results of that investigation very closely. I
would say that we are suspending military and
economic assistance to this country until the
government can give us a satisfactory response
regarding the abuses of human rights that have
taken place and what measures they are going
to take in order to cope with them. I think that
it's up to them to make their own decisions as
to how they're going to relate to us—but we
have the right to ask of our partners certain
standards of conduct.

"In the next few days," Pat Lasbury remembers, "there
was this team appointed by President Carter, led by William Rogers and [William] Bowdler who came down to
seek evidence. They did not get much cooperation from the
military. The military was very cordial to them, gave a
dinner for them, but acted as though—well, what can we
do? In a country where there's so many murders, we don't
know any more about this murder than about the hundreds
of others that have taken place.

"In subsequent days White had daily conversations

---

* Commander of the army garrison in Zacatecoluca and responsible
for all security forces in the region.

with the minister of defense about whether or not he had discovered any evidence, and it was like hitting your head against a stone wall. For that whole month there was nothing, nothing."

In keeping with Maryknoll tradition Ita and Maura were buried among the people for whom they worked and died in Chalatenango. There, in the small, overgrown and overcrowded country cemetery that lies at the bottom of the hill leading into the town, their bodies were laid to rest beside Carla's on Saturday, December 6.

On the same day, the bodies of Jean and Dorothy were flown home to their families in the States. But not before the people of La Libertad had an opportunity to say their own goodbyes. On the evening of Friday, December 5, after the celebration of the joint funeral mass for all four in San Salvador, Paul, Chris and Ken brought Jean and Dorothy back to La Libertad one final time. A wake was held through the night in their own parish church. At four-thirty the following morning, Paul celebrated a second funeral mass. When it was ended, and Jean and Dorothy's coworkers lifted their caskets and prepared to carry them from the church to the waiting limousine, the people inside the crowded church lined up to take their places. As the two caskets passed through the crowd, from hand to hand, from shoulder to shoulder, the congregation climbed onto the benches and started to applaud.

Outside in the early dawn the applause was picked up by the waiting crowd. In the square beyond the church, along the street outside the windows of Jean's apartment, and down the narrow streets of the port, the people of La Libertad and Zaragoza, of Santa Cruz and the surrounding communities, had arrived to line the route leading out of town to the airport road. They loaded the caskets. Then the small cavalcade of vehicles started out along the final stretch of Jean's and Dorothy's Salvadoran journey, moving slowly through the dense lines of defiant, triumphant applause.

CHAPTER XII

"A Bitchy Day"

You would do her an injustice to say that you understood her, because I suppose none of us are fully understood. We're all very mysterious people. But instead of trying to understand why Jean did what she did, we should just hear her message. The message of her life is a challenge, I think, not only to those who loved her, but to all Americans, that there are people on the other side of the American continent who are our brothers and sisters; and if we take our Christianity seriously they should be part of our family, of every family. I think that's what Jean was saying with her life.
—Father Michael Crowley

ON WEDNESDAY, DECEMBER 3, 1980, NEWS OF THE TRAG-
edy in El Salvador began reaching the homes of the families in the States. It was early evening when the phone rang
in the Donovan home in Sarasota, Florida. Jean's mother
picked it up.

"I answered the phone that day and a Spanish-speaking
operator said, 'El Salvador is calling you.' And asked if it
was our number. I said yes, and Paul Schindler's voice came
on the phone. And I knew Jeannie's voice should have been
on the phone. So I said, 'Where is Jeannie? Has anything
happened to her?' And he said, 'Get Ray on the extension.'
And I said, 'Please, Paul, tell me what happened.' And he
said, 'Put Ray on first and then I'll tell you.' So Ray got on
the other end and Paul said, 'Jean and Dorothy are missing.'
And then he said, 'Jeannie has gotten many people out of
situations like this, and we feel in a day or so, you know
. . . we're working on it. . . .'

"I guess we kind of went to jelly inside. It's a terrible
feeling not to know where your child is."

On the following day, it was Jean's father's turn to
receive the call. "I recall we were sitting right there in the
den and the phone rang and I picked it up and it was Paul.
He said that he was still at the parish house, but they had
gotten a report that they had discovered four bodies in an
unmarked grave; and he said he was going out to see . . .
but he was quite certain that he knew who he'd find. All I
could think of was: She's gone. . . ."

In Danbury, Connecticut, it was around eight o'clock
in the evening when Michael Donovan, Jean's brother, got
the news. "I remember very vividly. We'd just finished dinner. I was sitting at the table in the kitchen with my wife,
and the phone rang. It was my father. And he told me that
Jean and Dorothy had been kidnapped. I think my only . . .
my only response to that, I just simply said, 'Damn!' on the
phone, and after I got off the phone I remember my wife,

Ellen, saying to me that she thought my grandmother had died or something, just from my reaction."

Michael called Maryknoll for more information and was advised to try and reach as many politicians as he could to enlist their help to make calls to the State Department to put pressure on the Salvadoran government. So he began making phone calls.

"At about ten o'clock, I managed to reach a guy called John Blacken at the State Department who was the director of the Central American Office or something. He said, 'Yes. We have a report that some American citizens are missing in El Salvador, but we don't know how many, and we don't know who, and we don't know any of the circumstances.' I'd just talked to Maryknoll so I knew Ita and Maura were missing too. I had called him to ask for information and I ended up giving him information. Looking back on that night, now that I'm somewhat more informed than I was then, I sometimes doubt whether Blacken was really so ill-informed.

"The next morning I started phoning everywhere. When you get into that sort of situation—even though you've thought through the whole thing previously, because you figured something like this was going to happen—it's still a shock. And when it happens, until you hear that she's dead, you're still almost desperately hopeful that something can be done. When it really does happen, you just can't bring yourself to believe it until somebody actually says, 'Yes. She's dead.'

"I called back the State Department several times the next morning, to try to talk to this guy Michael Barry, the Salvadoran desk officer, but he was not reachable. I called Senator Weicker's office; some woman there told me the senator could not take any statements over the phone. I'd have to write him a letter. I do remember asking her why then did he bother to have an 800 number; and she said, 'I just work here,' and hung up.

"Then Senator Kennedy called and offered to do anything he could to help.

"And then my Dad called—to say they'd found her. He was crying.

"After I got off the phone with him, I was just sort of in shock. I remember there was a couch in my office; I was sitting on the couch trying to think, well, what shall I do now. And I just sort of sat there for a while, trying to think what I should do. And then I thought, well, I guess I should go home. So I told my boss I was going home, and I left. And on the way home in the car, there was a report on the radio that they were dead.

"They had the films that evening on the network news —pictures of the burned-out minivan and digging up the makeshift graves that they were in originally. My wife was with me, and there was an ABC camera crew there in our living room. They'd come to do an interview, but they hadn't started the filming at that point. It didn't really hit me until I saw it on the news. That's when I really broke up."

Bill Ford, Ita's only brother, is a Wall Street lawyer. He and his wife, Marianne, were celebrating the birth of a son in his New Jersey home when there was a phone call from Sister Melinda Roper, the president of the Maryknoll Sisters. At the time, while Bill was devoted to Ita, and although he and Marianne had been to Chile to visit her a couple of years before, he had very little notion about the reality of her life in El Salvador, and he had neither met Sister Melinda Roper nor indeed even knew who she was.

"We'd brought a new baby home from the hospital the day before. I remember we were all in the room, watching him being bathed and changed, when I got the call from Sister Melinda Roper of Maryknoll. She told us that the chances of the women ever being found alive were extremely remote and we should be prepared for the worst."

In Bay Ridge, Brooklyn, Ita's youngest sister, Rene, got the news from her brother. "It was very late at night and my brother Bill had gotten a phone call from Maryknoll and he called me immediately because he lives in Jersey and I live two blocks from my mother. He told me what had happened—that they were missing—and told me to go immediately to my mother's house because it would probably be on the news that night and no one wanted her to hear it on television.

"So I did. I went. And I walked up the stairs and I looked at her and said, 'Mom, Ita is missing.' And she just shook her head and walked into the kitchen and began to talk and cry and that was it. That's how we found out.

"I never believed that anything would happen to Ita. I mean she would tell us about the horror that was going on in Salvador and the people who were missing and murdered, but you never really think it would ever happen to her, no. No, not in my wildest dreams.

"I can remember seeing the films. We had a mass for Ita on Saturday—the day that she was actually buried in San Salvador—we had a mass in the living room of my mother's home. And we spent the day there, and we went home that night, my children and I, and the kids turned on the television, and on the news, as soon as they turned it on, they were burying the caskets in Salvador. And my daughter Jennifer said, 'Mom, look, they're burying Ita.' And it's like—you turn on the television and it's cartoons and fairyland. . . . They were actually . . . I actually saw them burying her that day. I remember that."

Not far away, in Rockaway Park, Queens, John and Mary Clarke, Maura's parents, did not know anything was wrong until the morning of Thursday, December 4. That day their younger, married daughter, Judy Keogh, had planned to drive over with a couple of old school friends from her Long Island home near Manhasset to spend the day visiting family and childhood friends in Queens. Her mother had prepared a large old-fashioned Irish breakfast for the visitors and was looking forward to their arrival.

"I remember I was expecting my daughter Judy and two of her school friends. I was always awfully glad to see them when they'd come back again, now that they were all gone and on their own, and I felt very excited that I was going to see them—very happy about it.

"So Judy came. And she told us both to sit, that she had something to tell us. I thought it was something, some big change they were going to do—that they were going to sell their property and move away. Something serious, anyhow. But she told me then that Maura and the people with her were missing.

"So whatever I had read about El Salvador, I didn't feel at anytime good about it. And I felt very upset—very bad—not knowing how they might be treated—tortured or mistreated. Then the phone kept ringing. And the news came from Maryknoll. The bodies were found. And it was a strange relief when they were finally identified as being the bodies of the Sisters and the young girl, Jean. It was a strange relief. It reminded me of a friend I have whose son was lost in a river and wasn't found for six weeks. She was so happy when his body was found. So I suppose it must have been a relief of that type that came to me. That they hadn't just disappeared as many people do down there, and nothing is known of them."

"She never cried," says her daughter. "She put on that iron coat. Did everything perfectly. Maryknoll wanted to know whether they would like Maura's body brought home. My parents said she would want to be buried there. She belonged where she was. They said her body won't help us any. All her life Maura tried in so many ways to make people aware of Latin America. It was her whole life. She never accepted that you couldn't have change."

In Cleveland, at the home of Dorothy Kazel's parents, the news from El Salvador reached Mr. and Mrs. Kazel on the evening of December 3, as they were preparing to hold a small supper party. "We had a couple coming over for supper and to play pinochle," Mrs. Kazel recalls. "We were going to have a little card game. And Father Al Winters of the Cleveland diocese called up and said that Dorothy and Jean were missing, they'd had no word of them for the last eighteen hours or something like that. We were all shook up. Everybody just holding their breath."

They had talked to Dorothy on the phone just one week earlier. She had called them on the Tuesday before Thanksgiving to wish them a happy holiday. Her father simply could not believe that she was not going to extricate herself from whatever difficulty she was in. "She was a little fearless," he admits, "but usually she got away with it, and when that happened I said, 'She'll come up with something.' Dorothy always knew how to get out of a tight spot. But those killers. I guess they had their orders."

In Cleveland, too, the news from El Salvador came as a devastating shock to Jean's friends. One year later her cousin Colleen, and her former roommate and friend Debbie Miller, were still struggling to come to terms with the violent loss of someone who had played such a central role in their lives and then, mysteriously, had changed and withdrawn her intimacy.

"I was watching soaps," Colleen recalls, "and it was like a flash . . . they said four missionaries had been . . . were missing. And I knew. I don't know why I knew. Maybe because I hadn't heard anything about anybody being kidnapped in El Salvador who had made it back. So I figured that was it. I just had a feeling. Then Uncle Ray called me after they had found out.

"And even now, I can see Jean being pulled off the road by a bunch of army guys or whatever, and her saying, 'How dare you? Do you know who I am?' I can see her—facing a band of guys with machine guns and saying, 'You don't know who the hell you're talking to. How dare you. I'm Jean Donovan. I'm working with the missionaries. Let that woman go! . . .' I can just see her, trying to take control, trying to get a hold of the situation and boss people around—and getting her head blown off for her trouble. It was a bitchy day."

"Ah, . . . it was a real unreal day," Debbie agrees. "Somebody else died down there. Somebody I didn't know. And we haven't been able to bury her. She could be down in El Salvador still, for all we know. Hiding out. Playing golf."

Fighting to keep control of her feelings, the hurt and the anger still too raw, too close to the surface, Debbie begins to laugh through her tears as an image of her friend, an image of the playful, occasionally outrageous Jean Donovan—the Jean with whom she had shared good times and bad, whom she had laughed with and fought with and never ceased to love—flashes suddenly before her and makes its presence felt around the kitchen table where we have been talking about her. "Someday," says Debbie, "Jean's going to come walking in, and she's gonna say, 'Wasn't that a Great Adventure!'"

Epilogue

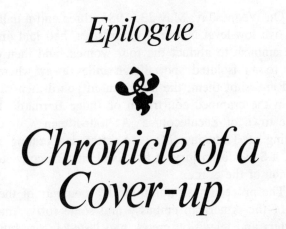

Chronicle of a Cover-up

IN ONE SENSE THE STORY OF JEAN IS OVER. IN ANOTHER
it is very much alive. On December 2, 1980, four Americans were murdered by agents of a foreign government that
owed its existence to the support—political, economic and
military—of the government of the United States. Though
Jean's story ended with the bullet in the back of her head
that blew her face away, it is necessary to ask the question:
what do the American people and their government make
of such a tragedy? How do Jean's fellow citizens and their
official representatives deal with a death such as this—one
that exposes the conditions of life and death in a country
ruled, as one visiting American described it, "by a terrorist
government," one which also happens to be our ally?

In their lifetime, Jean and her companions personified
those principles of idealism, generosity, effective energetic
service and commitment to the common good that generations of Americans have striven to uphold. Yet, since their
death four years ago, their own country has become ever
more deeply involved in support of the Salvadoran rulers
who thus far have been incapable or unwilling to investigate
documented evidence of a well-orchestrated, high-level
cover-up of the circumstances of their murders. Rulers
whose officially directed death squads have, in the interim,
murdered three more American citizens and massacred a
further thirty-five thousand of their own citizens.

On Wednesday, May 23, 1984, three and a half years after five low-level National Guardsmen had laid an elaborate ambush to abduct the four women, and then driven them to an isolated spot fifteen miles away where they raped and shot them, the five accused guardsmen went on trial in the cramped courtroom of Judge Bernardo Rauda in the town of Zacatecoluca. At four-fifteen A.M. on the morning of Thursday, May 24, after deliberating for an hour, a Salvadoran jury of five local citizens convicted the five men of the crime.

The proceedings, monitored by members of the legal staff of the American embassy and some forty American reporters and television crews, had lasted in one-hundred-degree heat for nineteen hours. Originally, Judge Rauda had planned to call a recess at midnight. But word reached American sources that the commander of the army garrison in Zacatecoluca—a colonel who has himself been implicated in the murders of two other Americans, labor advisors working with the agrarian reform program—planned a rally by his troops in front of the courthouse during the night to intimidate the jury. After consultation with U.S. Justice Department lawyer Carlos Correa, who had worked intensively with the judge coordinating the final stages of the preparation of the case, Judge Rauda changed his mind. Consequently, after nine hours of testimony and four and a half hours of arguments by the prosecution, it was half past midnight by the time the three court-appointed, unpaid defense lawyers—two of whom claimed to have never met or spoken to their clients before they walked into the courtroom—began the presentation of their defense.

They spoke for less than seventy-five minutes, and what they left unsaid was more interesting than the lackluster, disorganized presentation they made in behalf of the defendants. Although Chief Prosecutor Geronimo Castillo had depicted the guardsmen as vicious renegades acting solely on their own authority, the prosecution had never developed a motive for the crime. Yet the defense made no attempt to argue that the guardsmen might have been acting under orders, although one of the defense lawyers did make an oblique reference to such a possibility: "If they did it, they did it on orders," he said, "because in the National Guard if someone does not obey an order of this type . . ." He left his sentence unfinished.

The verdict was the first successful prosecution of any members of El Salvador's security forces who had been charged with responsibility for the murders of more than forty thousand Salvadoran civilians since October 1979. As such it created a historic precedent and was widely hailed as a first step in the restoration of respect for human rights and the rule of law. But sources close to the case could not help but recognize that, like every other manifestation of public life in El Salvador today—from the conduct of the war to the design of the agrarian reform to the running of the elections—this conviction owed more to American pressure and American management than it did to the efforts of the Salvadoran government. Security in the courtroom was in the hands of a special Judicial Protection Unit, formed and trained in Glencoe, Alabama; the jurors were driven to the courtroom in the morning and returned to their homes after the verdict in bullet-proof American embassy vehicles; meals and camp beds were provided by the embassy so that if necessary the jurors and the staff of the court could sleep overnight within the protection of the guarded courthouse; and when the electricity failed, just as the prosecution began to make its presentation, light was restored by means of hurricane lamps delivered by embassy staff.

"The press is going to say that this day it is possible to have justice done in El Salvador," one of the prosecutors exulted at the end of the trial. Yet one of the more ironic anomalies of this trial of the killers of Jean and her companions is that the verdict carried a multimillion dollar price tag—19.4 million dollars—which had been frozen by the U.S. Congress in November 1983 pending a resolution of the case. Within twenty-four hours of the conviction of the guardsmen, the State Department, announcing with relief that "justice has been done," released these millions to the very man who was the commander of the National Guard at the time of the killings, and whose name features prominently in a State Department Investigative Report on the initial cover-up of the killings by high-ranking Salvadoran officials—Minister of Defense General Carlos Eugenio Vides Casanova.

Writing on the Op-Ed page of the *New York Times* one week later, Bill Ford, brother of slain Maryknoll Sister Ita Ford, voiced another of the central questions raised by the verdict: "It remains to be seen," he wrote, "whether this decision will open the way to convictions in cases where the victims are Salvadorans." So long as it does not, so long as this trial of the killers of four American women remains an American-sponsored affair for the benefit of congressional critics of unconditional aid to the Salvadoran Army, the claim that "justice has been done" will ring hollow. And until further investigation is made of the charges that these men were acting on orders, the trial itself must be seen as one more step in the cover-up of the real circumstances of these women's deaths. If the failure to investigate the motive for this multiple murder and the refusal to search out the source from which the order to eliminate these women originated persist, the story of Jean and her companions will continue to haunt the conscience of a large segment of the American people, and their deaths will continue to plague the official policy of support for their murderers.

The story of the background struggles which led, finally, to those nineteen hours in the courtroom of Zacatecoluca, and the history of the original cover-up by Salvadoran government officials of the circumstances surrounding these murders—a cover-up sanctioned and concealed by the American government, acting in accordance with the demands of official American policy—are the subject of this epilogue.

The story begins during the first days following the tragedy. As the families of the murdered women struggled to cope with their grief, their anguish was intensified by the bewildering realization that the United States government was, in fact, protecting their murderers. From their earliest contacts with the State Department, they encountered a pattern of official evasiveness that would characterize the conduct of two American administrations in relation to what has become known as "the case of the four American churchwomen."

"The realization that the State Department was not interested in pursuing the case was something that dawned on us gradually," Bill Ford says. "As I went through my personal crash course about what was happening in El Salvador, it became clear to me that the death of the women was just an inconvenience to American policy. The American government, both under the Carter and the Reagan administrations, has a fixed policy in Salvador, and that policy will not bend to reason, or eyewitness, or anything else.

"Initially, it's a terrible personal tragedy, but gradually there intrudes upon the sense of personal tragedy the surrounding facts, and it was like a growing, horrible realization: we were supporting a government; that government had killed my sister; and my government didn't care."

In the months after the killings the families—parents, brothers and sisters of the murdered women—watched, with mounting outrage and anger, as their own government attemped to discredit the reputations of their dead.

On Friday, December 5, Patricia Donovan called her son, Michael, in Danbury to inform him that there were problems in El Salvador related to the return of Jean's and Dorothy's bodies to the States. TACA, the Salvadoran airline, was refusing permission to load the coffins on one of their planes, and Mrs. Donovan suggested to Michael that he call the State Department and ask for their help.

Michael was put in touch with a Ms. Joyce Gunn in

Citizen's Emergency Service, who called back within two hours to inform him that all arrangements had been made for the return of the bodies on the following day. Jean's body accompanied by Father Paul Schindler and Sister Christine Rody would go to Sarasota; Dorothy's, accompanied by Father Ken Myers, was going straight to Cleveland. However, according to a chronology which Michael later prepared for the House Foreign Affairs Committee at the request of Congressman Clarence Long, the next day he received two further calls from Ms. Gunn.

I. Telephone call received later Saturday: "Will you please get the hell off our backs." I asked who this was—Joyce Gunn of the State Department.

I don't know what she's talking about.

a. Congressman Gilman has been at the State Department all day, "Raising hell with everyone because you sent him here!"

b. I did not send Congressman Gilman to the State Department.

c. I told her: "If Congressman Gilman is raising hell at the State Department, then I am sure he is doing so of his own volition." I hung up without waiting for a reply.

II. 1. Several hours later, I received a telephone call from Joyce Gunn. State Department unsure if body should go to Danbury or Sarasota.

2. I reply that the body should go to Sarasota.

3. State Department will send me a bill for $3,500 for its services in the return of my sister's body to the United States.

There are two separate aspects to the cover-up that followed Jean's murder. The first concerns the efforts of the Salvadoran government to shield the murderers—the men of the National Guard unit which, under the immediate command of a subsergeant stationed at the airport on the night of December 2, apprehended, abducted, raped and murdered the four women. The second, more sensitive aspect of the case, concerns the issue of higher involvement in the crime. The question of whether the decision to kill the four women was taken by an individual National Guard subsergeant acting on his own initiative, or whether he was, in fact, obeying an order, and if so, from whom and how far up the chain of command the order to eliminate the women originated.

While the whole story has not yet been told, and may possibly never be known, there does exist, after nearly four years, a body of evidence that provides a documented chronology of the efforts of the Salvadoran government to protect the murderers, and of the attempts by the State Department of two American administrations to conceal this cover-up from the relatives of the murdered women, the Church, the Congress, and the American people.

On Friday, December 5, 1980, the administration reacted with outrage to the scenes from the gravesite in that remote Salvadoran field—scenes that had dominated the nation's television screens the night before. At the daily noon press briefing, the State Department made the following announcement:

> Overnight in San Salvador, our Embassy
> has confirmed that the four American women
> who disappeared Tuesday evening are dead.
> We are shocked and dismayed by those brutal
> murders. Pending clarification of the circum-
> stances of the killings, we are putting a hold on
> all economic and military assistance.

In San Salvador on that same Friday, the military also issued a communiqué:

> The Armed Forces of El Salvador deplores the brutal and useless assassination of U.S. citizens Ita Ford, Marina [sic] Clarke, Dorothy Kazel and Jean Donovan, and condemns, before local and international public opinion such an action which is opposed to the postulates of its 15 October 1979 proclamation which it is defending with much honor and sacrifice.
>
> Reiterating its policy in defense of human rights, it announces its decision to use all available means in the investigation and to request cooperation from an international investigation commission, to solve this inhuman crime. In this way the full weight of the law can be applied to those who are really guilty.

On the following day, President Carter dispatched a high-level, bipartisan Presidential Mission to El Salvador to investigate the circumstances of the crime and to report back to him personally with their findings.

The mission was led by Mr. William Rogers, former under secretary of state for economic affairs and assistant secretary of state in the administration of President Ford, and Acting Under Secretary of State William Bowdler. They spent three days in San Salvador and returned to Washington on December 9. Two days later they presented their findings to President Carter in the form of a report, which the State Department refused to release.

During the weeks following their return, in the absence of any visible progress in the investigation into the deaths of the women, there were those who began to suspect that the true purpose of the Rogers-Bowdler mission had more to do with negotiating a restructuring of the Salvadoran government that would facilitate the rapid resumption of American aid than it had with the stated objective of insisting on a "complete, thorough and professional investigation" of the circumstances of the women's murders as a necessary prerequisite for the restoration of such aid. According to Raymond Bonner in his book *Weakness and Deceit: U.S. Policy and El Salvador*, his examination of secret State Department cables acquired under the Freedom of Information Act confirms the view that the investigation into the killing of the women took third place on the list of American conditions for a renewal of aid; according to Bonner the priorities were a restructuring of the Salvadoran government and a commitment from the military leaders for the transfer of certain high-ranking officers, whose involvement in death-squad activities were well known to United States officials.

Yet three years later Mr. Rogers told me of his personal disappointment and dismay that Washington had failed so completely to follow up on what he regarded as the real objective of the delegation that he had led. According to Mr. Rogers, while he acknowledges that the delegation members had not viewed their mandate as limited exclusively to the investigation of the killings of the four Americans, since their murders were seen to be part of a much larger problem, yet "the prize" as he puts it, that he believed the delegation members brought back with them to Washington, was a real commitment on the part of the Salvadoran leaders to conduct an immediate and thorough investigation. "The clues," says Rogers, "were lying all over the place." It was his belief, one that he now acknowledges to have been naive, that the promises the members of the delegation received from the Salvadoran government, which included an agreement to permit the participation of the FBI at all levels of the investigative process, constituted a guarantee for the rapid and successful prosecution of the crime.

Subsequent events, as they proceeded to unfold in both

San Salvador and Washington, demonstrate that the Salvadorans' interpretation of their discussions with the members of the visiting delegation was a far different one.

In San Salvador, on the day after the members of the Presidential Mission returned to Washington, the junta announced plans to restructure the government. Four days later the State Department announced the resumption of economic aid to the new Salvadoran junta.

In fact, according to the director of the Council of Hemispheric Affairs, Laurence Burns, the decision by Carter's State Department to resume economic and military aid to El Salvador "was made at the very moment that the suspension was first announced." Speaking to the press a few weeks later, Mr. Burns said, "The evening of the day that that suspension was announced [December 5] I met a State Department official and in a discussion with him he told me that the suspension would be in effect until public outrage would die down because policy requirements demanded that the aid be restored."

By December 1980, a lame-duck administration in Washington was in possession of intelligence reporting an imminent guerrilla offensive in El Salvador. From the perspective of President Carter and his closest advisers, the policy requirements in El Salvador consisted of a single imperative: to prevent a military takeover by Salvadoran guerrilla forces before the new administration of President-elect Reagan came into office. If the people who "lost" Nicaragua were to stand by while leftists took over another Central American country, so the argument went, whatever future remained to be salvaged for the Democratic party after the conservative landslide in the November elections would be irretrievably lost. The decision to support the Salvadoran military, announced by the American government just twelve days after the women's grave was opened in that remote Salvadoran field, was taken in the interests of American domestic politics and was justified thereafter in terms of an East-West conflict.

Meanwhile, for the benefit of the concerned citizenry

and the members of the women's families, the fiction was maintained that present and future aid was connected to progress in the investigation into the deaths of the women. Declaring that "our economic assistance is critically needed to maintain the Salvadoran economy and avoid food shortages," the State Department's release concerning the resumption of aid states:

> Last weekend, the El Salvadoran Government was restructured and a civilian, José Napoleón Duarte, was named President. A new cabinet is being named. We consider these positive developments which can bring greater efficiency and stronger, more unified civilian control over the government.
>
> The Salvadoran Government's approach to the investigation of the death of the four Americans and these other developments have clarified the situation sufficiently for the United States to resume its economic assistance. The resumption of military assistance awaits further developments in El Salvador.

Within the American embassy in San Salvador, the evaluation by Ambassador White and his staff concerning the Salvador government's approach to the investigation was a good deal less optimistic than that reflected in Washington. On the same day that restoration of aid was announced, Robert White sent a cable to the State Department:

> San Salvador, December 17, 1980
> Subject: Report to the President
> I recommend that the White House release the Rogers/Bowdler report to the public. My reasons are the following.
> The friends and families of the murdered women have a right to know the results of the investigation. It makes little sense to announce

273

with great fanfare the dispatch of a Presidential commission and then not make their findings public.

Release of the report will assist the civilians and the moderates in the military in their efforts to reorganize the Armed Forces in ways that will ensure discipline and respect for the citizenry. By releasing the report we will assist the investigating commission to do a professional job and follow up on leads it might otherwise ignore.

Meantime, the content of the report was leaked to the press, and in an article headed, "The Government Stonewalls a U.S. Investigation," *Time* magazine reported in its December 22 issue that the Rogers mission had found "circumstantial evidence of possible security force involvement," and went on to say:

> After days of stonewalling, the Salvadoran government belatedly named a "high-level civilian and military commission" to "find the guilty people and punish them." But the three military members of the new four-man commission included two close friends of Defense Minister García and a first cousin of Police Chief López Nuila.

When the mission's report was finally released on December 23, it revealed that the members had put together a substantial body of circumstantial evidence pointing to Salvadoran security force complicity. A statement attached to the report claimed that "the text released is identical to the original except for minimal changes required to protect sources and avoid prejudicing the on-going investigation by the government of El Salvador with our assistance." In fact, in the final section of the report, the deletion of several key sentences robbed the published document of the most specific recommendations contained in the original:*

> *We entertain no illusions . . . the processes of law and civil justice are not very evident in El Salvador at the present time.* But, so far as we could tell from our inquiry, we are prepared to say that the authorities are now doing about what we can rightly ask at this moment.
>
> The United States should provide the maximum cooperation to the effort . . .
> *We urge that [the FBI] participate directly in the work of the Commission, help shape the course of the investigation, preserve evidence, search out witnesses and record their testimony, and review the overall performance and prosecution of the case. Doing so would enhance the prospects of its legitimacy as well as its chances for ultimate success.*

One day prior to the release of the mission's report, Michael Donovan and Bill Ford, together with representatives of the Clarke and Kazel families and the president of the Maryknoll Order, had attended a meeting at the State Department with Secretary of State Edmund Muskie and the members of the mission.

In the course of that meeting Secretary Muskie stated that the department had received no progress reports on the investigation since the return of the Presidential Mission on December 9. In fact, as the families later discovered, during this entire period Ambassador White had been filing cables almost daily, reporting on the mounting evidence of a cover-up by the Salvadoran investigative commission.

Though the families left the State Department that day with assurances about what would be done, one month

* Sentences in italics deleted from the published release.

later Michael Donovan and Bill Ford were back in Washington to hold a press conference at which they went public with their frustration. In his opening statement Bill Ford explained:

> On December 22 of last year, representatives of the four families met with State Department officials, including the Secretary of State.
>
> We were personally and specifically told that military aid would not be resumed until the United States government was satisfied that a serious investigation would be conducted. The families who were there protested that, in effect, the murderers were investigating the murderers. But we were told it was the best that could be done.
>
> We were also specifically told that as the United States government got information that it would be passed on to the families. We were told that we were entitled to such information, that it was the least they could do for us. Despite these specific promises, we've heard nothing from the State Department. Speaking just for the Ford family, not one telephone call that we have made to the State Department has been returned.

During the preceding weeks a number of things had happened in El Salvador. On December 28, American freelance journalist John Sullivan arrived in El Salvador. One of his assignments was to do some "investigative reporting" on the case of the four dead churchwomen. Sullivan, a native of New Jersey, checked into his hotel room at the Sheraton at around four o'clock and was seen leaving the hotel three hours later. He disappeared. Unlike the families of the four women, John Sullivan's family had no powerful lobbying group, such as the Catholic Church, to rally behind his cause, and to this day, although his skeleton was finally identified and returned to them more than two years later, they do not know how he died.

On June 6, two more Americans, AIFLD/labor advisers Michael Hammer and Mark Pearlman, were shot down in cold blood in the coffee shop of the Sheraton Hotel together with the Salvadoran director of the Institute of Agrarian Transformation, Rodolfo Viera.

On January 10, the guerrillas finally launched their long-awaited "final offensive." Militarily and politically their assault was a fiasco and was swiftly crushed by the Salvadoran Army. On January 14, President Carter announced the resumption of that portion of the military aid that had been temporarily suspended after the death of the women on December 5. Once again this decision was related to progress in the investigation into the deaths of the four women; the text of the State Department's official release cited the Salvadoran government's "commitment to a thorough, professional and expeditious investigation into the killings." Three days later, on January 17, following intelligence—later proved erroneous—reporting the landing of "boatloads" of Nicaraguan arms and volunteers to the Salvadoran guerrillas, Carter authorized an additional $5 million in emergency military aid, and this time, the official statement referred to "positive steps" taken in the Salvadoran government's investigation. This decision to release the aid had, in fact, been taken by the State Department as early as New Year's Eve, without consultation with either Ambassador White or Human Rights Commissioner Patricia Derian. Her memorandum, dated December 31, 1980, and addressed to Secretary of State Muskie, stated the case for withholding such assistance in the clearest of terms:

> Subject: *Resumption of Military Assistance to El Salvador*
> I do not agree with the decision to resume military assistance to El Salvador. This decision is contrary to what the President decided

following the murders of the American missionaries and is contrary to what we have told the public. Suspension was precipitated by possible security force involvement in the murder of the nuns and was to remain in effect pending clarification of such involvement. There has been no clarification. . . .

Nor are the security forces cooperating. They have refused to provide the investigatory commission with lists of units in the area at the time the nuns were murdered. Clearly the conditions upon which the phased resumption of military assistance was to be authorized have not been met. . . .

There are, however, compelling reasons to maintain the suspension. It originally was set in place pending clarification of security force involvement in the deaths of the American nuns. Resumption will imply USG exoneration of security force involvement, thereby prejudicing the outcome of the investigation. . . .

Finally, I would note that this decision has been taken while our Ambassador is absent from El Salvador and without any effort to solicit his views.

As for Ambassador White, his protest was heard loud and clear within days of the official announcement. On the weekend that the State Department released the military assistance, a congressional delegation was visiting El Salvador, whose members returned to Washington with reports of the ambassador's displeasure. On January 21, White sent the following cable to the State Department:

I have received various telephone inquiries today from journalists asking me about statements attributed to me by Congressman Studds. I have just telephoned Congressman Studds and

told him that I stand by my statement to him
that in my opinion, on the basis of the evidence
available to me, there is no serious investigation
being undertaken by the government of El Salvador into the deaths of the American churchwomen.

On January 21, 1981, the administration of President
Reagan was twenty-four hours old, and new officials of the
United States government began giving their views on the
case.

In the course of an interview with the Washington correspondent of the *Tampa Tribune* on December 16, Jeane
Kirkpatrick, President Reagan's choice of ambassador to
the United Nations, gave her views on human rights issues
and Latin and Central American policy. In response to the
question: "Do you have any doubt that the murder of the
nuns was a right-wing plot?" the ambassador-designate
answered as follows:

I think it's meaningful to ask: Do you
think the government [of El Salvador] was
responsible or brought about the murders? The
answer is unequivocal. No. I don't think the
government was responsible.

The nuns were not just nuns. The nuns
were also political activists. We ought to be a
little more clear about this than we actually are.
They were political activists on behalf of the
*frente** and somebody who is using violence to
oppose the *frente* killed these nuns. I don't
have any doubt about that and I don't think
those people are in control of the government.
The death squads are not agents of the Salvadoran government.

* Farabundo Martí National Liberation Front.

Jeane Kirkpatrick's statement did not receive much attention at the time. But some weeks later Michael Donovan received a clipping of the article from a friend. He attempted to contact the ambassador. His letters went unanswered. He tried to get an appointment to see her, but to no avail. Finally, he drove from Danbury to New York and called in person on the U.S. Mission at the U.N. He was still unable to speak with her.

Kirkpatrick's opinion regarding the "political activism" of the dead women was the first such statement by a member of the new administration, and the fact that she should have given public utterance to such views within ten days of their funeral gave an additional callousness to her remarks. She was not to be the last. In late February, commenting on the case in a radio interview, Reagan's designate to the post of human rights commissioner, Ernest Lefever, told CBS news:

> There is a difference between religious leaders being involved in theological thought and nuns and clergy engaging in activities against the government. Some religious orders have overstepped their bounds.

Later on in the same interview Lefever made a reference to "nuns hiding guns beneath their habits."

Then, on March 18, in testimony before the House Foreign Affairs Committee, Secretary of State Alexander Haig was asked a question about the investigation by Representative Dante Fascell:

Mr. Fascell: Mr. Secretary, it seems that the Salvadoran government is prepared to make a finding and a decision with respect to the murders of the Americans fourteen weeks ago.

Can we expect a report on that anytime soon?

Secretary Haig: Let me assure you that the dialog between our Federal Bureau of Investigation and the Justice Department and the investigation underway in El Salvador with respect to these heinous crimes—and I use that term without reservation—has been continuous. We have had our representatives down there. We have had the benefit of their investigations.

I would like to suggest to you that some of the investigations would lead one to believe that perhaps the vehicle that the nuns were riding in may have tried to run a roadblock or may have accidentally been perceived to have been doing so, and there may have been an exchange of fire. And perhaps those who inflicted the casualties sought to cover it up. This could have been at a very low level of both competence and motivation in the context of the issue itself.

"On Capitol Hill fascinated spectators called it 'The Day the Nuns Attacked the Soldiers,' " T. D. Allman wrote some months later in *Harper's* magazine, and in San Salvador on the following day, when besieged by the American

press corps, President Duarte took refuge behind some
theories of his own:

> Q: Could we ask you again about the
> comments the secretary of state has
> made about the possible way the nuns
> may have died? Have you heard what
> he said? Do you find what he said
> plausible?
>
> Duarte: I would say that this is one alternative
> out of one hundred . . . there are a
> hundred possibilities . . . there might
> be, might be people from the Left too
> . . . is not so easy yet to pinpoint the
> responsibility . . . so let's wait until
> we find out. And when we find out
> we'll let them know.
>
> Q: How long do you think that will take?
>
> Duarte: I don't know, but Kennedy's death . . .
> they're still looking around. . . .

A fortuitous piece of timing brought Michael Donovan
and Bill Ford to Washington to attend a briefing at the
State Department, arranged on their behalf by Senator
Kennedy, within twenty-four hours of Mr. Haig's statement
to the Foreign Affairs Committee. The two men and a
representative of the Maryknoll Sisters, arrived to meet with
Deputy Assistant Secretary for Inter-American Affairs
James Cheek and FBI representative Harry Brandon. Their
meeting that day was a stormy one.

Bill Ford remembers that "when we told Cheek what
Haig had said, his initial reaction was irritation that we
were baiting him. He thought that we were putting words
into the mouth of Alexander Haig. Then he consulted with
some of his State Department aides and was apparently
told, much to his surprise, that Haig had indeed said these
things. The terrible thing about what Haig said," Bill adds,
"is that whatever little physical evidence exists it points in
the opposite direction of what Haig was saying. Haig talked

about an exchange of gunfire and the FBI told us there were no bullet holes in the van. Haig talked about the women being shot as they ran away from a roadblock, the FBI told us the next day that the women were killed execution style —being shot in the back of the head at close range. It is frightening to think that the chief diplomatic officer of the United States was lying to the American Congress about how these women died."

Michael Donovan's version of the meeting reports:

> After quite some discussion of the matter, Mr. Cheek finally stated to us that "the State Department has no document, either classified or unclassified which states, or in anyway suggests that the four women ran a government roadblock, that the four women ever had weapons of any kind, or that the four women had ever engaged in any activity inconsistent with being peaceful religious missionaries."
>
> Mr. Brandon, of the FBI, then stated that the FBI had no evidence to suggest that the women had run a roadblock, or that they had ever had weapons, and that they did have evidence to suggest that the women had not run a roadblock. "For instance," he said, "there was not even one bullet hole in the van." Furthermore, Mr. Brandon pointed out, the roadblock theory does not explain the sexual attacks on the women.

But the efforts of the brothers of the murdered women to extract a public retraction of his statement from Mr. Haig were no more successful than their efforts to reach Jeane Kirkpatrick.

On March 25 Bill and Michael wrote a letter to Mr. Haig, with copies to President Reagan, Richard Allen of the National Security Council, and Ambassador Kirkpatrick, requesting a meeting at his earliest convenience to review whatever evidence existed to support the theory that their sisters had run a roadblock: "If there is no information to substantiate your charges," they wrote, "we ask that you provide us with a clear and unqualified retraction of your remarks and an apology."

They never received any reply from Haig, but the copy of their letter to Haig sent to Ambassador Kirkpatrick did elicit a form reply. "Dear Mr. Ford and Mr. Donovan," the ambassador wrote,

> Thank you for your recent letter concerning the United States role in El Salvador. . . . The Reagan Administration believes the fundamental problem we face in El Salvador is to maintain the pace of economic and political progress in the face of deliberate efforts by left-wing insurgents to disrupt that progress and to force the Government of El Salvador into a preoccupation with security concerns. . . .
>
> The United States in its dedication to certain founding principles, recognizes the need for and supports peaceful and democratic evolution in El Salvador. Again, thank you for sharing your thoughts with me on this vital issue.
>
> Sincerely,
> Jeane J. Kirkpatrick

It was not quite the last word from the ambassador.

Following testimony by Michael Donovan at hearings before the Senate Foreign Relations Committee on April 9, 1981, Mrs. Kirkpatrick received a letter from the chairman of the committee, Senator Percy, and the ranking minority member, Senator Pell to which she did reply.

> Dear Senators Percy and Pell:
> I am happy to respond to your letter concerning my comments about the American churchwomen killed in El Salvador. As I ex-

plained on "Meet the Press," that comment was taken out of the context of a broader discussion of the character of the struggle in El Salvador. I was discussing the ubiquity of violence in a society in which some 13,000 Salvadorans and non-Salvadorans had died in the previous year. My point was that order had broken down in El Salvador, that murders were being committed by traditionals, murders were being committed by revolutionaries, murders were being committed by simple criminals and that more and more people and institutions were polarized and drawn into the civil war. . . .

Thus, Archbishop Romero's statements about politics in El Salvador made him an activist in the eyes of murderous partisans of other positions. Thus the nuns, two of whom I said were reported to have just returned from Nicaragua and to have ties in the Santanista [sic] junta, were perceived not just as nuns teaching school children but as political activists on behalf of the *frente*. . . .

I think I have some sense of Mr. Donovan's anguish at the death of his sister, and I am happy to take this opportunity to assure him and you that my words, spoken as a political analyst attempting to describe dispassionately a tragically violent scene, were in no sense intended as a smear.

Since I do not know Mr. Donovan's address, could you please ask someone in your office to forward the enclosed copy of this letter to him?

Sincerely,
Jeane J. Kirkpatrick

By mid-April 1981, from the perspective of the families, the investigation into the deaths of their loved ones was going nowhere. Ambassador Robert White, the only official from whom they had received any sympathy or support, had been replaced by Secretary Haig on February 1, and testifying in Congress on the government's original decision to suspend military aid to El Salvador, White had been very specific in his charges:

> ... the agreement that was reached was that we would wait a month and then decide whether a serious investigation was underway or not.
>
> During that time, our reporting from the embassy consistently showed that there was no such—there was no serious investigation into the death of the nuns, and as far as I am concerned there never has been and I know of no evidence to say that that situation has changed.

The contradiction between the testimony of White and the information provided by the State Department in the only document that they made available to the families, a "Chronology of the Investigation into the Deaths of the American Churchwomen," was flagrant. The entry for December 19, 1980, read:

> The Embassy's evaluation of investigation Commission's work to date is that it is progressing reasonably well.

On January 5:

> An FBI assessment of the efforts being made to date by Salvadoran officials in the investigation, and on the FBI examination of physical evidence, indicate that the Salvadoran Commission is pursuing the investigation in a professional and penetrative manner.

And on January 21 it was reported:

> The Minister of Defense and Commander
> of the National Guard advise us that they want
> the investigation carried to its conclusion and
> the guilty parties found and punished.

Then finally, three months after the killings, the State Department had hard news to report:

> Feb. 27: Salvadoran Investigatory Commission provides FBI representative fingerprints of suspect National Guardsmen for comparison with those taken from the nuns' van.
>
> Mar. 2: President Duarte brings physical evidence discovered by the Attorney General's agents to the FBI representative for study by FBI labs in the U.S. The evidence consists of 7.62 caliber cartridges and bullets, along with a tooth fragment.

Missing from the State Department's public record, however, is any mention of the fact that the Salvadoran Investigatory Commission, appointed by the junta on December 8, had been dissolved on February 27 without filing any report on the results of their investigation. The entry in the chronology for February 27 concluded with the following:

> The Commission says it believes that, after the FBI's comparisons (of the fingerprints) the investigation should be carried on by the Attorney General's office, since that office has the powers of indictment and subpoena which the Commission lacks.

It sounded fine, except for one important and never mentioned detail: the attorney general's office had no authority to act against the suspects (all members of the National Guard) until it first received an investigative report directly from the National Guard itself. A report it could not receive since it did not exist.

On April 26 CBS News reported from El Salvador that it had acquired conclusive evidence that six members of the National Guard were involved in the killings. Citing FBI and diplomatic sources in San Salvador, CBS said that the six National Guard members would be arrested "this week."

The following day the high command held a rapidly convened press conference at which Colonel García, minister of defense, and Colonel Vides Casanova, director general of the National Guard, denied all knowledge of any new information on the case. But on May 7, during a television interview on the local CBS station in Rochester, New York, Robert White confirmed the story:

> A cover-up is precisely what is taking place. We have known for weeks if not months . . . not only that the security forces are responsible, but who in the security forces are responsible. The six men who are now under arrest. I don't know if that is public yet, is it? If it isn't, it is now. The Salvadoran government, the military, are holding six National Guard enlisted men as those responsible for the crime. All this talk of an investigation is nothing but a big charade because they knew from within three days who was responsible.

The next day in San Salvador, President Duarte addressed the press:

> I have not received any specific information from the FBI at this date.

I have no information specifically on this
that no member of the National Guard has
been detained because of the nuns' assassination. Because at the moment that we have evidence, information, we will detain whoever it
is. It doesn't make any difference where he is.
In what condition he is. If he has something to
do and we have the evidence we will detain
them and send them to the judge.

Twenty-four hours later, Colonel García called yet
another press conference in which he announced:

Apart from whatever the ex-ambassador
may have said—who must have his own reasons for intervening in this manner—I can tell
you that yes, there are certain people under
provisional arrest related to this painful case
of the American nuns. Certain people, belonging to our military institution, have been detained in relation with certain suspicions.

Our hands are clean, and we are conscious
that we are acting honestly and correctly. It
does not matter what comes out of this. What
matters is to do justice; what matters is to
demonstrate the truth; and above all, to say to
the world, on behalf of those who have been
identified as those who may or may not be
guilty, that they also have the right to defend
themselves, and it will be up to the trial to
determine whether or not there is any basis for
their guilt.

The State Department issued its own statement:

We are encouraged by the action of the
Government of El Salvador in detaining six
persons suspected of involvement in the tragic

killing of the four American churchwomen in
December.

> This action demonstrates that the investi-
> gation is making progress and shows the firm
> determination of the Government of El Salva-
> dor to act against wanton violence whatever its
> source.

Questioned by the press about the status of the case
three months later,* the minister of defense pointed out that
it had taken "the best equipment and the best personnel"
(presumably the FBI) months to come up with "indications
of proof." During the months that these "indications" have
been available, he continued, "they have been analyzed and
discussed. As members of the Armed Institution," he continued, "we are concerned with safeguarding the honor and
interest of the armed forces and do not want, through having acted too rapidly, to make lamentable errors."

Earlier that month Bill Ford had addressed an appeal
to some fifty members of Congress, asking for their help:

> My family has been given virtually no
> information by the State Department.
>
> We have not been told the names of the
> six men who were arrested, the units to which
> they belonged, and the immediate chain of
> command over these men. The State Depart-
> ment knows about radio transmissions from the
> airport in El Salvador about the arrival of the
> women in El Salvador, it even knows the names
> of the men who made the transmissions, but
> State does not know if anyone has bothered to
> question the government personnel at the air-
> port.
>
> Despite obvious signs that the murder of

* Press conference, San Salvador, August 26, 1981.

> my sister Ita and the other three women was
> ordered by officials of the El Salvador army or
> government, our State Department shows no
> interest in pursuing the matter. The arrest of
> six men at the scene apparently ends the matter
> as far as State is concerned. State does not
> know when or if the men will be tried, or
> whether the evidence is sufficient for conviction.

In early September, a UPI story from San Salvador reported that the six suspected murderers in detention in the National Guard barracks in San Salvador had been released "under their own recognizance" and that one of the six men had reported back to duty.

At this point the cable traffic between Washington and San Salvador developed a new tone of urgency.

> From Secretary of State, Washington, DC
> To Embassy San Salvador Immediate
> Subject: Churchwomen and Sheraton Murders
> We consider it essential that the suspects
> in both these cases remain under detention
> while the investigations continue, and you
> should continue to emphasize this point to Col.
> García and other GOES officials in the strong-
> est terms.
>
> Haig

There was a new ambassador in El Salvador by this time. On June 1, Deane Hinton, a tough-minded, outspoken supporter of the Reagan policy had taken up residence in San Salvador, and after four months in his new post, the tone of his dispatches to the State Department began to reflect something akin to the frustration and pessimism that his predecessor, Robert White, had known. In a cable dated September 17, Hinton wrote:

Subject: Murders of U.S. Churchwomen

Summary: We have arrived at a moment in our seeking justice in the murder case of the four U.S. citizen churchwomen when we think it is highly desirable, even essential, if convictions are to be obtained to put a USG professional investigator or investigating team, possibly from the FBI, to work on this here and, incidentally, on the Sheraton murders case as well.

In the last ten days of September, President Duarte, accompanied by Colonel Vides Casanova, commander of the National Guard, was visiting the United States to lobby for additional economic and military aid to the Salvadoran government. During his visit the president and Ambassador Hinton met with representatives of the families of the slain women.

Bill Ford and Michael Donovan, who had come to the meeting, in Michael's words, "loaded for bear," found the Salvadoran president to be forthcoming, warm, and, as Bill later admitted, "he showed more decency and sensitivity than we had seen in our own State Department." Nevertheless, the meeting raised more questions than it answered.

For the first time the families learned that the government of the United States knew the names of the six people who had been arrested but had agreed not to release them. "We pressed Duarte for the names of these people," Bill Ford recalled. "Duarte gave a very confusing and complex explanation as to why the names could not be released. The explanation essentially made no sense, and it was clear to me, listening to him, that the army had asked him not to release the names.

"They appeared to be befuddled by what to do with these men, because the murder of civilians by military men is not a military crime in Salvador. If a Salvadoran soldier kills a civilian for any reason it is not against military law. Duarte said you must understand that Salvadoran law is not set up to protect the innocent, it is set up to protect those already in power from the consequences of their actions."

The families were surprised at how frankly President Duarte spoke of the political situation, though nothing that he told them was in the least reassuring. Michael Donovan recalled that at one point during their discussions, "One of the participants asked Duarte, if the investigation led to a person who was prominent in El Salvador, would he— Duarte—pursue the line of investigation? And Duarte stated that yes, he would. And then the follow-up question was, and would you bring such a person to justice? And he said, as a practical matter, that could never happen. He said there would actually be no possibility of finding a judge in Salvador who would ever try this person. It would be impossible to come up with someone who would have the case in his court."

Then, as the meeting drew to a close, the Salvadoran president made an open admission of the limits of his power. "He said you must understand that I am not in charge," Michael Donovan recalled. "That I cannot make decisions on my own, and that the decisions that had to be made with regard to certain requests that we made of him—he said I will have to return and bring these up with the board of directors of the junta."

The meeting with President Duarte took place on September 30. At its conclusion the families had learned no new facts, knew no more about the status of the investigation than they did before. This was not surprising, given that no investigation was underway. Yet ten months of persistent and unremitting personal efforts, ten months of lobbying for support among senators and congressmen and their aides, writing endless letters, spending hours on the telephone, piecing together scraps of information and misinformation, all this was beginning to show results. The unsolved case of the four American churchwomen refused to go away. It was still very much alive in the public consciousness— most particularly among church communities, the press and certain circles of the Congress, among whom these four American women's death had brought the horror of the brutality of government security force behavior home in terms that the statistics about anonymous Salvadorans being tortured and murdered daily had not.

In September, when the United States Senate voted fifty-four to forty-two to require President Reagan to certify twice a year that the Salvadoran government was making progress in the area of human rights and political reforms, as a condition for receiving further economic assistance from the United States government, progress in the investigation into the murders of the four women and the two American labor advisers was the one clear specific incorporated into the language of the bill.

Over the next two months nothing changed. Eleven months after the murders had taken place there existed only two pieces of physical evidence against the six men under arrest, all of whom had consistently denied any participation in the crime: the fingerprint of one of those arrested had been found on the women's van; and a bullet fragment found at the murder site had been identified as having been fired from the rifle belonging to one of the other suspects in detention. It was this evidence, compiled by the FBI, that had led to the provisional arrest of the six men back in April—what the minister of defense had referred to as "indications of proof." In a letter from Ambassador Hinton written in early November 1981, copies of which were circulated to all the members of Congress who had responded to Bill Ford's appeal for help, the ambassador stated that the Salvadoran government was still engaged in the effort to develop further evidence. Yet eight months later, in July 1982, when the families finally received certain documents relating to the case, for which they had filed under the Freedom of Information Act more than a year earlier, they were able to read a succinct summary of the situation in the form of an internal memorandum of the CIA. Dated November 25, 1981, under the heading, "Investigation of the Murders of U.S. Nuns in El Salvador at a Standstill," the document said:

> Investigation into the murders of four U.S. churchwomen in El Salvador is at a standstill because there is insufficient evidence at this time to charge anyone with the crimes under Salvadoran law. The judge in charge of the official investigation has stated that the case is still "technically open" but there is nothing more he can do unless new evidence is received.
>
> Opinion among U.S. officials is divided as to whether the six soldiers will ever be prosecuted. Some believe that the Salvadorans will be forced to act because of pressure from the U.S. while others believe that senior army officers will stonewall any further investigation.

The first anniversary of the deaths of Jean and Dorothy, Ita and Maura was marked by an outpouring of ecumenical support throughout the religious community in America. Memorial services and candlelight vigils were observed in cathedrals and local churches all across the country. From Washington, D.C., to Seattle, from Florida to Chicago, from Texas to New York, the American Catholic Church, represented by their pastoral leaders—cardinals, bishops, priests and nuns—joined with the leaders of all the major Protestant denominations to pay tribute to the women and what they stood for, and to demonstrate solidarity with their relatives.

On January 26, 1982, just two days before President Reagan was required by law to certify that good faith efforts had been made in solving the murders of American citizens, if El Salvador's junta was to receive another $135 million dollars in economic and military aid, Defense Minister García made an announcement that the six National

Guardsmen under arrest for the previous eight months would go to trial "within a very few days."

Ten days later, the commander of the National Guard, now General Vides Casanova, dismissed the six suspects from the National Guard and two days after that he remanded them to the jurisdiction of the First Criminal Court in Zacatecoluca, together with all of the evidence collected against them during the course of the investigation of the case as conducted by the National Guard.

On the evening of that same day, President Duarte went on national television in San Salvador. Flanked by the entire junta, the defense minister, and the commander in chief of the high command, President Duarte announced that having personally examined all of the evidence and all of the testimony relating to the six former National Guardsmen, he was now in a position to state his firm conviction that there had been no involvement of higher ranking officers in these murders: "They [the arrested guardsmen] are the only and the true guilty ones," he concluded.

Yet, according to the official "Status of the Prosecution" report, handed to the families at a meeting with Assistant Secretary of State Thomas Enders in the State Department on February 17, the situation was far from being as conclusive as President Duarte had stated. According to this State Department document:

> Under Salvadoran procedure, the evidence which the National Guard forwarded to the criminal court does not constitute proof of the guilt of any of the defendants. The evidence provides rather a guide for the judge to follow in pursuing the case on his own.
>
> At this juncture, a substantial amount of evidence remains to be gathered by the court. Because so much remains to be done it is impossible to foresee how long this phase of the prosecution will require.

The families were also handed a ninety-two-page document containing the English translation of the report of the preliminary investigation conducted by the National Guard between December 12, 1981, and February 8, 1982. The testimony included the confession by a single guardsman, who related the sequence of events on the night of the abduction, rape and murder of the four women, in which he and four of his colleagues participated under the command of their immediate superior, Subsergeant Colindres Alemán. According to the depositions, the murders of the four women were portrayed as a wanton, motiveless act, executed by a small group of low-level guardsmen.

The meeting with Assistant Secretary of State Thomas Enders that day lasted approximately four hours, and the families left the State Department worn out with exhaustion and frustration. In an attempt to buttress their own perceptions of recent events, they had brought with them a statement made by Archbishop Rivera y Damas in the course of his homily in the San Salvador Cathedral on the previous Sunday. As reported in the *New York Times,* the archbishop had said, "I hope that this investigation is not simply a gesture to please, to gain publicity in order to promote further United States economic aid." While noting that it was possible that no senior Salvadoran officers were involved in the murders, the archbishop continued, "But there is one thing that worries me. And that is: how a sergeant could give orders unless beforehand, at least in a general manner, someone had not opened the way for a decision of this nature to be taken."

When Bill Ford quoted the archbishop's remarks to Thomas Enders, the assistant secretary replied that the cleric did not have the information that was available to the authorities. This information turned out to be the answer from the accused Subsergeant Colindres Alemán to one question in the course of the polygraph examination to which he was submitted by the FBI. According to the State Department, Subsergeant Colindres Alemán was asked only one question about orders from superior officers. The question was: "Did you receive instructions or orders to assault those women?" (The verb used by the investigator was *atentar*, which in Spanish is frequently used to describe rape.) Colindres Alemán responded, "No," and the polygraph machine noted no deception in his answer.

In the memorandum of the meeting with Enders prepared subsequently by Michael Posner,* director of the Lawyers Committee for International Human Rights, he described the substance of their discussions on this issue:

> [Colindres] apparently was not asked any other questions about his contacts with officers. We were told that he was not asked whether he had orders to kill the women, or to stop and search their vehicle. Nor was he asked if he had simply communicated his involvement in the killings to anyone before or after December 2. The State Department people were very uneasy talking about this. It was also apparent that they were not informed as to exactly how the investigation had been conducted.

Bill Ford, testifying at hearings before the House Inter-American Committee one week later, referred to this meeting with Thomas Enders in which

> the State Department was so eager to convince us that it was just the five men who had done it and we should in effect forget and get on with our lives [yet] there were many facts which they could not or they would not explain.
>
> For instance—in the document shown to us there is reference to the fact that after the murders, some of the guardsmen had large amounts of American currency, thousands of

---

* Lawyer for the families and the Maryknoll Sisters.

dollars in excess of the amount that the women would have been carrying. Where did the guardsmen get such money if not from the people who ordered them, who paid them to commit these murders?

There have been three judges assigned to this case in El Salvador. Two of them have resigned, supposedly out of fear for their lives. If the only committers of this vicious act are five low-level enlisted men, why should the Salvadoran judges fear these people?

As we understand the documents given to us by the State Department, there has been no questioning, no investigation into any person in Salvador, higher than a subsergeant.

Between February and November of 1982, the investigation conducted by Judge Rauda did indeed focus exclusively on the involvement of the five guardsmen under arrest. Under Salvadoran criminal procedures it was the responsibility of the National Guard to make an inquiry concerning superior orders and provide the judge with the information; but since this was never done, the judge was not at liberty to initiate an inquiry of his own or to extend the nature of his investigation of the crime beyond the scope of the preliminary report supplied to him by the National Guard.

In November Judge Rauda completed his reexamination of the evidence. He appointed three lawyers to defend the guardsmen and moved to send the case to trial. The defense immediately appealed the judge's decision, arguing that there was insufficient evidence in the record to put the five men on trial. Owing to a technical error (the judge had failed to notify the lawyers of their appointment in writing) the appellate court rejected the appeal and all further proceedings were "put on hold" for another four months.

In January 1983, Bill Ford, accompanied by Michael

Posner and Scott Greathead of the Lawyers International Committee visited El Salvador to try and find out for themselves what was going on. They had meetings with the judge, the attorney general, the American ambassador and members of his staff, the former president of the junta, José Napoleón Duarte, Archbishop Rivera and other members of the Salvadoran Church. They also interviewed a number of Salvadoran lawyers in an effort to assess whether there was any advantage to be gained by the families in hiring their own lawyer to assist in the prosecution of the case.

Before returning to the States they took a day to drive to Chalatenango so that Bill could pay a visit to his sister's grave, and accompanied by the Assumption Sisters, who had worked so closely with Ita, he also visited the refugee center on the grounds of the seminary and met and talked with some of those whose lives the four women had helped to save.

Describing his interview with one of the Salvadoran lawyers whom they had hoped might be able to assist the prosecution, Bill wrote: "He told us something of the difficulties that we could expect to encounter in the Salvadoran legal system. He said it would not be unusual if the defense tried to bribe or intimidate the juries and that one of the functions of an *Accusador Particular* [private prosecutor] was to offset the bribing or the intimidation of the jury by doing it himself.

"His wife came into the meeting and set forth the difficulties a lawyer would have working on the case, such as the police or armed men arriving in the middle of the night and dragging you off, never to be seen again. She said that there was no recourse against such events and said that her husband would want $100,000 to work on the case and another $50,000 just to conduct an investigation."

On their return to New York, Scott Greathead laid out for the families his conclusions of what had been learned in El Salvador:

The Fiscal General's office is indifferent to an expeditious and successful prosecution of the individuals responsible for this crime, including the five accused guardsmen. The Fiscal General's office is generally disinterested and shockingly unprepared for the trial of this case.

The Fiscal General's office has made no effort to investigate the culpability of higher ranking National Guard officers, despite the existence of evidence indicating that the five accused were acting pursuant to higher orders and the fact that death threats were received by two of the women shortly before the murders. It can only be concluded that the Fiscal General is deliberately ignoring this and other evidence of the involvement of higher officials because of incompetence, fear and/or political reasons.

The U.S. Embassy concedes that the Fiscal General has not seriously investigated the existence of superior orders or the involvement of higher officials, and that there is some evidence of higher orders in the record. Nevertheless, the Embassy stated in a December 1982 cable to the State Department that "the overwhelming weight of the evidence before the court indicates that the guardsmen were not acting on orders higher than those of Sergeant Colindres Alemán.

The Embassy refused to ask the Fiscal General to investigate the involvement of higher officials or a cover-up.

Yet all the while the administration was publicly upholding the myth of an upcoming trial for the five accused guardsmen, and as twice a year the date for the certification process rolled around, the predictable announcements of "significant progress made" were heard.

In the spring of 1983, in response to pressure from the Subcommittee on Foreign Operations of the Senate Appropriations Committee, the administration agreed to appoint an investigator to conduct "an independent and high-level review of all of the evidence available to the United States Government pertaining to the churchwomen's case." On May 23 former Federal Judge Harold E. Tyler was appointed to carry out this assignment.

Six months later, on December 2, 1983, the third anniversary of the women's death, Judge Tyler submitted his findings to the secretary of state. His report was immediately classified by the administration. The reason for the refusal to release the report to the families of the dead women, as stated by Deputy Assistant Secretary of State James Michel to Bill Ford, was that release of the report would "affect the integrity of the judicial process in El Salvador." To Bill Ford this argument had all the validity of "some kind of obscene joke." In fact, like every other aspect of the State Department's handling of the case, the timing of the eventual release of this report—within hours of the conviction of the five guardsmen and long after it had already been leaked to the press—was a political, rather than a judicial, decision.

The judge's findings give great credit to the efforts of individual members of the American embassy staff in San Salvador for developing and pursuing the evidence that eventually led to the arrest of the six guardsmen in April 1981. In the introductory section Judge Tyler writes:

> Representatives of United States agencies have been vigorous and effective in pressing the Salvadorans to investigate and prosecute this crime. . . . At least one United States Government officer has repeatedly exposed himself to great personal danger to obtain evidence crucial to the investigation. We believe the American public, and the families, can ask no more than that from their representatives.

Regarding the controversial question of possible involvement by higher ranking officers in these murders, Judge Tyler's report sheds no new light on the issue.

> The question whether Colindres Alemán was ordered to commit this crime by higher-ups is a troubling one. To the extent the Salvadoran authorities have investigated this matter, their enquiry is not nearly as complete as we would have liked. There is some evidence suggesting the involvement of higher-ups. . . .

the report notes, yet it goes on to conclude:

> Although it is unlikely that a dispositive answer will ever be known, we record here our best judgment: on the basis of evidence available to us, we believe that Colindres Alemán acted on his own initiative.

It is important to point out that the key phrase here, "on the basis of the evidence available to us," refers to evidence accumulated by investigators who had never searched for any connection to higher ranking officers. Nevertheless, inasmuch as the judge substantiates the State Department's position on this issue, their refusal to release the report is all the more puzzling.

Perhaps what troubled the State Department is the clarity with which Judge Tyler reveals the criminal nature of the Salvadoran men who have become the cornerstone of American policy in El Salvador. At the very outset of the report, the judge refers to "highly confidential information collected by the United States Embassy through the efforts of an Embassy official at great personal risk."

It is this "special Embassy evidence" upon which Judge Tyler frequently draws to set forth his findings regarding the cover-up of the crime by the Salvadoran authorities.

The first reaction of the Salvadoran authorities to the murder was, tragically, to conceal the perpetrators from justice. Evidence available to the United States shows beyond question that Colindres Alemán confessed his involvement in the crime to ranking members of the National Guard within days of the murder. They responded by concealing this fact from the outside world, and ordering the transfer of the killers from their airport posts and switching of their weapons to make detection more difficult.

According to Judge Tyler the cover-up was premeditated and functioned very smoothly.

Within days of the murders, Salvadoran authorities commissioned two investigators, one public* and one private, both with apparently the same objective: to create a written record absolving the Salvadoran security forces of responsibility for the murders.

. . . The murderers made no attempt whatever to conceal their culpability from other National Guardsmen. Not only had several guardsmen witnessed the churchwomen's abduction, but the defendants repeatedly conceded their guilt to their colleagues following the killing. For instance . . . within days of the murders . . . Sergeant Colindres Alemán approached his immediate supervisor, Sergeant Dagoberto Martínez and reported that "the problem with the nuns is me." Martínez advised Colindres Alemán to be silent about the crime,

---

* The public "investigation" was led by army Colonel Monterrosa, head of the much-heralded special investigative commission announced by the Salvadoran government on December 8. The National Guard's private investigation was conducted by Major Lizandro Zepeda Velasco.

but to admit his role if questioned by a National Guard officer. . . . Colindres Alemán followed precisely Sergeant Martínez' recommendation.

When questioned in the days following the crime, he confessed his role in the murders to the National Guard investigating officer [Major Zepeda Velasco, who] did not betray Subsergeant Colindres Alemán's trust. Rather, he undertook a course of action in the winter and spring of 1981 to protect Colindres Alemán and the other killers. . . . Although we have no direct proof, we think it is quite possible that Major Zepeda informed his superior, then Colonel Vides Casanova,* of his activities. Vides Casanova appointed Zepeda, and Zepeda reported directly to him.

And Judge Tyler continues:

It seems unlikely that a mid-level officer like Zepeda would have undertaken the obstructive actions he did without approval or encouragement from someone higher. Moreover, when we interviewed now General Vides Casanova, we found him evasive; he professed a disturbing lack of knowledge of Zepeda's investigation. In his answers to us, General Vides Casanova attempted to distance himself as completely as possible from all investigations of the crime.

The cover-up of the killers did not, of course, end there. In April 1981, the American embassy decided to confront President Duarte and Defense Minister García with the information it had developed through "special Embassy evidence." It handed over the names of six guardsmen,

---

* Now General Vides Casanova, minister of defense, since the fall of 1983; reappointed to this position by newly elected President José Napoleón Duarte in June 1984.

and demanded their arrest and the seizure of their weapons for delivery to the FBI technicians for ballistics tests. It was at this point that Salvadoran officials, the American press, and former Ambassador Robert White became embroiled in a series of conflicting statements and counterstatements that finally resulted in the admission by Defense Minister Garciá on May 9 that six men belonging to "the Armed Institution" had been provisionally detained. According to Judge Tyler, assurances to the contrary,

> although the cover-up had been thwarted, and evidence of the defendants' guilt produced, the military apparently remained ambivalent about the extent to which it would cooperate in the prosecution. Major Zepeda remained in charge of the National Guard's internal "investigation," and the disclosure of the true facts apparently did little to deter him from his course of concealment.

On July 1, 1981, Major Zepeda delivered the results of his second investigative report to Colonel Vides Casanova, in which he once again concluded that it was impossible to determine the guilt of the guardsmen because ". . . of the 'difficulty' in resolving a case so 'delicate.' . . ." This, then, was the report, the reading of which prompted Ambassador Hinton in mid-September to cable Washington that "if convictions are to be obtained," the embassy now felt that "it is highly desirable, even essential to involve a professional United States Government investigative team —possibly from the FBI to work on this here. . . ." According to Judge Tyler, for "political reasons" which he does not explain, any "serious investigation" would still have to come under the aegis of the by now totally discredited investigative commission headed by Colonel Monterrosa and it took an additional ten weeks to produce an agreement whereby a joint Salvadoran-American investigative effort was finally launched in December 1981.

Judge Tyler is full of praise for the thorough and persistent efforts of Major Medrano, which finally resulted in the confession of one of the participants in the murders in the first week of February 1982, and in the deposition of one guardsman who, while not a party to the killings, participated in the abduction of the four women and witnessed the torching of their van. Yet critics of this, the first serious investigation attempt undertaken by the National Guard one full year after the crime occurred, point out that the majority of the details revealed in the ninety-two pages of testimony accumulated by the investigative group basically serves only to confirm and fit the facts as they had already, in large part, become known through the efforts of investigative reporters and Church and human rights sources within El Salvador. The echo of Bill Ford's complaint, voiced in January 1981 concerning "the murderers investigating the murderers," had not ceased to haunt all aspects of the investigation.

Judge Tyler's prognosis, in the winter of 1983, of the chances for a meaningful trial of the six accused men concludes on a pessimistic note:

> Whether a jury can be assembled in El Salvador today that will have the courage to convict five former National Guardsmen of murder is an open question, and one that has concerned us greatly.
>
> Skeptics have told us that a successful prosecution depends entirely upon the will of the military in El Salvador. In this view, if the military thinks it is to its advantage for the defendants to be convicted they will be convicted; if the military thinks otherwise, they will be acquitted or never go to trial.

In November 1983, the U.S. Congress passed a law that withheld 30 percent of all U.S. military assistance authorized for El Salvador in fiscal year 1984 pending a verdict in the case, whereupon the Salvadoran military found the will to proceed with the trial. By this time it is worth noting that two key witnesses, National Guardsmen whom Judge Tyler, in the fall of 1983, had recommended be brought back for further questioning concerning the issue of "superior orders," were neither one any longer available to the prosecution. The guardsman who testified to having made the phone calls from the main airport terminal to Subsergeant Colindres Alemán, to inform him of the presence of "suspicious women," and who subsequently halted all traffic leaving the airport to allow the white Toyota van to proceed unmolested on its way into the waiting roadblock set up by the murderers, was reported "missing in action" shortly after making his original deposition to Major Medrano in December 1981. The corporal, who was second in command at the airport on that evening, and who arranged to send a pickup truck to fetch the murderers home after their jeep had broken down, has been killed "on active duty."

As the judge so neatly puts it: "The record from which we have had to work is not as complete as we would have liked." In the introductory section of his report the judge states:

> Since May [1983] we have had access to pertinent State Department files, both classified and unclassified, including numerous cables that had been transmitted between the State Department and the United States Embassy in San Salvador on this matter. . . . No documents necessary to our enquiry have been withheld from us.

Among the cables to which Judge Tyler presumably had access was one sent by Ambassador White to the State Department in the first days of December 1980. This cable reported the information (acquired during the course of extensive conversations between members of the embassy staff and the justice of the peace who had presided over the burial of "four unknown women" in a common grave during the early hours of December 3, 1980) that the recipient of the official report of this clandestine burial was a certain army Lieutenant Colonel Edgardo Casanova, who, from his headquarters in the army garrison of the town of Zacatecoluca, had overall command of all the security forces within the airport—La Libertad region at the time of the killings. Lieutenant Colonel Casanova is a first cousin of Minister of Defense Eugenio Vidés Casanova.

In the official files on the investigation there exist several significant pieces of information relating to this army colonel.

First: According to Ambassador White's statements to the press on the afternoon of December 5, when he telephoned Minister of Defense García to request an all-points alert for the missing women, one of the first actions taken by García was to telephone his regional commander in Zacatecoluca, Lieutenant Colonel Casanova, to transmit the alert to all of the army, police and National Guard posts within his region.

Second: According to the Rogers-Bowdler report, on the morning of December 4 at about eleven-thirty A.M., while the ambassador and the consul were driving about in the hills above the town of Zacatecoluca searching for the burial site,

> a political officer at the embassy, seeking information, telephoned Lt. Col. Casanova, the garrison commander in Zacatecoluca. . . . Col. Casanova told the political officer he had only learned of the killings of the four American churchwomen from Church representatives a few minutes before.

Third: When Father Paul Schindler called at the barracks of the Treasury Police in the small adjacent town of San Luis Tapla on the morning of December 4, the commander of the post had received no information regarding either the missing women, or the existence of the burned-out wreck of their Toyota van, which had been abandoned on the side of the road less than three miles from his barracks for over thirty-six hours.

Fourth: A few weeks after the crime, and within the same period during which the National Guard was hastily transferring Subsergeant Colindres Alemán and his companions away from their posts in the airport, the army also transferred Lieutenant Colonel Casanova from his command post in Zacatecoluca to a different region.

Nevertheless, despite these indications that Colonel Casanova had, at the very least, knowledge of the death of the women prior to the discovery of their bodies—knowledge that he covered up and denied; despite his failure to pass along the alert to the security forces under his command—as promised by Defense Minister García to Ambassador White; despite all this, neither Judge Tyler nor any other investigator, Salvadoran or American, has ever had so much as a conversation with Colonel Casanova. By way of explanation of subsequent refusals to investigate why the "all-points-alert" failed to reach the security forces within the very region in which the women disappeared, the official State Department position attributes this "failure of communication" to "lamentable errors and confusion."

Three and a half years later, when a former Salvadoran military officer of high rank defected and turned informant on his colleagues, the name of Lieutenant Colonel Edgardo Casanova resurfaced. On the evening of March 21, 1984, Walter Cronkite presented an interview on the "CBS Evening News" with a nameless, disguised man whom he introduced as a "former high military official from El Salvador. Our source," Cronkite explained, "was in a sensitive post in the top ranks of the Salvadoran security establishment. Our informant," Cronkite informed the audience, "said D'Aubuisson was directly involved in the murders of Archbishop Oscar Arnulfo Romero and two American labor advisers. However, he said the murder of four American churchwomen was not the work of the death squads. Five National Guardsmen were charged with these murders," he continued, "and our informant claimed a superior officer ordered the nuns killed."

Cronkite: Who was the authority . . . who gave the order?

Informant: The officer was Colonel Edgardo Casanova.*

Cronkite: Casanova is a cousin of the present minister of defense, Vides Casanova, who at the time was head of the National Guard. He must have known as well, right?

Informant: Perfectly.

Cronkite: And he's covering up the assassination of the nuns?

Informant: Yes. . . . Because of family ties.

Cronkite: The president of El Salvador at the time was José Napoleón Duarte. . . . Did Duarte know about the cover-up of the murder of the nuns?

Informant: He had to know about it.

Cronkite: Why?

Informant: Because he was a provisional president of the country and he had to be asking strongly what was —what happened in the case of the nuns.

Cronkite: So, in other words, the cover-up went broadly through the government.

Informant: Yes, sir.

One afternoon in May 1984, some two months after this broadcast, I spent an hour and a half in a secret loca-

---

* Colonel Edgardo Casanova has publicly denied his involvement in these murders, to both the *Miami Herald* and the *Los Angeles Times.*

tion with this Salvadoran officer, seeking personal confirmation of the charges he had made to Mr. Cronkite. His story of what happened on the night of the murders of Jean and Dorothy, Ita and Maura still does not fill in all of the details. He cannot point to a precise notation in a logbook of the communications that took place between Sergeant Colindres Alemán at the airport and Lieutenant Colonel Casanova on that night; or of communications between the National Guard barracks at La Libertad and the guard post under the command of Colindres Alemán at the airport. He only knows that such communications indeed took place, and in the case of the conversation between Colindres Alemán and Colonel Casanova, he claims to know quite precisely the language used by Casanova in response to Sergeant Alemán's request for instructions.

His story still does not shed any light on the activities or the whereabouts of the murderers and their victims between the hour of approximately seven-thirty P.M. when the patrol headed by Sergeant Alemán boarded the women's van outside the airport, and the time, three hours later, when peasants living beside the dirt road leading to San Pedro Nonualco heard a vehicle drive past their shacks and continue up the hill. Moments later some reported hearing gunshots; then all saw the white van returning with its lights blazing and the radio blaring.

The absence of such specifics is not surprising. In a country where so many people are killed daily without any motive or cause other than the general suspicion or rumor that they are "subversives," it is futile to expect that any formal record of the bloodshed would exist in any file or logbook or memorandum. There are no record keepers of the slaughter. Furthermore, this lack of documentation goes much deeper. It extends both to the deliberately vague, ambiguous manner in which "orders" are "transmitted" before the fact, and to the total lack of interest and consequent absence of any postmortem after the deed has been committed. In an institution that is as hierarchical and as autonomous as the armed forces of El Salvador, there exists a system, a code of behavior, whereby the wishes of the highest ranking officers are made known to their subordinates, who understand and execute them without any questions asked, without—and this is the key—the need for anything as formal as a specific order, either written or verbal.

It is this systematic, all-pervasive complicity that protects the murderers and explains the scale of the repression. Certain major assassinations that come under the category of "political" decisions—assassinations like that of Archbishop Romero, of the Attorney General Mario Zamorra, of the leaders of the FDR—are handled differently. But for the tens of thousands of corpses that litter the roads and end up in the public garbage dumps all across the country, there exist no death warrants, no death certificates.

It is against this background that I present the account of the killing of Jean and her companions given to me by this former intelligence officer turned informer (a man whom I refer to only as "the Colonel"). In judging his account it is important to bear in mind that while he has broken with his former comrades for a number of personal and professional reasons, he remains today what he has been all his life—a member of the armed forces of El Salvador; a staunch conservative; a traditional, middle-class Catholic to whom the ideas and beliefs of the liberation theologians are anathema. Seen from his perspective, the attitudes, beliefs and activities of the American missionaries in his country—as personified by the Maryknollers and the members of the Cleveland mission team—represent a threat. Consequently, from his point of view, the charge that Jean and Dorothy, Ita and Maura were "subversives" is something he accepts without question.

At the time of the murders of the four women, as a former head of the Intelligence Service of the Salvadoran Army General Staff (ANSESAL) "the Colonel" was an adviser on intelligence matters to the Salvadoran high command. On the night of December 3, 1980, he received a call at his home from a high-ranking army officer whom he will not name (for the man is a friend of his). This man called him up to say: we have a problem. Someone has killed some Americans. In answer to the question who was responsible, his caller replied: that idiot, Edgardo Casanova. To the next question, how did this happen? "the Colonel" received the following explanation:

On the previous day, his caller told him, the commander of the National Guard post at the airport had received word from his colleagues in the National Guard barracks of Chalatenango that two American nuns, whose names had recently been listed on the official intelligence report of the Central Bureau of Army Intelligence under the classification "subversive," would be landing at the airport on a flight from Nicaragua. According to the National Guard in Chalatenango, these two women—Ita Ford and Maura Clarke—were couriers (or worse) for the guerrillas, and might well be bringing messages to the guerrilla leaders in Chalatenango from their Nicaraguan counterparts. Therefore, the sergeant at the airport was to see to it that the women be intercepted and not reach their destination.

That evening, two other religious American women— Jean Donovan and Dorothy Kazel—both of whom were currently being kept under surveillance by the National Guard in La Libertad because "they had had contacts with civilian elements in that area who were members of a guerrilla group"—had driven to the airport to pick up their friends. When Jean and Dorothy left to drive to the airport, the guardsmen in La Libertad telephoned the guardsmen in the airport to warn them that the women were on their way.

When the flight from Nicaragua landed, the guardsman who was on duty in the customs hall telephoned his superior, Sergeant Alemán, and advised him that the two "subversive women" had arrived, whereupon the sergeant alerted his subordinates to be prepared to go out on an assignment. Having made his plans to intercept and arrest the women as they left the airport, the sergeant then telephoned the commanding officer of the region, Lieutenant Colonel Casanova, in Zacatecoluca. He informed him that the women were in the airport and that he was about to apprehend them and asked what he should do with them once they were in his control. According to "the Colonel," Casanova replied, "Why are you asking me? You know what to do—*Denle*." Literally: "Give it to them." A phrase that Sergeant Colindres Alemán understood all too well.

From that point on "the Colonel's" information is sketchy. He believes that Alemán, seeking further confirmation, drove the women to Casanova's barracks in Zacatecoluca, and either met with or at least talked on the telephone again with Casanova, from the little town just outside Zacatecoluca, known as San Rosario de la Paz, where, according to several testimonies in the record of the investigation, Alemán entered the National Guard barracks and spent some time. "The Colonel" is adamant on one point. Casanova himself wanted no part of the women and told Alemán to get them "the hell out of here."

In response to my question, "Why were Ita's and Maura's names listed on the intelligence report?" "the Colonel" gave the following explanation. Some weeks earlier, in a small town in the province of Chalatenango called Arcatao, in a confrontation between the guerrillas and the National Guard, a guardsman was killed. Arcatao had a strong Basic Christian Community with which Ita and Maura had close contacts, and in the aftermath of the guard's death, the intelligence-gathering service of the National Guard in Chalatenango forwarded information to the National Guard headquarters in San Salvador, accusing Ita and Maura of collaborating with the guerrillas. This "information" was duly processed according to routine intelligence procedures and reappeared a week later in the columns of the weekly intelligence report that is circulated by the Central Bureau of Army Intelligence to every garrison and barracks in the country. "The Colonel" explains that the publication of an individual's name in this document under the heading "subversive" is tantamount to a death warrant.

According to his own story, early on the morning following his receipt of this information, "the Colonel" paid a visit to the army chief of staff to impress on him the urgent necessity that Lieutenant Colonel Casanova, as the responsible party for this mess, be charged with the killings "for the good of the country." "The Colonel" claims that at the time he was sufficiently naive to believe that the failure to cope adequately with the situation created by the murders of these four American women would inevitably result in a fatal loss of American support. Nevertheless, as the days passed and his advice was ignored, he recognized that because of the influence of Lieutenant Colonel Casanova's first cousin, commander of the National Guard and member of the high command, Vides Casanova, the opposite had, in fact, occurred. The highest echelons of the junta and the high command were involved in the decision to protect the guilty man and cover up all traces of the murderers' activities on the night of December 2.

"The Colonel" knows, but will not tell, the identity of the person to whom Casanova allegedly confessed his role in the crime. Was it to Defense Minister García when he called on the afternoon of December 3? Was it to Police Chief Colonel López Nuila? To his cousin, Vides Casanova? Or to "the Colonel's" own friend and informant? He will not say. But on one thing he is clear. On the evening of December 3, a full twelve hours before the clandestine burial site had been discovered, the entire military hierarchy, from Defense Minister García on down, knew precisely what had happened to the four women on the previous night, why it happened, and who was responsible.

I asked "the Colonel," "Why did Colindres Alemán bother to contact Lieutenant Colonel Casanova for instructions? Why, in light of the intelligence that he had, and the urging he received from his colleagues in Chalatenango and

La Libertad, did he not act on his own initiative?" He looked at me as though I were slightly demented. "But they were Americans," he said. "No sergeant would take such an action against four Americans without checking first with his superior officer."

About the Author

Ana Carrigan was born of Irish and Colombian parents and grew up in Ireland and South America. She has had a distinguished career in film and television as a student and collaborator with Marcel Ophuls, as a producer for "20/20" on ABC-TV, and as the producer/director of "She's Nobody's Baby," for which she won a Peabody Award in 1982. The film she coproduced on Jean Donovan, *Roses in December,* was selected by *Time* magazine for their "Best of Ten" list in 1982, and received both an Emmy nomination and the Christopher Award. She was the associate producer of the NBC-TV Movie of the Week on Jean Donovan, *Choices of the Heart.* Ms. Carrigan has been a resident of New York City since 1965.